MOVING ON DOESN'T MEAN LETTING GO

MOVING ON DOESN'T MEAN LETTING GO

A MODERN GUIDE TO NAVIGATING LOSS

GINA MOFFA, LCSW

balance

NEW YORK   BOSTON

Copyright © 2023 by Gina Moffa
Cover design by Hayley Warnham. Cover image by Shutterstock.

Balance
Hachette Book Group
1290 Avenue of the Americas
New York, NY 10104
GCP-Balance.com
Twitter.com/GCPBalance
Instagram.com/GCPBalance

First Edition: August 2023

Balance is an imprint of Grand Central Publishing. The Balance name and logo are trademarks of Hachette Book Group, Inc.

The publisher is not responsible for websites (or their content) that are not owned by the publisher.

The Hachette Speakers Bureau provides a wide range of authors for speaking events. To find out more, go to hachettespeakersbureau.com or email HachetteSpeakers@hbgusa.com.

Balance books may be purchased in bulk for business, educational, or promotional use. For information, please contact your local bookseller or the Hachette Book Group Special Markets Department at special.markets@hbgusa.com.

Library of Congress Cataloging-in-Publication Data
Names: Moffa, Gina, author.
Title: Moving on doesn't mean letting go : a modern guide to navigating loss / Gina Moffa, LCSW.
Description: First edition. | New York : Balance, [2023] | Includes bibliographical references.
Identifiers: LCCN 2023010117 | ISBN 9781538740668 (hardcover) | ISBN 9781538740682 (ebook)
Subjects: LCSH: Grief. | Loss (Psychology)
Classification: LCC BF575.G7 .M638 2023 | DDC 155.9/37—dc23/eng/20230412
LC record available at https://lccn.loc.gov/2023010117

ISBNs: 9781538740668 (hardcover), 9781538740682 (ebook)

Printed in the United States of America

LSC-C

Printing 1, 2023

Mom,

This book is *for* you and *because* of you.

Through space and time, you are always here.

To my courageous clients: I am so deeply grateful and privileged to be your traveling companion on one of the most important inner journeys you will take.

And to those who show up here with me, to the grief and unknown, and who keep showing up—my heart is with your heart.

Grief is alive, wild, untamed and cannot be domesticated. It resists the demands to remain passive and still. We move in jangled, unsettled, and riotous ways when grief takes hold of us. It is truly an emotion that rises from the soul.

—Francis Weller, *The Wild Edge of Sorrow*

Contents

MOVING ON DOESN'T MEAN LETTING GO

Introduction

When Josh first came to see me, he was a twenty-four-year-old, self-proclaimed "grief mess" who was in such distress, he struggled to explain why he was even seeking therapy. His girlfriend, Rebecca, had died a year earlier in a car accident that he had survived, unharmed. They had been headed to dinner to celebrate both of them getting the jobs they'd been working toward, when they were sideswiped by a drunk driver and slammed into parked cars on the side of the road at 55 mph. Rebecca got the brunt of the impact and was unconscious at the scene, passing away later at the hospital. It was coming upon the year anniversary of the accident when Josh decided to reach out for help.

Sitting on my couch, trying to catch his breath, Josh confessed that he felt frozen in his guilt around still being alive. Grief, he said, was "infiltrating everything" in his life: his relationships with friends and family, his new dream job—which he felt unable to show up for even though it was the work he had always wanted to do—even his sense of the world itself. The trauma and grief of that accident was continuing to give him flashbacks, intrusive thoughts, and nightmares. He was coping (or, well, *not* coping) with a tremendous amount of guilt and shame by drinking to curb the intrusive thoughts and symptoms, but that only made him feel worse.

He felt stuck, jostling around in a disconcerting limbo not entirely in the past, but not quite in the present, either. Everyone around him had encouraged him to try to move on from the accident and Rebecca's tragic death, but his body and heart just couldn't.

He wanted help, but he was also struggling to accept support, adding that he still felt too attached to Rebecca to "just let go."

That made sense to me.

I've heard from a lot of Joshes over the years. People who have lost someone or something incredibly important and tried to get over it and keep it moving, only to find themselves feeling like an alien in their own life. Distant and disconnected emotionally, feeling out of sync with the world by a few beats, and genuinely confused by what's happening at times. Mind, body, and spirit, the people who reach out to me are desperate for healing, but unsure how to move forward after losses that have shattered their world even, and perhaps especially, when nobody else seems to see the full extent of the damage.

As a grief and trauma therapist for more than a decade, I have seen the way that grief sits at the root of so many mental health challenges, from post-traumatic stress disorder and major depression, to substance use disorder and anxiety. A study done before the pandemic by AmeriSpeak found that 57 percent of Americans were grieving the loss of someone or something important.[1] That means every other person you see is grieving—and, yes, "is" grieving in the present tense; grief never truly goes away. Spring of 2020, COVID increased that number, bringing loss to millions more doorsteps.

There is no escaping or outrunning loss in our lives, individually nor collectively. Loved ones, friends, pets, identities, pregnancies, homes, health—the many losses that come with life might just be a matter of fact if we had any real clue how to cope when they come, but we struggle. Even many of my colleagues tell me they either do not feel comfortable working with grief or are not well equipped clinically. Grief and loss classes weren't offered as a part of any mandatory clinical curriculum and even now, at best, it's still just an elective.

If only grief were equally elective.

You Are Not Alone

The people who sit on my couch are courageous. Some of them would shudder to hear me call them "brave," but it's true. Grief may be one of our most universal emotional experiences, but that doesn't erase how isolating, confusing, and profoundly painful it can be. It takes a lot to look at your pain head-on, to see what's under it. Josh struggled with that kind of vulnerability for a long time. He had always had a hard time expressing his emotions, and he'd pull himself up short every time he wanted to cry over his loss, telling me that his father always told him to stop crying and grow up. That forbidding voice echoed in every person who had told him to get over it or move on. After hearing it so many times from so many different people, it made perfect sense to me that Josh hadn't yet figured out how to be where he was in his grief experience. He was living between the shock of his loss and the expectations of others.

Then one day he came into the office, sat down, looked me in the eyes clearer than I had ever experienced, and said he was ready to do it my way.

"*My way*, huh?" I shrugged. "Thing is, Josh, my way is for *you*. So, it's *your way*, too."

Which brings me to this moment right here with you. If you are reading this book, it's likely that you're enduring a loss, maybe for the first time. Maybe you've lost a parent, grandparent, another family member or loved one. Maybe you're grieving a beloved pet, or a friend you used to call every day but haven't spoken to for years, and you're not sure why. Maybe you're going through a major breakup, enduring chronic illness, or are struggling with painful fertility challenges. Or, maybe you picked up this book for a different type of loss. Your grief may be very fresh or you may now be ready to process a loss that happened years ago. Our losses can be ambiguous, such as those of miscarriage or dementia, and even expand to things like loss of expectations, hope, a future, safety, identity, and so much more. Or, maybe you've endured losses that seem to have compounded. Maybe it was a traumatic loss or maybe it feels traumatizing to *you*.

Whomever, whatever, and however you lost, I am sorry.

I am so, so sorry.

And I'm glad that you found this book.

While no book can substitute for one-on-one therapy or specialized grief support, I hope that these pages can become a safe space for you—just you and me in this vault with no judgment, no secrets, and no societal or ancestral rules, a space to come closer to our truest selves and gather tools for healing wounds, old and new, one step at a time.

To that end, I want you to make me two promises: First, that you won't judge yourself while you're here with me. And second, that you won't rush yourself through this book. The healing process isn't a Netflix series to binge so we can hurry up and learn what happened to Judy on *Dead to Me*. The only thing harder than our losses is the pressure we feel from ourselves and others about how long we can grieve (spoiler alert: not very!) before we need to "just move on." I think you already know, just from the feelings that have brought you here, that our *entire* equilibrium is thrown off balance when we suffer a loss, and as much as I wish it to be true at times, we can't just click our heels and find ourselves safely back in bed realizing it was all only a dream.

Loss can leave us adrift, feeling alone and terrified, without any real sense of direction in a land we never wanted to visit. I often imagine a strange and painful opposite land, where we don't know what we want or what we need and every time we get a clue about those things, they change on us, and then we want something else. Maybe we want company, then we want to be alone. Maybe we want to go home and cry, but then we find something funny that was left behind and find ourselves bowled over in laughter. We sometimes feel guilt for a million things—and especially that first moment of happiness after our loss. We want to feel peace; we also want to go back in time and try again. It's a strange and wild ride. And, I see you.

Grieving When We Don't Know How

Grief can feel like a nasty tug-of-war between what *was* and what *is*. And, let's be honest—we aren't the same as we were before our loss. Like the worst version of Google Maps, our brain is busy "recalculating" itself as we try to find a way through the world and our future that doesn't feel utterly traumatizing and terrifying. Feeling so profoundly disoriented, some of us shut down emotionally, too overwhelmed to manage how we feel and how others say we're "supposed to" feel. I know the confusion and desperate need for something to hold on to that comes with loss, and hell, even the instinct to just keep tossing things and relationships away after loss. I know the anxiety that's grief's sidekick, looking around in fear, wondering who or what will be taken from us next. And yet, we still have to go on, only now looking closer at all we have left around us in our life, try to make sense of it all, and keep going...somehow.

It can feel unpredictable at times, especially if you're experiencing grief for the first time. But there are a few truths about grief that can help start the process and give you a sense of agency during an experience that can threaten to take you down. (1) It shows up in ways that are both obvious and more subtle. (2) It is *nonlinear*, meaning, there is no beginning, middle, and end to our grief, no timeline, and no real order to how things will come up for you. And (3) Grief is a full-on, full-body experience that exists on a spectrum. How grief shows up for you is based on the day, the circumstances, the level of exhaustion you feel, grief triggers, anniversaries, relationship struggles, and your emotional baseline. It's important that you can know and name this for yourself, because when we misunderstand what grief is, we dismiss it and, in the process, belittle its place in our lives, as well as its impact on our health and wellness. Grief is so much more than a feeling.

After loss, in our own time and ways, we all try to regain a sem-blance of normalcy and control. I know how hard it is to feel people really *get it*, that anyone other than you really understands what you're going through. How could they? Did they know your loved one? Did they see the way your (now ex) husband used to look at you? Did they stay up all night talking with your friend, sharing all your secret wor-ries and the joy of your accomplishments right up until the day they moved across the country and got a new best friend? Did they hold your pet's paw, telling them it would be all right when what you were really saying was goodbye? Did they get on their hands and knees and pray to God to heal or keep someone around, because they couldn't imagine living without that person and maybe didn't even know *how*? Did they know what it was like to have to tell people the baby you posted online about for nine months was no longer alive? *How could they know?* How could anyone really know what a loss means to some-one? We can't.

So if you're thinking that grief is a singular feeling you just have to feel your way through and get right back to yourself again, I'm so sorry to be the worst of all messengers: This is an experience that will require your endurance, emotionally, physically, and yes, even spiritu-ally, because your loss has changed your life.

Seeking out support and guidance during this time is courageous, and, I am sure, also exhausting and terrifying. I see your opening this book as reaching out and searching for connection during the hardest, maybe most confusing moment in your life. I know I already said it, but I'm really glad you're here.

A Little About Me

So, who is this person asking you to trust her with your heart and your hurt? Well, I am a psychotherapist with nearly twenty years of experi-ence working in different types of institutions in New York City, from

Mt. Sinai Hospital Center to 92NY (formerly the 92nd Street Y). I began in various social work roles and worked my way up to director positions, working with many different groups of people. This includes, in no particular order, Holocaust survivors and older adults in life transitions, low-income, inner-city populations struggling to attain basic daily needs, teens and adults deeply challenged by addiction of all kinds, and trauma histories, people enduring severe mental illness diagnoses in inpatient (and outpatient) hospital settings, as well as asylum seekers trying to escape further trauma and harm—people from all walks of life, grappling with the most challenging life (and death) circumstances. These courageous humans have been my teachers. I have been immensely privileged to journey alongside them during their darkest moments. My clinical expertise after years of being in the trenches with hundreds of clients is in the heart of these pages. A note on my social location: While, yes, I have worked with a wide variety of populations over my decades as a clinician, I am a white, cis female therapist who has a private practice on the Upper West Side of Manhattan, without the lived experience of being racially or culturally marginalized. For the purposes of this book, I will be speaking *specifically* to the clinical grief experience, while wanting to acknowledge the diverse racial and cultural needs and grief experiences that exist, and that also come through my door.

In addition to my work, I am also a motherless daughter, who in the same horrific week her mother died also had to struggle with losing her home, her job, and her health. At other points, just like so many people, I have lost partners, friends, loved ones, and several versions of myself that I treasured. I don't share this to compete in the Grief Olympics. (A) Those don't exist. (B) Nobody's loss is *ever* the same as anyone else's. Your loss is yours in the way your love is yours. It is sacred; nobody can take it from you. I share these losses with you, though, to assure you that I've also been around the block a few times, and that I may be able to help you find your way, too.

One of the many reasons I wanted to write this book was that during the pandemic, there weren't enough hours in the day to help the number of grieving people who needed it. Week after week, I would speak with people from different states who were desperate for a grief therapist but did not have access to grief therapy for a variety of reasons. As the pandemic wore on, more and more calls came in from a younger crowd inquiring about grief and trauma therapy after loss. Some called because they'd lost friends and family to COVID-19, or their pet died during the pandemic, which sparked grief for all of the family. But many others reached out because they were in the midst of major life transitions like breakups, job loss, home transitions, and more. I was heartened seeing so many more people taking their mental health seriously and wanting to understand more about what they were experiencing. I was heartbroken not to be able to help more of them personally. My hope was that this book could be a hand reaching out to say, *I'm sorry, I see you, I am here, and I care.*

What I Hope You Get Out of This Book

I cannot promise that this book will fix your pain, but I *can* promise that it will be a steadfast companion. The road through grief is fraught and lacks comfortable accommodation, but I do have a well-worn map that shows the different routes you can take to find what you need: a sense of safety, understanding, courage, peace, and guidance, to name a few. If you allow your experience to unfold in its own ways, the words on these pages may help you shift that pain. It may also bring up memories or experiences that may feel initially uncomfortable. I'm sorry about that. There may be triggers that come out of the blue, too. We will go there, into the grit of your grieving.

My goal with this book is to offer a sense of agency over an intolerable, unpredictable, and exhausting experience. Although I do not subscribe to the five stages of grief in how they have evolved since Dr.

Elisabeth Kübler-Ross created them for the terminally ill patient, I do believe in having a semblance of structure and some gentle guides to prevent you from flailing in a dark abyss. You should not be left to grieve indefinitely without a sense of relief. Perhaps counterintuitively, the path to that relief comes from tenderly facing your loss. This means I will challenge you to make contact with your most vulnerable feelings, dig deep for self-compassion in the toughest moments, and listen to your body's innate wisdom (you may not always be happy with that!). We will also identify different kinds of boundaries that aim to help you meet your needs and help others to help you, too. As unbelievable as it may feel at times, there is a way to move forward *with* your grief in a way that doesn't render you helpless or at the mercy of ever-shifting emotions. My promise is to be right beside you as we work toward taking the sting out of your daily grief experience a little at a time.

In these pages, I'll offer you some new ways of viewing your loss (and your life), practical tools, many reflections, and some stories from inside my therapy room that you may relate to, including my own story of loss and grief. By the end, I hope you'll have picked up some new ways to befriend and contend with your grief, and that you feel just a little less alone.

Grief is the deepest human wound there is, and it's everywhere. Even in places within our lives we didn't notice it. It deserves more than one-size-fits-all bits of advice. This book will ask you to open up your heart and peruse your painful memories and perhaps look more deeply at those wounds. It's no easy endeavor, even if you're eager to jump in. Where you go next and how you begin to find shreds of light and hope in your life again are the cornerstone of what's inside these pages.

In many ways, this is the book I wish I'd had when I was grieving the death of my mother. Perhaps I could have been gentler with myself through the clumsy moments that were really just me trying to push through it, deny it, see it, but then conveniently not have time for it... before inevitably answering the damn door and inviting that grief in. Trust me, though, like many of you reading this right now, if I could have drop-kicked grief in those early days and gotten back to my life with my mom still in it, I'd have done it. Instead, I warily dragged myself to the bookstore and searched for books that spoke to me, that I could point to and see myself. Sadly, I didn't see much of myself in those aisles.

Maybe I was picky. I wanted a book that spoke to my actual emotional experience and lifestyle of being a thirtysomething in a relentlessly fast-paced world with nonstop social media notifications and navigating friendships and a love relationship with this new, gaping wound. Not to mention that, at the time, not many people I knew had lost someone close to them through death. It felt lonely and exhausting. I wanted to learn how to better ask for what I needed, and sometimes, how to even know *what* those needs were. I was so used to working and caring for others' needs for so long, I hardly remembered how to take a deeper look at my own.

Grief can unravel us and we are then left standing over our lives trying to figure out how to put the pieces back together. Sometimes, it takes everything in us just to figure out where to start.

Now's as Good a Time as Any to Begin

There is never a "good" time to do grief work, or a time we may willingly throw open the doors to our soul and bare the pain and fragility and yearning within. Not usually without a really compelling reason, am I right? Yet, here we are, and here we will begin—not my way or your way, but *our way*.

So, right here and right now, I invite you into my office, asking of you only what I ask of my clients: Show up as best you can, and tell the truth.

That truth you share in the exercises or simply notice coming up as you read will inevitably be the gateway to your emotional freedom and a stronger sense that you can, indeed, get through the worst of what has happened. Facing it all, head-on, at your own pace and with my guidance and gentle support, is a courageous step toward healing, even when it feels like falling apart.

You will hear me say in different ways that grief is a unique experience and very individually processed. The flip side of this is the fact that we find the path *through* grief by shared experience. As a result, being witnessed and having your feelings and experience heard and honored is the path toward reconnection. The stories—both my own and those of my clients—are my way of offering you that.

Humbly, this book is an invitation to be with your shattered heart in a quiet place, here with me in the pages that will be all about you and your experience. I'm sorry to be the jerk who says that time doesn't heal all wounds. It doesn't. What it does do, though, is help to make space for new understanding, new normals, new connections, and new experiences—all of which come with both the bitter and the sweet.

As impossible as this may now seem, I assure you that you *can* learn to live with grief's flow and rhythm. And you can become empowered by the very thing you think might swallow you whole.

PART ONE

THE INNER GRIEF JOURNEY

CHAPTER 1

The Griefall

Griefall:
The freefall after loss.
The compass that both loses and finds you.
Nothing is ever the same.

"She died! She died!" my father said frantically on the other end of the phone. "She died while I went to pick up the phone to talk to you a minute ago!"

Time immediately stopped. I momentarily left my body.

I heard his words, but as I stood on a busy street in New York City, I couldn't make sense of what he was saying. I'd just hung up with him a few seconds earlier, when she was still alive.

My mother just died.

Full stop.

I told my dad I'd be on the next train back home, and hung up as my body began to shake from the shock. I was on the corner of East Seventy-Seventh Street, stuck in a loop of horrific information. I watched the street crossing sign change. White. Flashing. Red. And again—white, flashing, red. I willed my body to take a step, to cross the street, to move anywhere at all, but it was frozen in place. I looked around for someone with whom I could share the most important, devastating news, some stranger to witness my loss. I needed someone to give me a reference point. My world was shrinking around me, and fast. I felt disoriented and untethered to my surroundings. I felt like I was free-falling—but, to where?

But there was no one. On this otherwise ordinary Friday morning in early December, there wasn't a single human nearby. It was so weird. I mean, it's Manhattan. There are *always* people, especially during the weekday morning rush hour. *Where are all the people?! This doesn't even feel real. Maybe it isn't? But, wait, my mother died. My mother, who had celebrated her sixty-fourth birthday with family and friends twelve days earlier, looking healthier than she had in some time... is no longer.* This is real. Yes, it is real.

Now what?

I felt dazed, but aware enough to stifle any emotions. How could I navigate my way through the subway if my eyes were blurred with tears? I began to make my way to the Metro-North train at Grand Central to ride an hour up the river to the Hudson Valley to my hometown. I was careful not to cry, because even in my shock, I was still vain enough not to want to snot all over myself in public. Once on the train, I spent an inordinate amount of time practicing what I'd say if a stranger tried to sit next to me. "I'm sorry, you can't sit here, because my mom just died and I need space to quietly lose my shit if I have to, thanks." Or, "I'm sorry, but I'm saving this seat for my mother, who will be here any moment, I'm sure (even if not visibly)." Was anything *not* totally bizarre to say? Surveying my inner dialogue, I realized I was an emotional wild card weirdo at the moment. I had to embrace it, though—it could be no other way. Luckily, no one even tried to sit near me, so my train-riding reputation remained intact, and my relief was overflowing for my hour of aloneness.

I felt like I was disconnected from real life, but I knew when I got off that train I'd have to help to get the preparations for her funeral started. I needed to keep it together, so I stared out the window at the Hudson River speeding past, repeating the reality back to myself: *Mom died. Okay, she died.* Over and over I reminded myself of that simple, devastating fact, really trying to ground myself in that new heavy reality. The suddenness of her passing was too harsh to integrate. Loss is funny like that. Everything *feels shocking*, even if it isn't really a shock.

When it was time to get off the train, I felt myself clutching the seat. My body wanted to stay and avoid all that would inevitably come next with losing my mom. Funeral arrangements, calls to make, reservations to book, and many people to see in the coming days. I was already overwhelmed. I didn't want to face this first day without my mother alive or all the things I'd rehearsed in my head, preparing for this very moment. After all, my mother was sick with metastasized colon cancer and her oncologist had told us early on (a year and a half prior) that there would be no cure or remission. They'd caught it too late.

"Too late"—those words from my mother's oncologist will forever echo in my head. It's as if she had been instructed to show up to her cancer on time and was being punished for failing to be a good cancer student. Even as I exited the train, I, too, was *too late.* I had been staying with her for several weeks, and on and off going up to stay most weekends since her cancer progressed to the "it's only a matter of time" stage. This one night, however, I said a nonchalant goodbye to her, as I fully expected to see her the next morning after taking care of some things in the city. She died before I got back to her.

There I was on the platform wishing to avoid it all. I didn't want to see my dad's brokenhearted face or find her burial outfit or select a casket or write a goddamn eulogy when all I could think to say was *this fucking sucks.* There is just never enough time with people we love, is there? Fresh grief tossed me into the horrific limbo so many of you may understand, of not wanting her to suffer anymore, but really, really not wanting her dead.

゚〜゚

To this day, nearly seven years later, the rest of that afternoon and, honestly, most of the week is still a blur. Some details disappeared into the *grief void*, a mysterious and seemingly bottomless place. Where do our thoughts go during this time period? Where does our sense of time and place vanish to? What about our ability to form memories of painful yet significant moments? No one knows, just as we can't know where those missing socks go in the dryer. Maybe I'd willed my thoughts into the grief void unconsciously. Maybe that's just where they were meant to go. Maybe they will show up again one day when I am least expecting them. Or maybe they are gone forever.

This wasn't my first loss. I had lost other important people in my life, to death, as well as a harrowing divorce that I swore might take me down. I was also, at this point of losing my mom, a practicing grief and trauma therapist. Just a week earlier, I had a full work schedule. I ran support groups, I had sessions with clients feeling adrift and alone. The irony wasn't lost on me: I had worked with traumatized and bereaved people for more than a decade, ushering them through the most challenging moments of their lives. Yet, I realized I didn't know the first thing about grieving *this* particular loss. This time, it wasn't someone else's mother who was gone. *My* mother was gone. I felt consumed by my own grief, like the bottom had fallen out beneath me and I was racing toward the dark unknown. It's an experience I began referring to as my *"griefall."* That fall was just the start of my grief journey.

The Moment You Always Remember

So, that's how it all began. In under two minutes on a cold December morning, I went from being a therapist who worked with grief to being a full-fledged, card-carrying griever, and a woman without her mother. The entire train ride home, I kept ruminating over the last thing I'd said to my mother: "Do you have to go to the bathroom?" I mean, really?! Not what I would have wished for. Yet this is real life—and death.

You'll have your own entry point to the griefall—the moment you'll always remember. Maybe it starts through a conversation that ends in a breakup, a doctor's appointment, the first time your grandparent couldn't remember your name—a moment where you realize you can't go back to something you lost, for which you now yearn relentlessly. Maybe, like my own, it's the phone call where you get the worst news of your life and you realize that nothing will ever be the same.

However yours has looked, that griefall is like a thermometer in March—unpredictable at best. It's a profoundly untethered feeling, like a total free fall into a new reality you never wanted and certainly didn't ask for. There's nothing really to do here in that fall, except notice and be gentle with ourselves on the way down. Ultimately when it comes to this griefall, all you can do is stretch out your arms and surrender, knowing that when and where you land is anyone's guess. At times you may wonder, as I did, if you'll ever land. It's no wonder so many people hold on for dear life to anything along the way that can stop their fall into grief...

Sparkle-Covered Sadness and Emotional Bypassing

Sam's griefall led him into new and very uncharted emotional waters. Almost a year after losing his mom and the yoga studio he'd opened in downtown Brooklyn, he called me for a consultation, and immediately told me that he was okay. *Huh?* As you may imagine, I was utterly confused, but could feel that Sam wasn't used to sharing emotions, and in fact, seemed to be quite uncomfortable with them in the vague, roundabout way he described wanting to see me for therapy. He went on to tell me again that he'd lost his mom and his big dream, yes, but it was "okay." He just wanted to work through some things. Then he told me not to worry because he's not a problematic client and he'd be entertaining at the very least.

Whoa.

Well, this isn't usually how therapy works. As a therapist, I am there for witnessing, encouragement, and gentle nudging toward different viewpoints as needed. I am a mirror reflecting back what you show and share, a detective to help you see yourself from other angles. I'm also a supportive but savvy travel companion heading down whatever roads your healing takes us. What I am not? A quiet audience member looking to be entertained by a one-person show. There's Netflix for that.

During our first few sessions, Sam told me that he had spent so much time trying to jump through hoops to save his yoga studio that he hadn't been available much during his mom's cancer journey. He hadn't thought it would be fatal—he'd taught his mom meditation and helped her to adopt a more alkaline diet. Because his finances had taken a hit he was busy taking teaching jobs whenever they came up, and he'd stopped visiting his mom as often.

My heart cracked wide-open as he sat there reporting what he called the "most devastating events and losses of my life to date." He smiled as he spoke, but his tone of voice was flat and his eyes conveyed a thoroughly heartbroken soul. Nearly a year had passed since he lost his mom, but Sam's griefall was ongoing, intensifying each time he dared to get closer to the pain of her death.

"There has to be a reason for all this craptastic luck, right? Maybe I've been doing it all wrong. Maybe I was, like, mispronouncing the Sanskrit mantras or something!" Sam said, briefly faking a laugh. "I just started Kundalini meditation with this community. I see people blissed out and spontaneously laughing. I was freaked out at first, but then they started talking about all this success they have had since starting meditation, and I don't know. I wanted that, too. I heard that Kundalini is sometimes known to dredge up all the stuff that isn't working and bring it to the forefront to be cleared out. I didn't think it would bring THIS. I thought it might lead me to a new career or financial wealth, not *burying my mother and my business!*"

And there it was: classic emotional bypassing.

Sure, we all would love for the sting to be taken out of our pain, but what emotional bypassing does can be harmful in the long term. Attempting to avoid, gloss over, or sweep the pain under the rug only tricks us into thinking that if we don't feel it, well, maybe it isn't there, right? Nope. But I get it. Going through a major loss can kick up a whole lot of emotion within us, and that can be really terrifying. What emotional bypassing can do is make us believe that if we go toward the pain, it might make us feel even worse, and then what?! Maybe we think if we start to cry we will never stop or if we fall apart, we will never come back together. But it only prolongs our pain, I'm sorry to say. I hear some rendition of this a lot in my work: "I have no right to complain about my loss, because there are people who have it so much worse." Yes, *and* that doesn't make your pain invalid or unworthy of being felt and understood and honored, but it does make it scary to experience, still. Or, maybe the age-old classic bypass, "This happened for a reason and so I will see it as a gift!"

Whatever form your emotional bypassing takes, I want to remind you not to try to sidestep the pain that you have, do, and will experience because of your loss. It's all a part of who you are now and we can't cast it out. I want you to keep this in mind as you move forward throughout the book, so if you have any bypassing tendencies, you may see the importance of acknowledging your experience and your feelings as valid and as a vital part of your story and healing process.

So, with that understanding, I hate to be the bearer of bad news, but just because you pray or meditate or vision board in just the right way every day doesn't mean you're exempt from loss or grief or painful experiences. We really cannot use spiritual practices or positive psychology to sidestep the harder, more raw, and pain-stricken emotions that come with grief. We can use spiritual practices to help comfort, guide, support, and bring tenderness to our feelings of being torn open by our grief, but to use it as a shortcut? It just doesn't work—we cannot avoid the emotions and full-body experience that come with grief, at least not indefinitely.

And, look, I get it. We want to make it stop. We want to be back in control, to feel like we have some capacity to slow the agonizing vertigo of that griefall. To have a way to say, "Just kidding, false alarm, everything is still okay, nothing to see here." Our Western mindset shows us that getting "back to normal" is the ultimate benchmark of healing, and the sooner we can white-knuckle our way through our feelings as though nothing is wrong, the sooner the griefall will be over and we can get on with our lives.

But one way or another, those feelings will find us. We can't outrun them through comedy, or yoga, or work, or anything else. Alluring as the sparkles may be, there's still sadness underneath to attend to. In fact, the griefall ends the moment we embrace our experience and emotions and are ready to be with them with tenderness.

Having said all that, if you, like Sam, are holding fast to a set of beliefs that shield you from your emotional truths, I see you. Let me be clear: Trying to sidestep the pain of grief and inadvertently prolonging the griefall is all very normal. To feel the pain, to land in those sticky crevices where all the most trying emotions erupt and derail you? To dive straight into the realities that threaten to chew you up and spit you out into a million pieces? Most humans would be like, yeah, thanks, but *hard pass* on all that. I mean, it sounds as least as bad as it feels. Who *wouldn't* want to avoid feeling helpless and vulnerable! We crave the safety and certainty of whatever we can get our hands on, grabbing for anything to help us break our fall.

Important Note About Emotional Safety

Throughout these pages, you will hear me talk a lot about "safety." It may not be something you think much about, but it's vital when it comes to our lives and well-being. I will say this is a safe space, because my intention is to create a space within these pages where you can find consistency and tools, as well as a caring human here to be with you throughout. One of the first rules of doing therapy with a client is *creating safety*. Yet, I am not dense enough to realize that alone is enough or is simply a given. I cannot define what feels safe to you, nor can I proclaim this is safe here in these pages if you don't feel that way. So many people do not have a safe place to be themselves in the world, or within their families or communities, and so, it's important to me that this feels authentic to you.

With all of that in mind, here is where I am at that intersection: I will provide information and client stories based on my expertise, experience, and training. I will also share some parts of my own grief journey with you. But, more than that, I will be a consistent companion here with you. I invite you to come to these pages and meet me here however you can. If you need/want to, please feel free to underline, cross out, or just simply reread anything that jumps out to you as helpful, unhelpful, or validating or activating. Our reactions to things we see or read are related to our histories and past experiences, so I simply ask that if something feels hard or activating within you as you go through these pages with me, that you take the time you need to find that sense of safety in your body in whatever way works for you. If/when you're ready, I welcome you back. I will be here.

Barn Fires and New Perspectives

As my own griefall continued to unravel before me, there were no sparkles or inspiring quotes. Instead, it felt like I had tripped on the sidewalk and fallen headfirst down a bottomless void.

After the funeral, I returned to the city, where I learned that my apartment building, too, was being sold. The new lease included an astronomical rent increase. If I didn't sign it, I would have to move out within thirty days. Shortly after, the not-for-profit organization where I worked as a clinical director began to close its Manhattan location; thus I'd need a new job, too. I felt distracted and confused, like I was living in some alternate universe. The fear and sense of loss was endless, bottomless, and unforgivably cruel. I needed comfort. I needed love, nurturing, and supportive guidance. I needed my mom. I longed to call her and tell her all of this bullshit that was going on—about how scared and overwhelmed I felt, about how utterly groundless my life had suddenly become. I just wanted to rest in her comforting words and her reassuring pep talks. *But oh, that's right. She's dead.*

Just a few days later, I found myself in the emergency room in horrible pain, and was diagnosed with pancreatitis. The timing couldn't be better (eye roll). Treating pancreatitis is a waiting game that requires fasting until your pancreatic enzyme counts have gone down. Now between jobs, briefly uninsured, motherless, and soon to be moving, I sat in a hospital bed for days, literally being starved. When my enzyme levels did decrease enough for me to be released, I was forced to venture back into the wild where my grief process had yet to really begin. I was still free-falling.

I used to wonder why I wasn't feeling much past the initial griefall. The momentum of each successive crisis somehow kept me in a state of emotional suspended animation. But then I remembered: With all the foundations of my own life crumbling so quickly, I didn't have the luxury of crumbling with it. I didn't have *time* to grieve, to really get into the feelings or be present with the full-body grief experience that was banging down my door.

My situation, sadly, wasn't unique; many people have harrowing stories about grieving amid crisis or trying to grieve while needing to be back at work immediately after their loss. Sometimes, life demands so much, there's no time or energy for feelings—any feelings, let alone getting sandbagged by grief—so we push it farther down on our "things I need to do" list. And I get it, life doesn't just stop because we are enduring a loss (even if we wish it would).

Thankfully, a week after my former organization shut down, I was hired as the clinical director of an outpatient mental health and addictions program at a Mt. Sinai Hospital location, a major NYC hospital system—a job that brought the most amazing work family to me in my time of feeling so utterly lost. I swear they were sent by my mother sometimes, because this group of therapists and counselors that I supervised really saved my broken heart in ways that continue to bring tears to my eyes. I also had a small private practice, which had been growing at a surprisingly fast rate. I moved to a beautiful new apartment in a new neighborhood that bathed me in sunlight and beautiful neighbors who became dear friends. I helped my father, as needed, clearing out my mother's closet and donating most of it to Goodwill or family friends. Above all, I kept going. *Just keep swimming*, I told myself over and over again, taking a cue from Dory in *Finding Nemo*. That's what I needed to do at the time.

For months I swam quickly past anything emotionally challenging or even vaguely grief-related. I had a challenging new job to tend to, a private practice to grow, new health directives to heed. I got pretty good at swimming past my pain, even ignoring the extreme exhaustion, persistent headaches, and ongoing stomach issues I was experiencing. *I'm fine*, I told myself, confident that my intellectual understanding of grief would blur and soften the hard edges of my griefall.

But as the months piled up, my body began to feel badly weathered, beaten down by persistent physical symptoms. I'd been avoiding the crux of my griefall for so long that grief had begun seeping out of my organs. My thyroid was now a problem child I had to deal with after pancreatitis. I had hit my limit.

My education and training as a therapist were the lungs of my life, but I was still just a newly bereft daughter rebuilding her place in her own world, wondering how or when I'd find a sense of equilibrium amid all the changes I was thrust into.

Though in my capacity as a therapist I told people day in and day out about the importance of taking time to grieve, I had yet to take my own advice. I knew I'd have to face the heart-wrenching journey I help people navigate every day. Nothing about it felt easy or even remotely okay. It felt more like I'd swan-dived off a cliff only to hit every sharp edge on the way down. As hard as I tried to circumvent my own grief, nevertheless, she persisted.

One day while packing my apartment, I removed a magnet from my refrigerator that read:

> *Barn's burnt down*
> *now*
> *I can see the moon.*

It's from a poem by Mizuta Masahide, a seventeenth-century Japanese poet, and I'd looked at it many, many times. This time, however, it silenced my heart. With tears in my eyes, I thought, *Maybe this whole tearing down of my world will make sense one day.* Over the many months that followed, I slowly began to recognize that the bare elements of our human existence are about loving, connecting, and holding on to things and people we cherish—*while* processing the impermanence of it all and still loving, connecting, and cherishing anyway. Life is change, and to live a full life and love deeply means you will inevitably lose and grieve these losses, because everything is always shifting in some way.

I don't know what your griefall looks like, but however and wherever you land and begin the real task of grieving, I want you to know this: Showing up willingly to the emotions and holistic experience is an act of bravery, but also necessity. I realize that sounds like an enormous undertaking and uncertain as hell, but I promise you, we are in this together. There's no rush, there's no specific timeline, there are no expectations, and there is no societal "right way" here in these pages. It's just you and me—clumsily but courageously looking deeper into the painful, complicated feelings to see what treasures we can sift out to bring along the way. So, let's get to it, shall we?

Let's Check In: The Griefall

Hey. I want to check in with you, and have you check in with yourself.

Self check-ins are going to be vital for you in your day-to-day life while grieving, because they keep us present to our feelings, thoughts, and needs when all three of those seem to be shifting like some kind of deranged kaleidoscope. The better you know what you are experiencing, the better you can know what to do (or not do) about it. There is no rush to feel the feels. Nothing has to change right away, even if all you want is to feel better as fast as possible. It's about being as present and gentle with yourself as you can. I promise, we will get there, but slowly, at a pace that allows your grief the space it needs.

For this check-in, I'd like you to put your hand on your heart, noticing as you do how the world slows ever so slightly. Breathe in deeply, give your busy mind a moment to quiet, and let your emotions come forward if they need to.

With your hand still on your heart, ask yourself the following questions:

If you think about your loss right now, do you feel yourself still falling in that griefall or have you started to get to know your grief and invite it in for coffee?

Have you allowed yourself to acknowledge all that's coming up for you right now with gentleness and without judgment?

Do you feel safe to feel all of your feelings that may come up?

If not, is there something that can help you to feel safer?

Are you able to make a promise to be gentle with yourself as you navigate the unknown terrain of the grief journey?

I'd like you to revisit those questions from time to time while reading the pages ahead. Take note of what (if anything) shifts as you continue to learn about and engage with your grief.

But the truth is, we are not static, and watching how we change and grow and hurt and heal can give us a welcome sense of structure. Even if we veer off (and we will), having a part to play in meeting our grief where it's at can be such a powerful stance when we're in one of the most vulnerable emotional places of our life.

The griefall is, as I have envisioned it, the universal starting place for the grief experience, and so in the pages ahead, as we witness the fullness of all you've been experiencing, this is my plea to you to return your hand to your heart anytime you need to take a breath, take a beat, and give yourself a tender moment of presence. Remember, you don't have to do any of this alone.

CHAPTER 2

Honoring Life's Many Losses

"All the art of living lies in a fine mingling of letting go and holding on."

—Havelock Ellis

Right after my mom died, in need of friends and familiar faces I loved, I went to the beloved neighborhood restaurant I'd frequented every week for many years on the Upper West Side of Manhattan. Upon entering, John, the bartender, ran over to me. After expressing how happy he was to see me, he told me about a building code dispute. The restaurant, which had been the hub of my local community, was now scheduled to close *that very night*.

"Sweet Jesus, can I catch a break?" I remember sighing out.

I don't usually mention the Oceanic Grill when I tell my grief story since, well, compared to my mom, my livelihood, my apartment, and my health, it's rare that someone doesn't raise a cynical eyebrow at me for grieving a *restaurant*. But I was floored. For me, it wasn't just a restaurant. That place was my headquarters, my home away from home, my refuge. But no matter how long I wax poetic about the lobster roll or the way my inner circle of close people in my life knew to meet me there on Thursdays, the love that I felt for that sanctuary will always be personal. No one could ever really understand, which is the tricky thing about non-death losses. They don't seem like they should matter as much because, well, *no one died*.

At the core of all loss, though, is attachment. We form emotional connections to the people, places, pets, and things in our lives in ways that don't always make sense to other people. For example, think back to when you were a toddler: Did you have a favorite stuffed animal or blanket? Something that you couldn't bear to be without? Or maybe you have kids now and can imagine the hell that breaks loose when they've spilled chocolate milk all over everything and now Mr. Bear has to go in the washing machine and your kid screams like you've just murdered him. The question isn't "Does the blanket have the same inherent value as a human life?" The question is "What did that connection give you? What have you lost?" In its most essential form, what we are grieving is the safety, love, and connection we felt to what we have lost. Whatever or whomever that may be.

Only you know the depth of your attachment and, subsequently, your grief. How long or how intensely you grieve will vary because the attachment you have to what you lost is unique to you. Some attachments are stronger than others, of course, and only you know how strongly attached you feel to someone or something. It's not for me to judge.

Maybe you have loved an old book or a keychain or a specific bench in a park the way I loved the Oceanic Grill. Maybe you've never quite gotten over your first car and the freedom it brought you, or the way an elementary school teacher who passed away always made you feel seen. Maybe you're heartbroken over a friend who ghosted you, or grieving the apartment you had back when you were single, even though you're happily partnered. That's not chump change. It is meaningful and it matters.

To avoid the hurt and stigma of mourning a loss that others would brush off as "no big deal," we often dismiss these other losses, burying the very real grief they can cause. Truth is, no one can understand the meaning of our significant attachments, but comparison isn't actually the point. The point is that we cannot and should not hold ourselves to some universal standard. There's not some great Grief Table stipulating how much a given loss is allowed to hurt, or for how long, or in what ways, and whether it qualifies as a loss at all. The grief police aren't going to arrive on your doorstep and tell you you're doing it wrong (though I'm sorry I can't guarantee the same for certain friends or family members).

Losses are as deep and personal as the attachments we held, and should always be respected. After all, aren't the connections to partners and spouses, pets, friends, dreams, homes, jobs, imagined futures, communities, and so much more that make our lives worthwhile? When we lose those parts of our lives *of course* it hurts—sometimes quite a lot. No amount of denial, whether on an individual or societal level, can undo the very real pain. By disregarding our grief, we prolong and magnify its impact on our health, well-being, and relationships. So, right here, right now, let me be clear: *All* of your losses are valid. Your feelings are real, your experience matters, and we can sit with it together.

Maybe you've never thought much of these other losses. Maybe you've been talked out of grieving them or bringing attention to them. Maybe a recent loss is bringing up memories or latent feelings of loss you haven't fully considered.

In the rest of this chapter, let's take a moment to help you name the other life experiences you may not have initially categorized as a loss and make space to include them as part of your healing. We're going to delve into four different categories of loss—anticipatory, ambiguous, disenfranchised, and secondary loss—that are common but often under-grieved, to better understand the weight that we're carrying. After all, we cannot heal what we cannot see. So let's take a closer look.

Anticipatory Grief

With all the talk of grief following loss, it's easy to forget that, sometimes, we grieve *before* we lose. It can come with a painful health diagnosis of someone we love, or a job we love in a company that will be closing down, or knowing our pet is growing old and maybe has outlived their life expectancy and it's the "any day now" feeling of loss. Sometimes, we don't realize we are experiencing grief, because we are still in the adrenaline of the news, but when it all sinks in, like my own mother's cancer diagnosis, which included no cure or hope for long-term remission, the grieving process somehow already begins, whether or not we are actively conscious of it.

I've heard similar reactions from many clients over the years who have dealt with the painful blow of an end-stage diagnosis of someone they love that they have been living in grief, mourned already, and it's kinda done. Yes, of course that grief is and feels real, but it can also be complicated, because there can be a small piece of hope for their survival/longevity still weaving in and out of that grief. It can feel very up and down, because you're preparing for someone to leave over and over sometimes, depending on the diagnosis.

The confusing thing about anticipatory grief is that, even though the loss has not yet occurred, it feels so real to you that your brain and body begin that full grieving process in earnest. Trying to protect us from pain later, the brain gets a head start, trying to integrate what it will be like and putting us through the same emotional and physical roller coaster that typically occurs *after* a loss.

For example, I had a client recently talk about a friendship that had just been headed in a downward spiral since COVID. She felt she and her friend had grown so far apart that there was little common context or understanding left between them at this point. We talked about the potential future ending of the friendship and what that felt like, and she anticipated the feeling of grief, as this friendship was meaningful at a piv-otal point in her life. Yes, she was "anticipating" the loss, but she was also already grieving the changes in the friendship, even though the ending technically hadn't occurred yet. If the friendship could be saved, she'd have wanted that, but she could feel it was ending before it was official.

The stories of anticipatory grief run rampant in my practice, and it really speaks to the idea that we humans have *a lot* of anxiety when it comes to the unknown. We begin to mourn what may feel out of our control or not make sense or feel predictable in an effort to regain that sense of control and give ourselves a softer landing. It's "easier" to grieve ahead of time, and we think we can trick ourselves into being less sad when the loss officially occurs. If only it really worked that way. Sure, anticipatory grief can take away the element of surprise, but mostly, it can still be shocking when it happens, and it still hurts no matter how much we prepare.

I want to honor that preemptive grieving is a completely necessary human reaction to anticipated loss. We aren't naming this to discount it, or to say it's not "real" grieving just because another grief journey lies ahead. The reason to name this grief is to give yourself care, kindness, and remove the expectation that you should be "done by now" just because you got a head start. Leave room for grief to come up again whenever and however it needs to. Our hearts need more grace than that.

Ambiguous Loss

Much as we might wish it, not all losses have closure. This can be especially challenging when we've been taught that we need to be able to tie up big emotions with a nice bright bow. A definitive "end," however painful, is often cleaner for our brains and hearts to navigate, and without one we're often left seeking resolution that never materializes or, in many cases, just isn't possible.

The phrase "ambiguous loss" was coined in 1999 by family therapist Dr. Pauline Boss, who was the first to give voice to the idea that not every loss comes with a resolution or closure.[1] Common examples of ambiguous loss are when someone becomes psychologically absent even though they are physically present, the loss can come from estrangement or incarceration, or having a loved one with PTSD, addiction issues, chronic mental health issues, dementia/Alzheimer's, or other challenges that change the dynamic of the relationship such that it cannot ever continue as it was. The pain of these losses can sometimes sneak up on us because our brains are wired to be able to process a concrete loss. With ambiguous loss, it often takes time before the loss is apparent. For example, if we have a family member with cognitive decline, the grief from that loss becomes more apparent over time, as the person we love loses their ability to be who they once were to us.

Ambiguous grief experiences can feel excruciating and "crazy-making." We are creatures who crave a sense of resolution, and here, it is seemingly taken from us as we try to reconcile the dual reality that a person or a future is both here and gone all at once. Sophie, a client of mine, came to therapy not realizing she was suffering from ambiguous loss. Sophie lost several relationships with family members over political differences and could not seem to sort them out enough for any comfortable reconnection. Estrangement over politics is a valid loss experience that deserves the same tenderness and attention as any other death-related loss, even if the future of the relationships remains unknown.

In fact, I venture to say that these days, the socio/political/racial divides around us seem to have so many of us feeling a collective sense of ambiguous loss far more than we have in decades around the world. Thanks to COVID-19, millions of people were left in the unknown—symptoms without an anchor, a real sense of life never being the same again, questions about whether it was even real or not, but in the end, no real clarity or closure for any of us. We just sort of... went on.

In the "here, but not here" type of loss that is ambiguous loss, you may experience grief that can become complicated. It can feel like you're in grief limbo, not really having any sense of when it will feel better, because it's a loss that's ongoing. For many people, ambiguous loss can feel incredibly traumatizing, as it is the most stressful form of grief. Many of my clients who experience ambiguous loss talk to me about symptoms similar to post-traumatic stress disorder, as living in any unresolved circumstance surrounding loss can be really traumatizing.

We will talk more in depth about how trauma and grief overlap in chapter 5. I'd like for you to keep in mind as we journey forward together that enduring ambiguous loss will test your ability to withstand the persistent, ongoing grief experience. If you find this to be true for you, I want you to move at a slower pace if you feel overwhelmed or activated by the exercises and reflections in this book. Understanding together all the ways that ambiguous loss can occur in our lives can be overwhelming and inundating. Although I fully believe in the power of understanding our grief and loss to be able to navigate it, feeling more of a sense of agency over the experience, we are not in a rush— your well-being and self-care are my top priority.

A Special Note on Friendship Loss

A client once described to me that losing her best friend was worse than the day she asked her spouse for a divorce. This best friend started out as her neighbor and they grew closer over time. She told me she felt the loss of a confidante and a safe space for her to vent or trade memes on Fridays, confiding in her as her marriage began to fail. Worse, she said, the friend moved a short time later and the new neighbors mostly kept to themselves. She doesn't know if she and her former friend will ever reunite, but is feeling the grief fiercely. At times, losing a friend can feel harder than ending a romantic relationship because of the emotional intimacy between dear friends.

Friendships can be complicated at times. Needs and desires change as we grow and live a fuller life. Sometimes, the people around us aren't able to meet those needs, whether literally or emo-tionally. Sometimes, they have their own challenges. Those challenges can seep out in behavior, and sometimes in how they relate to us. Those shifts in friendship dynamics can cause people to grow apart, and that can hurt like hell. When these changes can't be fixed through two-way communication and connection, the loss can feel especially painful. Even then, though, no matter what others tell us or we tell ourselves, we haven't failed at anything.

Friendship loss in adulthood is common, but we still have a stigma around it, almost like we're still in high school, and people are pointing at the "weird" kid who doesn't appear to have any friends. My clients often say they feel ashamed of losing a friend, perceiving that it reflects negatively on them. Many of us feel unworthy when relationships grow distant or end because of poor behavior or incompatibility that was overlooked until, finally, it couldn't be any longer.

Though society doesn't (yet!) give the same weight or importance to friendships as it does to romantic relationships, the emotional intimacy, shared history, and long stretches of our lives we spend with our friends is undeniable. So *of course* the loss of that confidante, secret keeper, cheerleader, and everyday support system can feel crushing.

Disenfranchised Grief

Like we've talked about, there have been a lot of unspoken rules around grief—society loves to dictate how long we get to grieve or when it becomes too much, or how fast someone should "move on," but with disenfranchised grief, society takes their rules to a whole new level—this isn't about how we grieve, but about who has the *right* to grieve. In his groundbreaking book *Disenfranchised Grief: Recognizing Hidden Sorrow*, grief researcher Kenneth Doka explains that this kind of grief occurs "when [people] incur a loss that is not or cannot be openly acknowledged, socially sanctioned or publicly mourned."[2]

Communities and families will differ in their belief systems and what they deem as important and worthy of grieving over, so the kinds of losses that might engender disenfranchised grief vary widely. That said, some common examples are suicide, grieving an abortion, the grief of giving up a child for adoption, or losing custody of your children. Even losing a pet can be considered disenfranchised grief, because so many people minimize the powerful and loving bond we can have with our pet, and how at times, they are the only source of affection and love one may feel. Why does society get to dictate why these losses are important or not? All of our losses deserve to be publicly grieved and accepted.

What makes this type of grief so hard is that it's wholly dependent on the values of people around us and what they deem worthy of grieving over. Take, for example, the parent/s of a school shooter. We tend to point the finger or look at them in judgment, overlooking the fact that they, too, have lost a child: Even if that person survived the event, they may be incarcerated or, at a bare minimum, their sense of who their child is will be fundamentally different. Do they "deserve" to grieve, when their child caused so much harm and pain, and brought grief to so many others? These are tough issues of morality that we sometimes struggle with, but loss is loss, nonetheless. We don't get to choose whether or not someone is worthy of being missed and grieved.

Chris, a longtime client, lost his brother to suicide early in his life. It was never talked about in his small Midwestern town, or even within his family. People in his community would look down or away when they approached his family. It was a confusing and painful experience for Chris, who had to contend with the devastating loss of his brother, in addition to the loss of his friends and the family's close-knit community. Much to my own dismay, suicide is still continuously stigmatized. In some communities that judge death by suicide, grievers aren't allowed to have a proper burial and ritual, as the loss is clouded in supposed moral failing when it should be approached with sensitivity, tenderness, and love. Although Chris remained deeply affected by the loss of his brother, the accompanying shame and stigma poured salt in the wounds of a kid who just wanted some comfort and safety.

At the root of disenfranchised grief is marginalization, or social exclusion. And sadly, being excluded is hardly a new experience for so many people around the world, both historically and today (hello, sexism, racism, ageism, homophobia, transphobia, ableism, psychological, political, and economic marginalization, I'm looking at you all here!).

A particularly painful kind of marginalization happens when the person grieving is not recognized as a griever. In other words, your relationship to someone lost doesn't appear close enough for you to feel grief. For example, maybe you're grieving the death of an ex-partner or colleague from a previous job, or someone who you wouldn't be able to grieve openly because of what it may reveal about you, such as the end of an affair. Grieving a celebrity death, like Prince or Robin Williams, also falls into this category since, by definition, grievers do not have personal contact with those figures.

The defining factor in whether you are experiencing disenfranchised grief is whether your community and family systems are accepting of your loss or not. The more open and accepting a community is, the better able they are to validate your loss as "legitimate" and, therefore, give you the comfort and support you need to grieve and begin the healing process.

There are far too many instances where someone's loss experience has been ignored, dismissed, or minimized. It does far more psychological damage than we could qualify here, as it is invalidating one's most basic human experience. If you are experiencing disenfranchised grief, please know that the loss you are grieving is real. The pain of feeling unseen or outright dismissed is cruel; know that I see you and you can learn to honor your grief for yourself, regardless of what anyone else says.

Even if you yourself have not endured the experience of disenfranchised grief, understanding it could help you look differently at people and communities around you and perhaps bring about the opportunity for deeper empathy and connectedness. No one should ever have power over how we grieve or what is worthy of being grieved. I hope we can do better for all people suffering through loss so that none feel alone and shamed.

Secondary or Cumulative Loss

Many times, a loss we experience has a domino effect. The dominoes that fall after the first? Those are the *secondary losses*. For example, let's say that you got a divorce. Whether this feels like freedom or like hell, you likely don't live in the same home you used to. You may have lost some friends in the shuffle, along with the rituals or traditions you shared with a spouse. If you have children, you're likely sharing custody. Maybe your spouse kept the dog, or you're grieving the comfortable dip in that one cushion of your old couch. The first loss triggers a cascade of others and, as pieces of life shift and change, for some, they can fall hard. And they can be shocking. Those additional pieces are the secondary losses, and they can really pile up. This is why I will be telling you *a lot* to tend to your body, your heart, and your needs. Grief can be such a shock to the system, and when we begin to learn more about how losses can lead to more losses, it can be pretty overwhelming. Sometimes, what we are left with after multiple losses are huge gaping holes.

These holes in life are often painful, fracturing our lives in ways we can't always foresee. They are also not typically things that people around us will recognize as layers of our suffering. How could they, really? It's hard enough to get people to acknowledge and validate a primary loss. Sadly, there aren't going to be texts pouring in to acknowledge your loss of identity after being laid off from your dream job, or the sense of being needed when your kid leaves for college. When my client Jenny lost her partner Kenzie, she lost the person who paid the household bills (she didn't even know the passwords to the accounts!), and she lost the person she'd vent to after work, the person who would remind her to light the Sabbath candles at sundown every Friday even though Kenzie wasn't Jewish. These secondary losses would show up and seemingly pile onto the loss of Kenzie, which was already so overwhelming to Jenny. For the first six months after her loss, Jenny would come to therapy telling me she felt like she stepped on a new land mine every week, because there was always something else to grieve that was connected to Kenzie or their life together.

Secondary losses can show up at any time after your loss, which is part of what can feel so disorienting about them. Naturally, every loss is unique and so the way that secondary losses will show up is going to be very different for everyone, but I want you to know that, even though it may be a "secondary" loss, that doesn't mean you aren't entitled to grieve. These compounding losses can be incredibly overwhelming and deserve the same support and care as they come up for you.

Let's Check In: Feeling the Weight of Secondary Losses

That was a lot of heavy information coming at you. Learning about new types of loss can open up a proverbial can of grief worms. Let's take a moment together—hand on your heart, deep breath in...and slow exhale out...How are you feeling right now? While understanding and awareness are critical first steps on our healing journey, talking about these different types of grief can feel really hard, and may be just too overwhelming at times. That's okay. Take a break if you need to, go get a glass of water, take a walk, text a friend, or do whatever you need to tend to your heart and body.

The Many Layers of Grief

One of the invisible, insidious realities of grief is its many layers. Humans are really complicated! Loss may invariably feel like peeling an onion, revealing all of the nuances within. The layers reveal our lived experience before grief and all that our loss has left in its wake. This can look like secrets of an affair or lies long hidden coming to the surface after a spouse has died. Or a twin losing their other half, having lived a nearly mirrored life for many years. Layers of grief reveal the vicissitudes of our connections and their complexities therein. We linger in the nuance of the dynamics and patterns and only we can ever fully see, understand, or appreciate the imprint of what is left upon us in the wake of loss. Good, bad, our choice, or not—we live and lose, and all of those losses, their layers, and ripple effects deserve to be seen and understood so that we can grieve fully, and take the steps toward healing.

Sudden identity shifts can be particularly hard to reconcile, leaving us with questions we can't immediately answer: *Who am I without this job/relationship/title/home/etc.? What does my life look and feel like, both to me and to others, when I'm not CEO/spouse/best friend/marathon runner/parent/etc.?* Questions like these flow with abandon, but their answers are much harder to come by. We are forced to redefine, reimagine, rebuild, or release parts of our lives and ourselves. It all takes time, obviously, but first we need to do what many of us have been taught *not* to do—pause, in whatever ways we can, and allow ourselves to feel, to grieve the loss and its many layers, *including those that don't seem connected to the reason you picked up this book.* By acknowledging these unhealed parts of our abandoned grief, we can gain a deeper understanding that leads us toward healing rather than away from ourselves.

When Grief's Ripple Effects Multiply

When Shira first appeared on-screen, she was brushing her long brown hair and applying lip gloss in her camera. I smiled patiently, amused by this beginning to our first encounter. This sort of moment happens often over virtual therapy sessions. While in the midst of their lives, people haphazardly rush onto our video call, not yet done with whatever they were just doing. More often than not, these small moments make me miss the "old" days when I'd open my office door and see a client waiting patiently for their session, having spent a little time in the quiet of the waiting room. Then, by the time they'd sit on the couch, the calm would have already washed over them from their commute and the outside world, and our work could begin in earnest.

From our intake call, I knew she was battling a lot of anxiety. The torrent of words was still prominent in my mind, but the call had given me very limited information about what Shira needed or what she was looking for (two very different things in therapy).

It didn't take long, though, to figure it out because Shira had made a list, which she promptly turned toward the camera for me to read.

Things to Talk with Gina About:

1. *Anxiety over state of world/money/wedding/going outside*
2. *Safta dying and no funeral*
3. *Lost my job—who am I now?*
4. *Nikki's bad behavior/losing friends*

Seeing the list, I immediately knew why she'd called me. She was experiencing an overwhelming amount of loss, whether or not she was conscious of that yet. "Wow. That's a list of really important things. Do you want to start at number one or with what's at the top of your mind?"

Shira pondered my question for a minute and said she wanted to talk about losing her grandmother. All of the items on her list were important, but the loss of her grandmother felt particularly salient during a time of so much unexpected loss in the world. Her safta ("grandmother" in Hebrew) caught the coronavirus in her assisted living home. She got very sick right away and went onto a ventilator for two weeks before passing. As Shira told me the story of her grandmother's death, her face clearly conveyed her pain.

"I didn't get to say goodbye. None of us really knew what was going on and all of a sudden, we got a call that she'd been placed on a vent. The nurses put us on a FaceTime call, but Safta wasn't conscious. A few days later, she was gone, and we obviously couldn't have a funeral, so we did a Zoom funeral and shiva. Super weird. Suddenly, I'd lost my grandmother and all the cultural things that are meant to help give closure or something just weren't there. And now, she won't even be at my wedding." Shira spoke stoically, but as she spoke, tears filled her eyes.

I respected how easily Shira could access her emotions and, wanting to capitalize on the moment, I asked more about the relationship and the last time she saw Safta. After exploring her losses more—the loss of her safta and the rituals that might have helped her feel some level of peace—I wanted to know whether she had another place or community where she might find comfort, looking to get the full scope of her support system during hard times.

"Well, that's a whole other story. I've been fighting with one of my best friends. I didn't even tell her my grandmother died." I wanted to inquire more about her grief over losing her grandmother, but Shira was ready to talk about something else. I never worry about missing information; there is always a time where the exchange circles back to important topics.

"Is the Nikki on your list the best friend you're fighting with?"

"Yeah. She'd been a good friend, but over the past year, she has had these weird outbursts. She gets really mad at me, and I can't figure out what she's actually mad at. She just huffs and puffs and starts to cry and walks away. The first few times, it was over stuff like having my music too loud while driving with her, but she somehow couldn't tell me it bothered her. I try to talk to her about it, but she says she just sometimes does that, it sometimes gets her into trouble, but she can't help it. So, it's my problem now, I guess. I get to either accept it or lose the friendship, but it just keeps happening and I don't know how to deal with it. And, it's hard, because last year, my other dear friend, Kara, and I ended our friendship. She was always making snide comments about my weight. Once she told me that I should get a rebounder, because her sister got one and it helped her lose weight. She legit couldn't figure out why I was so hurt. Why does a dear friend have to always talk about my weight?! I kept telling her it hurt me and embarrassed me. She tried to gaslight me every time I told her I was upset by saying she was upset, too. I asked her to elaborate on that, but she never really could."

Shira shook her head, but kept going. I sensed that she needed to vent and really get it all out. I welcome that approach—put it all in a pile in front of us and take out the things that feel most important or necessary at any given moment. As therapy goes on, we add to the pile, take things away, or put things to the side, but always having it all present there with us.

"So, I'm losing close friends and it really feels embarrassing to me. Who loses friends as an adult? Aren't we supposed to be able to talk things over and move on?! Ugh, it's a lot, sorry."

"It's a lot of loss and it's not about being an adult, but about wanting to have people in your life who feel safe and trustworthy. There is nothing wrong with that and yet, sometimes the people we think can be that, just aren't able to be. That's hard and it's sad, too," I said back, thinking about how little attention is given to friendships ending.

It took several sessions to touch upon each loss in Shira's list and we found we had still more layers to explore together. For Shira, the pandemic kicked up some old relationship wounds, and left her wondering if she was marrying the right guy. The self-doubt kicked up some ancient grief, like the estrangement of her brother over the last four years. This played a role in her feelings of loss and abandonment and warranted significant attention on its own—the loss of her livelihood, as well as the ability to celebrate her wedding with her family—all of which made her other losses feel more devastating and harder to manage. Within a short period of time, her identity in the world had been severely shaken, leaving her feeling lonely and disoriented. All of that was then piled on top of the recent loss of her grandmother. Shira was seriously dealing with a lot of grief.

The more we explored together, the more losses we named. The more we named, the more we could move through together. The more we moved, the more she healed. See where I'm going with this? The way we begin to heal isn't by ignoring or invalidating our losses, but rather by seeing them fully, and acknowledging all the pain we carry—even and perhaps especially ones we didn't know were weighing us down.

The Power of Naming Our Grief

If you were a person on the planet in 2020, I guarantee that you've already experienced different types of non-death loss. Every single one of us lost feelings of safety around leaving our homes, being near other people, giving and receiving affection, and plans for the immediate future, as well as doing things that had always seemed relatively basic: shopping for groceries, going to theaters and restaurants, traveling, and on and on. The certainty of employment, too, as well as feelings of trust in our external surroundings were all abruptly stripped away, with little warning. For weeks that rolled into years, grief cloaked in our "new normal" spanned the globe in intricately woven layers. *No one was spared.* Loss infiltrated the most joyous occasions—college graduations, high school proms, engagements, weddings, and births all included. Loss itself wasn't spared, as in-person funerals were rerouted to the nearest server for online viewing only. Life as we'd known it had come to a screeching halt. Human existence—how to navigate it safely—was in a state of limbo. Terror and grief became common, everyday experiences.

Knowing all this, I want you to take a moment to make your own list, like Shira did. Imagine we're going to have a session. What would you want to talk about? What's bothering you right now? What feels hard? What would you want to talk about? What *wouldn't* you want to talk about? Write it all down.

To help get you started, you might consider the following list of losses, which are listed in no particular order. Notice if any stand out to you, and feel free to circle them so you can keep them in mind as you progress through these pages. As always, feel free to add your own, too. I want you to hold on to these in your mind as we learn more and process our grief together throughout these pages.

- Life transitions (e.g., parenthood, retirement, relationship status)
- Fertility challenges
- Divorce/separation
- Breakups
- Rejection of all kinds
- Chronic sorrow (associated with chronic illness and caregiving)
- Loss of friendships
- Loss of intimacy/affection
- Loss of livelihood
- Loss of home/moving
- Loss of purpose
- Loss of spiritual community
- Loss of resources
- Loss of time passing
- Loss of an identity
- Loss of hope

- Loss of health/mobility or chronic illness
- Loss of what could have been (potential)
- Loss of security and safety
- Loss of rituals (e.g., during COVID)
- Loss of parent/relative/friend to estrangement/dementia/ imprisonment

As you can see, there are so many ways we lose in our lives. Sometimes, more than we can really hold in our consciousness. It can feel like around every corner is another opportunity to lose someone or something dear to us. Grieving is hard even when we know what we have lost. Reading this chapter may have opened you up to seeing ways you have experienced grief, perhaps without knowing that it was grief. Like, "Oh, man, that was a loss, too, that I didn't realize or consciously grieve." That could feel like a lot, I know. If you learned something new in this chapter about your life and relationship to loss, I want you to carry it with you as we navigate how grief shows up for us—body and mind.

A little at a time, we will continue to explore together experiences you may have had that could affect the way you interact, avoid, or engage with your grief as it comes up. I want for us to learn how to allow our grief to be present, in all its forms and iterations, and use it as a way to get closer with ourselves and our sense of grief's place in our lives as we move forward toward healing.

CHAPTER 3

The Freedom to Feel
What You Feel

"Our feelings are our most genuine paths to knowledge."

—Audre Lorde

Want to know something that seems obvious, but isn't? No one really knows how to grieve. As author Francis Weller so aptly describes, grief can show up as "wild and untamed," and be relentless in the "riotous ways"[1] it can take hold of us, yet most of us just don't know how to let that grief express itself with such abandon.

With grief, there's no script, no recipe, and no instruction manual. From one moment to the next, one day to the next, it's always changing. By the time we get the hang of one feeling, it goes and morphs into something else, because, well, that's what feelings do. Honestly, that alone can be so disorienting. But grief is a lived experience that we have to engage with in all of its sticky rawness. Trying to ignore it is futile. Trying to skip it is futile. No matter how fast you run away, how determined you are to avoid grief, it will inevitably outrun you. (Sorry.)

For months after my mother's death, I told myself that I shouldn't need to grieve for too long because, for starters, it wasn't like it was a surprise and also because I was a professional therapist working on a daily basis with loss in my clinical work. But finally, the jig was up. I leaned into the emotions that flowed in, allowing whatever I needed to experience to come in for a cup of tea, and sometimes, lunch. They were not always good houseguests, often overstaying their welcome and leaving a mess in their wake. We had beautiful conversations, my grief and I, but it was painful and lonely at times. No one can ever really understand our individual experience of our loss, and that can feel isolating.

Over time, I came to understand what she—my grief—was looking for: tenderness, attention, space to be present. To step into the experience as best I could and allow what came up to simply *be*. My grief slowed me down and reminded me of the deep commitment and love I had for my mom, whom I missed desperately. It also reminded me of all the losses that came along with losing her.

I was at lunch with a dear friend one afternoon at an Upper West Side local favorite, French Roast, and as she asked me about the details of my mom's final days, I felt the tears swell up with such force that there was no way I could stop them. I sobbed, right there at the table. I have no idea why *that* was the defining moment that brought home for me that I had emotions that needed to be felt, but apparently, I was ready. *It felt so good to let. It. Out. To feel.* My grief finally needed me to slow down; it was time to go all in.

I went home that evening, cooked a dinner my mom would have loved, and made myself a "she went and died" playlist. Singing, and music in general, has always helped me connect with my emotions, hitting a place inside me that unlocks the gates and allows my feelings to flow. I was back to healing through music in that moment, it seemed. I appointed Sara Bareilles and Brandi Carlile "Patron Saints" of my mourning as, over and over again, their songs yanked me beyond my griefall and into the full force of my emotions. Singing along with them felt like I was connecting to my emotions in a way that I could only describe as a spiritual experience. It took time and making room for the many emotions that came to the surface, but eventually, I landed from that free fall, and, better yet, discovered I wasn't destroyed by the emotional outpouring, even if it was a bit touch and go.

The period after a griefall can feel like being trapped inside a snow globe that's grown dark and ominous. Even when we're grieving alongside others, no one feels what we do, how we do, when we do. We are each trapped inside our own griefscape right when it feels the most painful and exhausting. Most of us would do anything to break the glass and escape. But in that snow globe we're doing the hard work of cozying on up to the feelings that are trapped in there with us. The path that goes from the initial griefall to active grieving is the shift from shock to allowing for our feelings to come up and be seen.

The grief work ahead can be really uncomfortable, inconvenient, painful, and an often confusing task of feeling our feelings fully. As always, you don't have to go it alone, so we're going to talk about some of the reasons we don't feel our feelings, how our feelings manifest themselves to us in our grief, and look at some ways we can validate our own emotional truth.

Permission *Not* to Grieve

By the way, I want to say this right off the bat: I know I just went on a whole tear about how important it is to get in there and start feeling your feelings, but you have permission *not* to grieve, too. Well, not right now anyhow. There's a misconception that you have to grieve someone or something directly following the loss. That's nonsense. It comes when it comes. You may be busy making funeral arrangements, dealing with insurance claims, writing thank-you notes, raising kids, caretaking, having to get back to work, coping with a flare-up of a chronic illness, or maybe you're utterly exhausted from the too-muchness of it all. You may also not be in a place where you feel safe enough to fully embody your feelings. It may feel too dangerous to be fully present to your loss. And, it can be really scary, too.

I feel you. We've all been there in this place where the feelings wear you down, where you're too bombarded with life. Or your own emotions. Or physical symptoms. Confronting hard feelings with honesty isn't a walk in the park, and you get to go at your own pace. Sometimes that wild abandon of grief...is simply going to bed.

Particularly when we are in survival mode or are emotionally burnt out, shut down, or disconnected, our grieving process may become delayed. This is okay. Sometimes we may be in shock, or not have any social or emotional support; sometimes we may feel very unsafe or just not have the capacity to engage with our grief. I have had clients come to see me many years after a loss for grief work, as it is the first time since their loss that they are able to process the experience. If your grief is not present for you, don't push it. Don't force it, and don't pressure yourself to feel vulnerable when it is not the time, place, or circumstance. Remember that your safety comes first.

If this is you, take a step back and tend to what needs tending to in the moment. It's okay to put a pin in the grief in order to deal with what's in front of you. The grief will be there when you're ready.

Permission to Feel

Let's talk more about feeling the things...Perhaps the only universal truth about grief is that *eventually* we each must allow ourselves to feel whatever comes up. It's harder than it sounds; after all, who wants to wallow in pain? Who wants to surrender to the agony of loss and its deep, seemingly endless torment? Not many, I imagine, but this is exactly what we each must do and surrender to our emotions.

Emotions like: sadness, fear, anger, rage, devastation, overwhelm, nostalgia, wistfulness, relief, shame, guilt, distress, confusion, fatigue, remorse, panic, loneliness, heartbrokenness, disappointment, and peace. You may find yourself feeling exhaustion in all ways, worn out, anxious, stressed, worried, tense, frustrated, empty, numb, or sensitive to noise, bright lights, and crowds. You may feel less patient, tearful, weepy, waily, or absolutely withdrawn. It may feel shocking and like some out-of-body experience.

So, bearing that in mind, I want to say something loud and clear for you: Even as we go through "healing" activities and exercises intended to help you move forward with your grief, you are absolutely allowed (and expected) to feel however and whatever you feel at any given time indefinitely. Even if it's numbness. Even if someone tells you other-wise. Hell, even if *you* think otherwise. This isn't an endeavor for the mind, it's a journey of the heart. That sounds simplistic and cheesy, I know, but it's true. We cannot intellectualize our way out of or around grief—trust me, I tried! In the end, grief is always smarter than we are. We cannot deny our emotional needs for long without them banging against the walls of our whole being, calling out louder and louder to be heard in some way.

When we least expect it, a scent, song, memory, or event may yank us down a long, dark rabbit hole of sadness or longing or anger, shame, guilt, or regret—or perhaps several of these at once. Other seemingly random moments may inspire laughter and joy over the beautiful and funny moments that suddenly come alive inside us.

Of course, feeling our feels isn't a given for many people. Some-times, it can feel downright impossible to express what we feel. It can be so terrifying at times, too. Feelings signal something important to us. We will feel fear if our emotional or physical safety is threatened, sadness with the loss of someone or something significant to us. We feel anger in the face of injustice or mistreatment, guilt when we may have harmed others. If we reflexively move away from feelings, we will miss something meaningful that needs attending to.

Whether having endured traumas of all types, interpersonal rup-tures, loss upon loss, or various mental health challenges, your feelings matter, but there will be times we may not want to or feel safe enough to feel our feelings. For example:

- You may not have learned the temporary nature of emotions and that they don't last forever, and that you will survive them.
- Your parent/caregiver demanded you stop crying or expressing emotions when you were hurt, frustrated, or sad (or really any negative emotion).
- You were not modeled on how to feel painful emotions so didn't know what to do with them when they came up for you.
- You were taught that only weak people show sadness or fear.
- You were taught that feeling emotions won't "fix" anything and therefore is not useful.
- You feel afraid that if you begin to cry to express emotion, you may never stop.
- You picked up that if feeling certain emotions is unacceptable, then feeling them may make *you* unacceptable.

Did any of these ring true for you? Are any of them the reason you may be having trouble expressing your emotions around your loss? Sometimes, we aren't sure anyone cares about how we feel, or we were taught that our feelings were not welcome. But our feelings are a part of us, a part of our life experience as humans, and no matter what we learned or picked up along the way, they are important.

The goal is to allow whatever comes forward to ebb and flow into and through us without apology, censoring, or judgment. Our feelings, however challenging at times, are ultimately our guide, slowly but surely leading us back to the light of day. There is no right way to feel, and there aren't shortcuts. As we move forward together, I hope you can grant yourself the permission to feel without preconceived ideas of what your grief experience is supposed to look like. The path to emotional expression might be a little bumpy, but I want you to go at your own pace and respect whatever comes.

From Griefall to Grieving

"I don't even know how I am supposed to feel," Liv said, seeming exasperated as she took her sunglasses off and headed to the couch. "Like, I'm tired, I'm sad, I'm tired again. I am sad again. I cry a lot and then I have no tears. Is this even normal? I feel crazy!" I'd been seeing Liv for over a year when she lost her dad. She'd originally come to see me following a turbulent breakup and subsequent cross-country move to start law school in New York. She was fragile at the start of our work together, often arriving in tears that she'd try to hide behind dark sunglasses. When she'd take them off, I'd see a weary, emotionally spent young woman who was also courageous and determined. She always showed up and had an earnest eagerness to learn about herself following her breakup, even the dark, sticky stuff most people prefer to avoid. For better or worse at times, she'd say, she wanted to feel better for the long haul and knew she'd adopted some patterns she needed to change. We worked hard on those patterns for nearly six months.

Then one day she called me to tell me that her father had just died, a few days before her next scheduled session. During our call, she was all about scheduling and practical details until I finally asked if she felt like she could talk about what was going on inside of her. She went silent for a while. I thought we'd lost our phone connection until I heard her breathing.

Therapists have to be artful with communication—*when and how we speak*—especially since interrupting a silent moment may prevent a volcanic expression of emotion that could be beneficial to the work. Hearing her breathe, I stayed silent and present along with her, giving her space to fill if and when she felt ready.

When she finally did speak, she told me she was fine. I sighed internally even though it was the response I was expecting.

When she next entered my office, she closed the door behind her and grabbed the oversized pillow on the couch. "I got the tickets back home to LA, so I will leave tonight. I don't know what to expect when I get there. I talked to my mom over FaceTime on the way over and she told me to stop crying, because I looked like Kim Kardashian. What the fuck, Mom?!"

"Hey, she's comparing you to the most famous person on the planet!" By that point in our work together, I knew that levity was a comfortable way to ease into our session and relax her into sharing more. She laughed, relaxing her body and loosening her death grip on the pillow a little.

While Liv had always enjoyed an easy closeness with her dad, she and her mom had had a tumultuous relationship for as long as Liv could remember. Her mother's pressure to always be "fine" and to perform and be at the top of her game or class had pushed Liv into ongoing cycles of anxiety and depression. She struggled to trust in her inherent worthiness, which messed with her sense of security in relationships. She made bold decisions, but often in order to *run away* from something or someone than to *run toward* herself or her desires.

For so much of her life, Liv had made sure to keep herself busy. At first it was something her mother had done for her to help her become more "well-rounded," but over time Liv had adopted it for herself. Being in constant motion had the benefit of producing external results while also helping her avoid the painful emotions that tried to reveal themselves in the empty spaces of her quiet moments. I see this with clients fairly often, and, of course, I had also experienced it myself after losing my mother. For so many people, this might feel familiar. Feeling like there is a hamster wheel and if we step off, our entire world may come crashing down, so we keep moving, keep the wheel spinning, thinking it will keep us safe from the big, bad emotions that threaten to overtake us.

On several occasions, Liv had mentioned that she didn't know the first thing about grief or grieving. She said she'd never experienced it before her father's death. I always found it curious that no matter how much we spoke of losses in her life, she didn't seem to allow the grief experience to be acknowledged, let alone felt in any way. She had lost Milo, a beloved golden retriever, whom she spoke of incessantly with tears in her eyes. She had been through a terrible breakup with a guy she'd thought she'd marry. In her younger years, she'd lost all four grandparents. She'd been too small to remember three of them, she'd told me, but was close to her poppy, about whom she retold many joyful memories. When I asked her if she could remember back to how it had felt to lose her poppy, she didn't take the bait. Instead, she said that at the time she never experienced losing him as grief, at least not exactly. And so there it was—loss without recognition of experiencing loss.

Liv is not alone in this. At times, there may be no obvious intuitive leap within us that points the arrow from grief to grieving, so giving permission to feel whatever we feel may seem inauthentic and confusing. I get that. The thing is, grief can show up in lots of different feelings and experiences that don't necessarily always feel *griefy*.

How Our Emotions Can Show Up in Grief

Emotions are fundamental to being human, but it can be so hard to connect with them in times they feel the absolute biggest! Identifying our feelings and experiences can feel tricky, especially if we aren't used to doing that. Sometimes, journaling can help for those who aren't in a grief support group or therapy. It can feel really hard to distinguish what we feel when we feel *so damn much*. Let's look at some emotions right here and now together. Getting back to basics and seeing feelings pointed out can help you to connect with one if you're having a hard time.

But that doesn't mean feeling is easy. It's exhausting. It's terrifying.

At times it's so anger-inducing, it takes everything from us. I get it. It's a game of grief roulette where life keeps you guessing, *What version of my grief am I going to get this time?!* Are you going to wake up with heaviness so burdensome you can't imagine getting out of bed? Are you ruminating while sitting at your desk over all the details of your loss and the things you wish were different? Are you mindlessly scrolling social media looking for something that "speaks to you" to get a second of relief or connection? Are you walking throughout the day rageful over the fact that this loss happened and it wasn't fair or right?

Yet here I am, gently nudging you to let yourself go there as long as you can tolerate it. To let your emotions have their space and their time. Even if that time is inconvenient or embarrassing because it's at a friend's birthday party or while in line at the grocery store. What matters most is not indefinitely stifling the emotions that are calling to be let out and seen—even though we can't know what they will bring. That's true courage right there. And, what's also necessary? Taking a breather from the heaviness of your grief. Taking a break and allowing in distractions so that you can refill that internal endurance meter again. Sometimes, it will feel as though you are ping-ponging between feeling what you need to feel and also taking a breather and streaming Netflix shows. All of that is common. The goal is simply to allow, recognize, and affirm your own unique experience—however it shows up in any given moment.

Grieving takes so much out of us, and we are going to spend a lot of time here talking about all the ways that might be for you, and all the ways your own sense of boundaries and self-care will be needed at your side nearly indefinitely. Giving your feelings and grief experiences space and time will be necessary—even the ugly and uncomfortable moments where it all feels complicated and painful. Remember, this is YOUR grief, and you are allowed to process, feel, and experience it in your own time, and in your own way.

Let's Check In: Becoming More Aware of Our Personal Grief Experience

So, this is all pretty heavy. Can we check in? If you feel safe where you are, I ask that you close your eyes and put your hand over your heart. Take a deep breath in and exhale it out hard.

Do it again and add a vocal sigh if it feels right to you.

Does anything come up?

What sensations or emotions can you notice?

Maybe you can feel your heart beating—is it pounding or beating quickly?

Maybe you notice any stress you're holding in your body, and I ask that you just notice it and see if it lessens just with your awareness.

Maybe you feel a strong emotion just at the threshold of wanting to come up and be felt and expressed.

I want you to ask yourself these questions:

What do I need to feel that I may not have felt or let myself feel around my loss(es)?

What do I need to tune in to in my emotional world and just allow it to be there without trying to fix it?

These questions are not to force your feelings out, but to simply allow them to be felt and validated.

For as long as you feel able, allow the feelings to rise. This can be just by either keeping your hand on your heart while you breathe or putting your arms around yourself like a hug or whatever feels most comfortable to you as the feelings run their course. If you feel overwhelmed, I want you to open your eyes, look around at where you are, feel your feet on the ground, and take a deep box breath (inhale, hold, exhale, and hold for four counts each), to regain a sense of calm and groundedness.

Being Gentle with Ourselves

When we try to build a dam in the waters of our grief, it doesn't permanently stop the feelings from coming over the precipice. What happens is that the waters rise and fall according to life's reminders and stressors, as well as the memories that are activated, bringing you back to the shore of your loss. And some days, *you're gonna need a bigger boat*.

As we have talked about in earlier chapters, grief manifests emotionally and in the body. Both of those experiences can happen separately or simultaneously, and it can feel unbearable at times. When we don't accept our feelings and experiences as they are, our internal self-compassion muscle atrophies and it becomes easier to fall into the dark abyss of depression. This is why you will hear me continue to remind you that it's not only *okay* to feel what you feel, but that when you can, you simply *must*.

Your feelings will contradict one another at times. Let them. *Grief is the gray area*. It isn't always one or the other. It can be two or more experiences occurring at once. Your only job is to notice and allow for what comes up, including when it arrives with a wellspring of seemingly never-ending tears.

If you are experiencing any of these emotional symptoms below, please know that it is completely normal for them to come and go or to stick around for a long while. They may shift as quickly as a few different times in a day. Also normal.

Even with self-compassion and new understanding, you may feel sadness, irritability, confusion, anger, rage, tearfulness, detachment, numbness, anxiety, the inability to concentrate, listlessness, and a feeling that life is no longer worthwhile. You may also feel an inexplicable sense of dread of so many things—the future, the future without your person, the uncertainty, the practical things that have to happen, or just an all-encompassing, nebulous feeling of dread.

During the periods when your feelings and physical sensations are more overwhelming, I want you to imagine shrinking your world down so you only have to concentrate on a few things:

1. *Your basic survival, like feeding and watering yourself, and getting as much physical rest (and movement) as you need; even if it feels sleepless, at least your body is resting (if resting causes more anxiety, we will visit ways to ground and center your body in chapter 10).*
2. *Asking yourself what you need at any given moment and then asking for help in getting those needs met if you cannot easily meet them yourself.*
3. *Paying close attention to your boundaries. Hit pause on whatever feels like too much and check in with your mood and body to see what you can and cannot commit to.*

When we're in grief's foreign landscape, it's important that we hold on to something that feels anchoring. We will talk about more ways to "anchor" and what that looks like a little later in the book, but these three things are a way to care for yourself when it all feels like too much. It's okay if you feel too tired to get out your toolbox and do "grief work." Some days, it's going to be more than enough that you drink water, try to eat something nutritious, and take a nap.

If you were my best friend and you were going through a major loss, I'd sit with you and tell you to be tender with yourself. I'd tell you to write on Post-it notes and put them all around your house. Little notes that would remind you when you are overwhelmed and exhausted that you don't have to rush, that you don't have to force yourself to feel the feelings all at once, that you are allowed to have boundaries to protect your feelings, and well, that you're not alone in this. Grieving can make us feel like we are so far removed from the rest of the world and our life that it can take time to reacclimate to our surroundings.

Offer yourself gentleness. You and your grief are worthy of that tender care.

Allowing Our Grief to Be ... Whatever It Is

When Liv came back to New York and returned to therapy, there was a noticeable shift in her demeanor. She was warm, as always, but now there was a distance in her eyes. She settled on the couch, but in a different spot than before, a little farther away from me.

Hmm.

I have a terrifically shitty poker face, so I got straight to the point. "I'm happy to see you ... and I can't help but notice you're farther away than usual."

"Ah, I don't know. I guess I don't wanna be seen today. I didn't mention it on the phone, but the trip was a total shit show. My mother was playing hallway monitor for our feelings. Legit, we couldn't cry in front of her or she'd lose it. But she made some good points when I tried to call her out. And I agreed with most of it."

"Care to elaborate?" I don't tend to agree with anyone overseeing the emotions of another person, so I was thoroughly curious about what had shifted in Liv, and why.

"I ran away to New York. I didn't go back often to see my dad and I wasn't the best daughter. Or like, as good as maybe I thought I was. There's absolutely no reason I should be crying hysterically or getting all emo right now. Anyhow, I'm fine. I think she's right, my mom. I could have been a better daughter and crying about it now isn't gonna bring him back."

I felt like I was speaking with a body snatcher. The Liv who had been in my office before her father's funeral wouldn't have even said that, let alone have believed it. Then again, grief is so deeply unsettling that it can bring out new and different self-doubting dialogues. Liv's mom had evidently barged into that exposed and tender place, convincing her daughter to tamp down her true feelings because she was a "bad daughter."

"Do you really believe all of that?" She nodded, staring at the rug below. Then, she looked up and met my eyes. I could tell she was trying not to cry, her hands squeezing into tight fists as her nose scrunched up. I held up my hands to give her some options to choose from. "So, are you trying to not feel the feelings because they hurt or are you trying not to feel the feelings because you now feel ashamed about having the feelings?"

She chose door number 2: being gaslit and shamed into believing she didn't "deserve" to feel what she felt. My heart filled with empathy for her.

While being overwhelmed by loss, we're often confronted by our core emotional wounds, whether from childhood or previous trauma. For Liv that core wound was shame around her vulnerability and emotions, a debilitating lesson that was likely instilled in her from a young age by her mother. These kinds of emotional double whammies, like feeling grief and feeling shame for feeling such powerful grief, are incredibly confusing and painful and have a nasty habit of showing up at the worst possible time, but it's just a small example of the ripple effect of loss, and the secondary losses it brings in its wake.

After listening to her mother berate her for feeling sad, Liv now felt her only option was to beat everyone to the punch and deny, dismiss, and shove down her feelings. It's what she'd been taught to do and how she'd been expected to behave. Spending time with her mother had reminded her of all that.

When Liv finally began to cry, I felt heartened. However messy, her emotions could finally get the time and space they deserved. But then she stopped crying mid-sob, haunted anew by her shame. "I can't believe I'm crying like this. Ugh. I can't stand it when I cry. It's not like it does any good anyhow. I'm sorry, Gina. I didn't mean to use up all your tissues, now the next poor soul is gonna have to use their shirt."

Can I be real for a minute? I hate when people "should" their emotions. I will say this again because it bears a *lot* of repeating: You are allowed to feel whatever you feel. Period. We can't manufacture emotions based on what we "should" and "shouldn't" be feeling. That's not how feelings work. There's a difference between not having access to the feelings and not *allowing* them to come up. Feeling genuinely disconnected from your emotions after a significant loss is a survival response that protects you from potentially overwhelming feelings. We will get into those coping rhythms more in a later chapter but for right now, I want you to know that it's completely okay to experience a disconnect if that's what you're experiencing. Feelings will come and go, they will shift and morph, and they will vary in their intensity of expression. This is grief. My request? Just allow whatever you feel safe enough to come up, to come up.

Checking to See If the "Gaslight" Is On

Gaslighting—manipulating ourselves or being manipulated by others into questioning our reality—is a painful but common part of grieving. From a young age, most of us are taught to plow through our feelings in order to get back to the business of living. With that sense of impatience, we can experience deep incongruence with the world at large when we're spinning inside our griefscape.

To be clear, there is no shame in gaslighting our emotions or experience. It's a way of protecting ourselves that's tied to our survival instinct. That's why so many of us, Liv included, have been taught to self-gaslight—to protect ourselves from our bigger, darker emotions. The problem is that when we continue believing that our feelings and experiences aren't really happening or don't deserve our time and attention, real mental health mayhem can ensue. Ultimately self-gaslighting leads us away from self-empowerment, healing, and health and wellness, not toward it.

Identifying and working on self-gaslighting allows us to look more deeply at our self-limiting views and what we permit (or don't) in our emotional landscape. This may seem like a lot of extra work, or even an unnecessary tangent, but it's a critical starting point for witnessing our own grief behavior patterns, needs, and personal nuances in a healthy, open, and curious way. Once we can do that, we can meet our grief where it is and work *with* it rather than against it.

That said, many of us do tend to question our feelings and grief experience at some point, especially when we feel out of control and emotionally "all over the place." Not everyone will experience gaslighting or even self-gaslighting. But I believe it's a worthy endeavor to discuss it further, as there is a difference between being genuinely unable to feel what we feel, and either consciously or unconsciously talking ourselves out of feeling the feelings. If you see yourself in some of the questions below, it's a good idea to just give space to the fact that we are always influenced by society and there are times when we may close off what we are feeling or experiencing to make others feel more at ease. It's always good to know when and with whom this happens, and more, if we are doing it to ourselves. Inevitably, within a grief experience, there will often be a healthy amount of confusion and self-questioning, so I want you to remember that none of this is pathological and the only goal is to recognize and bring to light all of the potential barriers to our being able to fully and honestly grieve as our body, mind, and heart need to.

A Gaslighting Disclaimer

Gaslighting often starts with a trusted adult who emotionally manipulates you into believing that you are *not* allowed to have valid emotional experiences of your own. That can be a hard pill to swallow if you have been unconsciously self-gaslighting your entire life. If someone close to you used gaslighting as an emotional abuse tactic with you from an early age, shedding these false self-narratives can be a daunting endeavor—and one that we will not tackle to completion in these pages. I hope, though, that by gaining self-awareness, you may begin to identify those old beliefs. Just like naming your grief, naming any belief is a powerful step toward owning and embodying your emotions. If at any point you feel triggered, I encourage you to pause and reach out to someone you trust rather than trying to travel this (sometimes rocky, even dangerous) path alone. Feeling safe and nurtured emotionally is critical when you're doing this kind of inner work. If you're feeling safe and ready to move forward, let's take this next step slowly. We are in no rush here.

So, how do you know if you're gaslighting your grief? Let's start by identifying common self-gaslighting scenarios. Take your time here, because I do want you to think of times in your life when you acted as if your experience wasn't important or valid.

1. Do you question your memories? Do you change them around to make yourself feel worse?
2. Do you make excuses for people who don't allow you, or haven't allowed you, to express your grief and emotions authentically?
3. Do you think or call yourself "crazy" for feeling what you feel or experiencing what you experience within your grief?
4. Do you think you're too sensitive and therefore disregard your emotions when they come up?
5. Have you in your life, in general, frequently discounted or invalidated your experiences or emotions?

If you nodded your head or saw yourself in some or all of these questions, you may have a hard time really allowing yourself to grieve fully and authentically. Inevitably within a grief experience, there will be a healthy amount of confusion and self-questioning, so I want you to remember that none of this is pathological and the only goal is to recognize and bring to light all of the potential barriers to our being able to fully and honestly grieve as our body, mind, and heart need to. Whatever your experience, it's all okay and welcome here.

Affirming Our Own Emotional Experience

Honoring ourselves and our feelings is a *practice*. Like meditation, gratitude, or yoga, it's not a one-and-done, and it's not something we learn to do overnight. Especially if we weren't given much room growing up to feel what we feel or express ourselves openly and honestly, this can be a challenging process. However you experienced being able to express yourself, I want you to know that in these pages, you are safe to experience and feel whatever it is that is authentically coming up for you—now or later. Some activities that have helped my clients shift into a place of emotional self-acceptance have been the addition of affirmations. Sure, they can seem cheesy to some people, but there is data that positive self-affirmations can help with negative self-doubting thoughts and replace them with a more adaptive, kind self-narrative. Numerous studies by psychologists and neuroscientists have concluded that affirmations have far-reaching benefits in soothing stress and helping to reset a negative self-talk pattern. These are all present at times within a grieving experience, as we tend to judge our experience. The key to the affirmations being effective? What we say in each statement needs to be authentic and particular to our present experience.

The self-affirming statements can help you to confront invalidating thoughts you may have been carrying around about your grief. It may feel overwhelming to think about this right now, or maybe it doesn't feel like the right time to affirm and validate yourself. Come back if that's the case. I'll remind you of this over and over again: You have every right to feel however you feel. Your feelings are not a problem to be solved. You have every right to grieve in your own unique way, for as long as you need to, because only *you* know the meaning of your loss.

The goal is to repeat affirmations to yourself (especially the ones that hit a deeper chord with you) and slowly internalize a more loving and accepting voice. It's okay if you aren't feeling that now or at other moments, but posting affirmations that resonate somewhere you can see them every day can be helpful over time. Even if you don't believe it right now, you're planting the seed. Now, as always, you are worthy of your tender loving care and acceptance. Let that truth grow until it breaks through the surface and feels the light of day.

Affirmations for Allowing Yourself to Feel How You Feel

1. I will allow whatever feelings come up to stay for as long as they need to *without* trying to eradicate or judge them.
2. No matter how I've been made to feel, I do *not* have to go through this hard time alone.
3. I will *not* judge my experiences or my responses to them in a negative light.
4. I am doing the best I can and I will be *gentle* with myself.
5. I will allow myself to do *self-nourishing* things *without questioning why*.
6. I will *not* insult myself or call myself names, especially when I am down.
7. My grief experience is *all mine*. It is *valid and worthy* of my own tenderness.
8. I will aim to understand my experience with the goal of *less pressure* and *more empathy* for myself.
9. I am allowed to honestly express myself and my painful emotions.
10. I am not "too much" and neither are my feelings.

Letting Our Emotions Breathe

Over the next few months of her therapy, Liv gave her emotions time and space a little bit at a time. She often came to our sessions wanting to talk about what had come up after our previous session. Her grief crescendoed at moments, filling her with all her love for her father and all the pain of his loss. She expressed anger and sadness and talked about missing her poppy and feeling his loss even more since losing her father. A loss piled on top of loss, she said. More buried emotion was being set free and she dared to grieve fully, honestly, and authentically.

"Now I get it... all you were ever talking about with allowing in the grief, but also grieving all the little losses that came with losing my dad. Including now, grieving the relationship with my mother that I always wanted, but never had. Damn, that is sad. But, I guess that means we start working on all of that, huh? It kind of feels like I have this whole new understanding of my relationships and why I am the way I am. Like, why do I deny myself my feelings?" That's where the work really begins.

໑

As we go through these chapters ahead, I want you to imagine that I am going slowly along with you. If at any time, processing, feeling, or allowing in the emotions feels unsafe or overwhelming, remember to take a step back, and a step away from the too-muchness of it. Though we'd all love to just *get it done already*, the act of healing can't bulldoze its way through our lives. There are no miraculous shortcuts and there is no single, magical epiphany that changes *everything*—not even the ones that are posted on IG, Facebook, or TikTok for all to witness.

Take the time you need to rest, distract yourself (in a safe way), or connect with supportive loved ones before you return to the experience, as it will be there waiting for you, trust me. As we move ahead, we are going to talk about how this grief experience affects your brain and body. It may feel like a lot of information, and I want to remind you to keep taking your time. Grieving isn't running a sprint, that's for sure. We need the strength and endurance to show up as best we can to what comes up for us.

Deep, emotional healing follows no deadline and recognizes no straight and narrow path. Therapy, or any healing path you may choose, must be allowed to wind and rewind, unfolding in its own time and according to its own unwieldy path.

Go gently; feel your feelings. That's truly the best you can do right now.

CHAPTER 4

My Body Was Calling, but I Was on "Do Not Disturb" (and Other Ways the Body Calls While Grieving)

"Learn to read symptoms not only as problems to be overcome but as messages to be heeded."
—Gabor Maté, *When the Body Says No: The Cost of Hidden Stress*

Grief is often viewed as an emotional response to loss, but let me not mince words here: Grief is a FULL-BODY EXPERIENCE. Our feelings aren't just our emotions, they are also our physical sensations. The two kinds of feelings are linked etymologically and quite literally through the mind-body connection, and grief has a habit of showing up emotionally *and* physically. In fact, without us even noticing, our bodies can start to bear the brunt of our grief experience. We don't sleep the same. We find we're struggling with inexplicable pain. Our muscles hurt. Our digestion is weird. We're getting headaches all the time, or can't seem to shake that cold. No part of the body is unaffected.

I'm so relieved that we have entered a time in our history where the mind-body connection is not up for debate and we can have serious conversations around keeping the body and mind healthy and in balance together, without it feeling like just another wellness trend.

I want to talk with you about some important ways that grief affects our body, so that you won't be totally freaked out (like I was) when the body begins to participate in your grief experience.

When I say that grief can *get on our nerves*, I kind of mean it literally. Scientists have demonstrated repeatedly that the vagus nerve, one of the longest cranial nerves that connects our brain to our body, is the body's information highway. It is a main tenet of the parasympathetic nervous system, and one of the most important functions of the vagus nerve is afferent, bringing information of the inner organs, such as gut, liver, heart, and lungs, to the brain.[1] The vagus nerve is connected to our emotions and mood, our gut health, heart health, and immune system— some of the most important things we need to function. I like to think of it as our air traffic controller, overseeing all the moving "planes" in the air and helping to keep everything moving safely as they should. If we tried to land all the planes at once, what do you think would happen? Thankfully, the vagus nerve is there to direct our body-mind traffic.

When I bring up the mind-body connection in sessions, so many people say they've heard of it, but aren't totally sure what the mind-body connection looks like when it comes to mental health, or they ask how it all works outside of just meditating. It's a good question!

Just like we learned to do for our emotions in chapter 3, in this chapter, our goal is to learn to be more fully present to our bodies and our physical experiences, giving ourselves permission to notice the symptoms and sensations that our bodies share. The goal of learning to tune in to what our bodies are saying is to move toward our bodies with more care and awareness. Ignoring our bodies' needs or calls for attention, rest, or nourishment will leave us depleted and potentially very ill. At the very least, by silencing or overlooking our physical experience, we prolong our suffering and close ourselves off to vital information about our grief process. In essence, I want you to be better than I was when I first lost my mom at learning how to connect the dots between your physical symptoms and all of your grief and really begin to listen to your body differently. This starts with becoming more aware of your body, how it talks to you, and more importantly, in having an honest, curious dialogue with your body in times of heightened stress by checking in with it.

Ignoring the Doorbell

For a while after losing my mother, I overlooked a critically important element of the grief journey—listening to what my body was trying to tell me. It seems painfully obvious now, but at the time I just wasn't able to listen. I knew I was experiencing uncomfortable painful symptoms, but the immense exhaustion and other various physical symptoms I was feeling could be easily dismissed as "stress," and I, like many grievers, was paying more attention to getting through each day than staying quiet long enough to hear my body's cries for help. It happens often with grief. After all, with so much emotional overwhelm dominating our psyche, moving through the world requires so much energy that factoring in the body's needs is simply too much to bear. I didn't have space for anything else, so I didn't answer the door. It just seemed easier. In hindsight, I think I subconsciously knew that heeding my body's message would also mean facing the one truth I still wanted to run away from: *I was never going to see my mother again.*

Our bodies are always listening, even when our hearts and minds are distracted or closed off. Thoughts, feelings, beliefs, and attitudes can positively or negatively affect biological functioning. If we don't pay attention to the ways in which the body is talking to us, we may find ourselves fighting illness, exhaustion, and mental health manifestations of our grief.

Where the Mind Meets the Body

The mind-body connection is the relationship between our thoughts and feelings, with our physical body. One can't really be healthy and balanced without the other. This also means that some physical symptoms we may experience can be attached to an emotional element in some way. The mind, with its thoughts and emotions, can greatly influence our bodies, and vice versa. Think about a time when you were nervous and had "butterflies" in your stomach or something emotional that made you "sick to your stomach." What's happening is that your brain is communicating to your stomach that it's nervous and on guard. Or a time you are anxious over something going on at work and you get a migraine or tense, tight muscles. This is the relationship between your mind and body at work. I don't know about you, but that connection for me is really, really strong!

Let's Get a Little Nerdy Together

Let's get more specific about how loss can affect our body. According to a research review conducted by Dr. Mary-Frances O'Connor in 2019 for the *Journal of Psychosomatic Medicine*, "in the past forty years, the field of psychosomatic medicine has investigated biomarkers that may help to explain the relationship between bereavement and medical outcomes, including mechanisms in autonomic (particularly cardiovascular), endocrine, and immune systems."[2] Basically, what we keep learning is that loss impacts our bodily systems at every level, from our heart to our hormones, even to how often we get sick.

With so much emerging research in the field of psychoneuroimmunology (a fancy term for the study of the effect of the mind on health and resistance to disease), more and more research is identifying that loss as a critical cause of chronic health conditions. I'd love to see the medical research community (hi!) bring this information forward to the masses, so that more and more people will be able to understand how their emotions manifest before they wind up suffering without a clue of what's happening or how to help themselves.

In looking deeper at this mind-body connection, we have all heard of "broken heart syndrome" (also known as takotsubo syndrome), which occurs when an *extreme* emotional or physical event triggers a weakening of the heart muscles. This can lead to a heart attack, heart failure, shock, long-term heart rhythm abnormalities, and changes in blood pressure.[3] All the more reason someone needs significant support after loss: The body holds on to so much of the stress losing someone significant to us brings. Even though we have so much with which to contend after loss, making sure we tend to our body is often the most overlooked, but most necessary.

Multiple studies have shown that grief increases inflammation in our body, which can lead to increased health challenges or the exacerbation of preexisting conditions. It can also lower our immune response, which makes us more susceptible to illness, as we may find ourselves more easily catching colds or being exhausted. In fact, with many of my clients, being physically exhausted and finding themselves down with a cold are the common manifestations of their grieving. There have been occasions where someone speaks of heart-related symptoms, like palpitations or chest pains, which I attribute to the anxiety they are experiencing.

More often than not, the physical stress of grieving will cause us to lose our sense of balance and coordination. Think of your own life right now—you may find yourself bumping into things or falling more easily than you ever had before. Maybe you bump into the corner of a wall, like I did so much after losing my mom. It's like, my body just couldn't seem to navigate the outside world! After a major loss, we don't seem to function in our bodies as smoothly as we used to. Even small daily tasks that we do every day become harder to maneuver. Our brain and our eyes don't coordinate the way they did before our loss. We get more colds, because now our immune system is weakened from the stress. We may get winded and exhausted much faster than we ever have—this is the way that grief can rearrange our entire being. In every case, I always recommend being in contact with a medical doctor to make sure these symptoms are not the result of a serious medical condition.

Learning the Body's Language

Although the manifestation of emotions in the body is not a new concept, many of us think of it with some distance—as in, it's real and it happens…but mostly to other people and at other times. The truth is that, especially during an intense time like grief, the mind-body connection can act as a powerful guide, proving repeatedly the old adage "What we resist, persists."

Our bodies are wise and they will speak to us through any means possible. Most times, the better we get at listening, the gentler the communications. But when we're used to ignoring or overriding its messages, the body starts to speak through symptoms that may bring real discomfort or pain, shouting louder and louder to get our attention. Rather than waiting for your body to produce a crisis that demands your attention, I want to encourage you to listen to what your body needs as often as you can.

Each of us may experience different symptoms and sensations, but most of us will feel at least *some* of the following symptoms at some point. As you look over this list, keep in mind that there are twelve systems that the body uses to function—nervous, respiratory, digestive, endocrine, urinary, musculoskeletal, cardiovascular, renal, reproductive, lymphatic, hematopoietic, and integumentary. That's a lot to keep track of, right? Thankfully, we have the vagus nerve keeping an eye on things for us, but, inevitably, when one is off, that imbalance causes an imbalance in other bodily systems. As a result, seemingly simple symptoms like pain or abnormal sensations are good reasons to seek out a medical practitioner.

How Grief Can Affect Your Body

Head/Brain	Headaches, dizziness, change in sex drive, sleep changes, change in light sensitivity, brain fog, racing mind, being flooded with stress hormones, changes in concentration and memory, as well as cognition
Heart/ Upper Abdomen	Increased risk for heart-related disorders, palpitations, weakened heart muscles, racing heart, shortness of breath
Stomach/ Gastrointestinal Tract	Diarrhea, constipation, stomach pains, nausea, increased or decreased hunger/appetite, bloating, or gas
Full-Body Immune System Responses	Generally weakened immune system, fatigue, increased adrenaline, increased neuroendocrine responses, such as elevated cortisol (stress hormone), weight changes, frequent colds, cold sweats/chills, body temperature changes, sexual changes, dehydration, dry mouth, pain in the areas your loved one once felt pain (i.e., phantom empathy pains)
Musculoskeletal Response	Muscle aches, joint pain, backaches, tightness in muscles around the body, neck pain, general physical tension in muscles
Nervous System Response	Anxiety, physical shaking, increased sensitivity to loud sounds or bright lights, vacillating between fight-or-flight stress response, exhaustion, disturbed sleep, loss of appetite or increased hunger, shortness of breath, racing heart, dissociation

A Reminder About Patience

Please, please be patient and kind with yourself if your physical well-being has not been something you've been able to tend to. You have a lot on your plate right now, and so much on your mind. There are no expectations that you were already supposed to know this or know how to tend to your body's needs during this surreal time in your life.

All we have to do is learn and do the next best, most loving thing that we can to take care of our body at any given moment.

If, as you get to know your physical symptoms better, you notice a change and/or you find yourself experiencing anything like the above, please contact your primary care physician. While these symptoms may be related to your grief, they are absolutely real, valid, and deserving of medical attention.

When Anxiety Shows Up at the Door

It feels like everyone is anxious these days, and perhaps justifiably so, given climate change and the state of the world. We often think of anxiety as a mental thing—worrying, or panic attacks—but anxiety is also a natural byproduct of grief. Our brains will search for our missing person, pet, or thing, according to Dr. Andrew Huberman, a neuroscientist and professor at Stanford University School of Medicine and host of the *Huberman Lab* podcast. This can toss us into a place of relentless renegotiating and unsettledness in trying to figure out where to place this person or thing within our reality.

Anxiety is a fear-based response that lives in our body. It's a survival feeling that has stored the sense of alarm in our body. When we lose someone or something major to us, our fear alerts go off and along with it come physical sensations. A lot of them. And often.

Anxiety is a physical survival response that brings with it sometimes unbearable physical symptoms, and within grief, it's somehow overlooked so easily. Few people equate grief with anxiety, because for so many, it seems like an Eeyore type of emotional experience only (sadness and low energy). But anxiety is very common within grief, and I want you to be able to pinpoint some of the symptoms you may be experiencing now or have in the past, so that you can prepare for the moments anxiety knocks on your door. Try to remember that anxiety is a very normal reaction to stress and the chaotic, confusing, and vulnerable state that grief can toss us into.

Along with a general sense of feeling "on edge," you may also experience some or all of these symptoms:

- Insomnia or not being able to stay awake
- Muscle cramping and tightness
- Restlessness and fidgeting
- Irritability and lack of patience
- Excessive sense of worry
- Persistent sense of dread
- Trouble being around other people due to physical discomfort
- New fears that may arise around your safety and well-being
- Trouble concentrating or holding a conversation
- Memory challenges
- Dizziness
- Upset stomach
- Vision changes
- Involuntary shaking
- Panic attacks (shortness of breath, chest pain, unsteadiness, trouble breathing, nausea)

I have many clients who will tell me how hard it is to concentrate, to sleep, and how their appetite is so up and down. I had a client who suffered from frequent shaking in her hand since she had to put her dog to sleep, and did not associate it to her loss. I always either know or inquire about the last time they were in touch with a general practitioner, but it's also really helpful to simply educate people and help them to understand what they are experiencing. When we understand what we are experiencing, it can help to empower us to take actions that can lead in the direction of improved functioning. The more we listen to our bodies, the better equipped we are to give ourselves a stronger foundation from which to heal and move forward with our grief.

The Brain's Way of Making Sense of Loss

In the introduction to her book *The Grieving Brain*, Dr. Mary-Frances O'Connor shares that "after decades of research, I realized that the brain devotes lots of effort to mapping where our loved ones are while they are alive so we can find them when we need them."[4] She goes on to explain that the brain prefers habits and predictions over learning new information, and "it struggles to learn new information that cannot be ignored, like the absence of our loved one."

What grief asks of us is to try to renegotiate our world without someone who gave our life meaning and predictability. It asks us to try to hold on to the attachment, while knowing that we have to detach as well, from the predictable ways we are always connected to this person. It's a wild ride for our brain, if you ask me. It's a constant game of redirecting ourselves. I know I'm not alone when I tell you that it took me almost a year not to pick up the phone and call my mother when I had something to ask her. It was like my brain just didn't want to let go of the predictability that my mother always picked up at the other end of the phone line and I knew where in the world she was.

And on an episode of *Huberman Lab* called "The Science & Process of Healing from Grief" with Dr. Andrew Huberman, he asserts, "We experience a loss of someone we are really close with, a pet, or something very meaningful to us. This is our attachment. Our brain has been used to that attachment and the predictability of being able to know where our person/pet/thing is... Now, that person/attachment is no longer here and we are left to reconfigure (a) where the person/attachment has gone, (b) how we are supposed to move forward without them, and (c) how to also stay attached to them while forming a new understanding that they are not going to be connected to us in the same way."[5] That's a *lot* for the brain to take on. Little wonder, then, that we can become anxious, disoriented, and depressed while we navigate how to reintegrate our loss into our mind in a new way.

How Cortisol Plays a Part in Your Stress

During times of intense stress, our neuroendocrine system comes into play. It's impossible to talk about anxiety and stress without talking about cortisol. Cortisol is sometimes referred to as the "stress hormone," and within the first six months after your loss, this hormone may become elevated in your body, for obvious reasons—you're experiencing pretty overwhelming stress. Going through a significant loss of ANY kind can throw our body's stress regulators into high gear. Loss is one of life's great stressors and it's no surprise that when the stress of grief becomes more intense, so does our stress hormone.

Grief can activate a part of our brain where responses are integrated and increases the production of corticotropin-releasing hormones and vasopressin, which produce anxiety-like symptoms within our brain.[6] Emergency-mobilizing chemicals are then released. As our stress increases, the chemical levels increase, and our central nervous system becomes highly stimulated. The stress hormones cortisol and adrenaline will affect your breathing and lungs (quick breaths or holding your breath), heart rate (it may speed up or palpitate), circulation (you may get cold, clammy hands or feet, or sweaty palms, or even goose bumps), hearing and eyesight (these may each become sharper or more enhanced). You may experience a sudden burst of energy that allows you to move—fight or flee—faster than usual, or you may feel unable or barely able to move at all (freeze). Your eyes may dilate to allow you to see clearer all that is around you, and even your skin may become pale or have temperature changes to protect you from the environment.

Understanding how our body is affected and, in turn, responds to a loss is one of the things I believe has long been missing in our understanding of the grieving process, especially as we have gained more in-depth knowledge of how our nervous system participates in our experiencing of our grief. The more we understand about how every part of our body plays a role in the stress response that grief thrusts us into, the better prepared we can be to give attention, care, and nourishment to our physical needs along the way.

Learning to Befriend the Body

Grief is hard. Preaching to the choir, I know. It's so exhausting and it does such a number on our entire body. Maybe that sounds dramatic, but that's because it *is.* Grief is dramatic in the way it comes in and takes the wheel of our life, leaving us feeling helpless and powerless. Yet, as dramatic as it is, it's asking for us to drive along with it. It wants us to engage it, because it means we are paying attention to the effects our loss has had on our entire life—heart, body, mind.

Noah came to see me because he was having intrusive gastrointestinal symptoms after getting divorced. The symptoms, he said, were getting in the way of his daily life to the point that he would even have to reschedule our sessions because he would never know when he might be sick to his stomach and need to run to the bathroom. After a slew of different tests and blood work, Noah told me that none of the symptoms had a physical origin that could be placed beyond these symptoms, so it was ruled as IBS. Noah was applying to medical school at the time, and held a lot of anxiety and shame, as he told me he thought he might be able to figure out what was happening with him (I can understand that one!). We all have blind spots, and after suffering from major loss, our bodies carry a lot of the weight of stress, sometimes without our being aware of it. Noah was somehow cut off from the physical aspect of his grief, and the more he ignored it, the louder it got.

One session, I asked Noah whether he thought his symptoms might be undigested grief after the loss of marriage, or some aspect of the loss he wasn't able to fully take in as of yet. The symbolism of this intrigued him, and despite the GI issues still piloting his life, Noah and

I got to explore how the symptoms were connected to his loss and the fears and anxieties associated with the life transition he didn't choose. The great unknown was terrifying to Noah, and despite the fact that none of us know what the future will bring, we somehow go on every day able to stomach it (pun intended). That said, when Noah realized he was embodying all of his deepest fears and carrying those fears in his body, he was able to name his fears and talk about the loss of his marriage in a new way, a way that allowed him to be present to dynamics in his relationship that were unhealthy for him, body and mind together.

This is probably the part where you expect me to say his symptoms magically disappeared overnight. I'm sorry to disappoint, but that wasn't quite how it went. Remember, we're not learning to speak with our bodies just so that we can get them to stop talking; I'm not promising the miraculous resolution of all your physical ailments when you're feeling "healed" from the worst of your symptoms, or that you shouldn't seek medical attention because "it's just my grief." It's both, and, as I said earlier, it's always smart to be in touch with a medical provider who can support you when symptoms become intrusive or overwhelming, or who can investigate any contributing factors.

The goal here is to create a bridge between your emotions and your body. Listening to your body as it directs you toward emotional hurt, and what you might need.

Building Body Awareness

Tending to physical symptoms while grieving means being very aware of how our body responds to stress, and the best way to do that is through mindfulness. Mindfulness is an awareness of what is happening within your sense, body, or emotions in the present moment.

The word *mindfulness* has been tossed about in so many wellness communities that it often means different things to different people, but what I want to talk about is the aspect of mindfulness that can ground and center us, and how sometimes it brings along with it all the intensity of our emotions living just below the surface.

According to the National Institutes of Health, mindfulness-based activities have been shown over time to lower blood pressure, lower heart rate, reduce moments of acute anxiety, help to improve quality of sleep, improve GI-related symptoms and other physical discomforts, help increase distress tolerance with regular practice, and more.[7] These activities can offer relief from some of those symptoms we have been learning about in this chapter.

Mindfulness-based exercises can look like meditating, walking and noticing your surroundings, journaling, singing, free drawing, mindful breathing techniques, and so many more. Anything that keeps you focusing on the moment in front of you without judgment. There are so many great mindfulness apps out there now, I recommend you download one or two and see what feels good to your body. It's called a "mindfulness practice" for a reason—it's different every day depending on our level of stress or discomfort, and also because it can feel different to us each time.

A simple, effective exercise to build body awareness is to do a body scan.

You can try it with me if you'd like. Take a deep breath, and then another.

Place your hands comfortably on your lap or down by your sides and notice your breath. Focus your attention on each part of your body, beginning with your feet. Breathe in deeply through your nose and out through your mouth. Shift your focus from your toes, to your ankles, up and up, all the way to the top of your head, noticing any sensations or experiences, even feelings that may come up as you continue to breathe. Do not analyze or judge whatever may arise. This is simply a moment to be present with your body and notice the sensations. Put your hand on your heart and take another big, deep breath. Slowly exhale. Take note of how you feel after this activity or if there is any shift in your physical comfort.

Let's Talk About Self-Care

We hear "self-care" tossed around a lot. So much so that some of my clients roll their eyes when I mention it. And, I totally get it. Social media has taught us to imagine self-care as luxury or superficial acts of beautification, which totally misses the mark. Because self-care is just that: caring for yourself. I cannot stress the importance of self-care enough when we are in the midst of grief. We may not always know when our body is reacting to an emotional stress response, or even when it's exhausted (think: a million tabs open and apps running in the background kind of experience). As you've already read, our entire body plays a part when we are grieving, and making sure that we can be present to our physical needs and concerns is going to be the most important thing we do for ourselves. And I'm talking about the basics here: Water. Vegetables. A nap. I know, you're already exhausted, and having to expend more energy taking care of your body's needs feels overwhelming even just to think about, but your grief impacts your body, and your body impacts your grief. When we take care of ourselves, we create the best possible environment for our grieving process, however it comes up at any given moment. We can build from the bottom up, supporting our emotional well-being by listening to our bodies and attending to their needs as best we can. In the way that I am thinking and talking about it when it comes to loss, self-care = self-preservation.

When we are grieving, and especially when that grief feels fresh, our basic physical needs take a back seat. *Water? Too much work to go to the sink. Movement? How can I go for a walk when it feels like my body is encased in cement? Eating? Who's hungry anyway? Sleep? Ha!* I'd even venture to say, we nearly all forget about those needs at times altogether.

Tending to our physical needs helps us to stay more present, and helps our immune system regain and maintain its strength—because, remember, grief is an endurance sport. Not the kind we sign up for, the kind we wish we could avoid, but once we are "on the team," we have to try as best we can to keep our body healthy.

It might feel annoying to stop what we are doing to take inventory of how we feel and how our bodies are faring in the heightened state produced by painful times. Immediately after loss, most self-care goes out the window, mostly because your brain is inundated with stress hormones that make regular life feel like too much—which it is. Over time, the persistent lack of self-care can make grieving harder and more painful. Instead of treating self-care like a task list, I want to help you become more aware of it, and your need for it. We'll do that by looking at simple questions around the two basic areas of self-care: physical self-care and emotional self-care.

Let's Check In: Self-Care Inventory

Even and perhaps *especially* when it feels like too much, tending to your physical health can give you the extra support you need. These questions are here to help you assess how your physical well-being is faring. Please don't judge yourself if you find you've been neglecting some important aspects of your physical well-being. It's bound to happen. You've got a *lot* on your mind, and you don't need to address these all at once. When you are ready, take a tiny step in the direction of giving some loving care and attention to the areas where it's most needed. Let these questions also serve as *reminders* that your physical care and well-being need constant check-ins and attention!

- How are you sleeping? Do you have a sleep ritual or nap pattern that makes you feel more rested?
- Are you using alcohol or other substances to "relax"?
- What types of food are you eating? What makes you feel nourished?
- How much water are you drinking?

- Do you tend to move your body or stay still when you are feeling emotionally overwhelmed? Is there a type of movement you enjoy?
- Do you have any routines you adhere to? Are there rituals you rely on to start the day off right or wind down?
- When was the last time you had a checkup or physical with your primary care provider?
- Are you in physical pain, and if so, what are you currently doing to manage this pain?

Involving Your Body in Your Grief

If you feel it in your body, let's engage it in your body. Sure, cognitive behavioral therapies have a time and place that are very helpful, but a full-body experience deserves a full-body approach to processing and healing.

Although I use different types of talk therapy, including CBT work, I believe no clinical work can get too far without getting the body involved. If you are looking to enlist additional support on your grief journey, or find that your body has a *lot* to say to you, I recommend enlisting the help of somatic-based practices. In addition to individual or group therapy, coaching, or pastoral care, these modalities can offer a full-spectrum grief therapy (that also includes trauma-informed care, which we will talk more about in the next chapter):

Somatic Experiencing

EMDR (Eye Movement Desensitization and Reprocessing)

ART (Accelerated Resolution Therapy)

Yoga for Grief

Art Therapy/Sensorimotor Drawing

Music (playing an instrument or singing)

Dance

Interactive Journaling

Biofeedback

Psychodrama

Mindfulness Meditation

Energy Healing Modalities, such as Reiki

Acupuncture/Chinese Medicine

Reminding Our Brain That Our Body Matters

Loss permeates every part of our being, and interestingly, it remains a mental health burden that society still sees as an emotional response to loss. Well, you and I both know it's so much more than our emotions. You have heard me say this before (and it won't be the last reminder!), but making sure you get good sleep, eat nutritious meals, move your body, and connect with people who love you is imperative to getting through these times. Your body will thank you. There have been so many times my clients will come in and tell me that this is the first sip of water they had all day or that they haven't been able to keep food down. Inevitably, they begin with, "I don't know why, but..." To which I will give them a glance that says: *Are you sure you don't know why?*

It can be really painful, confusing, and exhausting when our bodies take on the brunt of the major stress from our loss. Especially when we don't realize what's really going on within us. Making sure we are nourishing our bodies with healthy food, getting enough water, movement, and adequate rest can be a tall order when we are in the throes of grief, yet grieving takes a certain level of endurance. Tend to your body's needs as best you can, whether through proactive self-care or body-based practices with a therapist or practitioner. Finding a way to engage with our grief, while also remaining present to the full experience it brings to us, is the way through the thick of the most intrusive symptoms.

If you're onto me by now, you know I want you to go slowly and at your own pace, that I want you to know you don't have to go it alone; in fact, I encourage safe, supportive connection as much as possible, and, of course, I couldn't let you go without reminding you once more to include your whole body in your well-being routine or ritual. It's hard to cope with the effects of our grief if we are suffering physically, or simply trying to ignore the body's calls, and it's hard to do any kind of emotional processing when we're sick or in physical distress.

Grief work can be wonderful in that it gives witnessing and validation to a very vulnerable and deep wound, but if it *only* focuses on the talking and the cognitive processing, then it falls short of getting to the deeper "heart" of the matter that can make the work more thorough.

It's so important that we begin to listen to how emotions and painful life experiences show up in our bodies so that we can set ourselves up to get the support we need to cope with the plethora of emotions that want a seat at the table, knowing we have a safe harbor in our bodies when the emotional storms threaten to take us down.

CHAPTER 5

Grief's Sister, Trauma

"Trauma is also a wordless story our body tells itself about what is safe and what is a threat."
—Resmaa Menakem, *My Grandmother's Hands: Racialized Trauma and the Pathway to Mending Our Hearts and Bodies*

I'd be willing to bet that when I say we're going to talk about grief and trauma, your mind goes to some pretty catastrophic situations. Wars. School shootings. Increased violence. Environmental disasters. Genocide. Plane crashes and train derailments. And on the one hand you're right: All of those experiences present an overwhelming shock to the system for those who suffered through them. What I want to talk about in this chapter, though, is something that I don't think we talk about enough, which is the way that a loss doesn't have to be traumatic to be *traumatizing*.

See, loss of any kind is a shock to the system. It makes us question what we know to be true about ourselves, our place in the world, and so many of the things that we take (or took) for granted. For some people, loss isn't just life-altering; it's life-altering in a way that changes the way our minds and bodies feel safe in the world.

In the last chapter, we talked about how grief shows up in the body, manifesting the emotional hurt in physical symptoms that can affect our immune systems, endocrine systems, cardiovascular systems, and more. When we're talking about the intersection of grief and trauma, what we're really talking about is how our *nervous system* reacts to the losses we've suffered.

Of course, not all loss catalyzes into trauma, much the same way that not all trauma becomes PTSD. But as a therapist who specializes in both trauma and grief, it would be impossible for me not to talk about the ways they overlap—our experiences of them, and how we heal, share some remarkable, useful similarities.

If trauma in your loss is not something with which you identify, you're welcome to skip this chapter or be here with me in understanding it more (just in case something pops out for you). For some, it may be a piece of the puzzle of your grief experience that you feel has been missing in your own understanding of loss. So, I invite you to explore more with me, if you would like to understand a little more about trauma itself, the relationship between grief and trauma and how this understanding can play a role in how you move forward in your healing process.

Especially since the start of COVID-19, so many of my clients have shared that they feel "traumatized" by their loss, telling me how it has brought them to a place where it's hard to function or find a safe landing, unable to cope any longer with the painful and intrusive symptoms. That was understandable as we saw the death toll rise into the millions and it seemingly took everyone equally in its wake. We were humans trying to figure out how to survive something unprecedented and terrifying, and there was no playbook on the best path of survival for quite some time.

It was no wonder that trauma became more connected with grief in the minds of people who suffered loss during the pandemic.

Because of the prevalence of clients wanting to understand more about why they feel so traumatized by their loss(es), it felt really important for me to spend time here bringing it more into the open. I want to dig in and help some of you who may feel your nervous system has been upended by loss to understand where that feeling and experience may be coming from, why, and where we go from here.

So, What Is Trauma?

I don't know about you, but I can't go online or walk down the street or listen to a podcast anymore without hearing the word *trauma*. It's the punch line of jokes, the topic of dozens of TED Talks and bestselling books and billions of TikToks; it's "Big T" and "Little t" (Hint: The loss of a loved one can be both)—but for as often as it shows up in our conversations, how many of us know what trauma actually *is*? What happens when we experience it, and how does it show up in the body? Before we explore the parallels between grief and trauma, let's look at trauma on its own and get a clearer idea of how it can affect us.

A trauma is an event/series of events, or a variety of experiences that occurs outside of our nervous system's ability to cope, meaning that the necessary inner resources to handle what is happening—namely being able to calm and ground the nervous system—are not available and it's just "too much." In other words, it's an experience that can render us helpless by what can feel like an overpowering force beyond us. Symptoms may show up for you right away or rise to the surface over time. Trauma creates a stress reaction that is so overwhelming that the nervous system will have trouble, and need help regulating itself to feel safe and grounded. The legacy of that activated, overwhelmed nervous system affects our emotions, perceptions, behaviors, thought patterns, and bodily sensations. This makes trauma both an experience *and* our full-body response to that experience.

Depending on what type of traumatic experience(s) you may have endured, trauma can really root itself within the nervous system. It's important to understand your experiences, so you can take the right steps toward your healing. There are three types of trauma that play a role in how we are able to metabolize certain life events and each can play a role in how we process traumatic events.

Acute trauma is a single event you have endured, such as assault, car accident, natural disaster, mass violence.

Chronic trauma is repeated or prolonged exposure to a painful pattern or traumatic event, such as abuse, domestic violence, bullying, war, chronic exposure to painful medical procedures, neglect, homelessness.

Complex trauma describes both children's exposure to multiple traumatic events—often of an ongoing, invasive, interpersonal nature—and the wide-ranging, long-term effects of this exposure. These events are severe and pervasive, such as abuse or profound neglect.[1] This is ongoing emotional or physical abuse, chronic neglect, abandonment, or medical trauma or exposure to chronic substance misuse by adults.

For some people, having gone through any of these can make subsequent loss feel much more complex and nuanced, and will require slow, safe, and caring support to guide you through when you are ready. According to SAMHSA (Substance Abuse and Mental Health Services Administration), trauma is defined as containing 3 E's—Event, Experience of event/s, and Effects of the event/s.[2] This helps us to understand and integrate our understanding of how trauma plays a role in overwhelming life events, especially following a major loss.

Understanding trauma and the ways in which it has been in our lives can help us to look at our loss in a more complete light. If we have endured traumatic life events, grief and loss can be harder to metabolize and process, because our nervous system will continuously be scanning for our next bout of danger around any bend. Though it may not or doesn't have to be that way for the long term, I want to honor that, and your life experiences here, however confusing, painful, or *traumatizing*.

Trauma's Symptoms and Signs

I am often asked why trauma is so hard to "get over." Why does this affect so many people for so long and how can it be so pervasive? The answer is not that simple, but the gist of it is that it is an experience or period of time when we are helpless, terrified, and are simply pared down to our human element: *survival.*

Many people who have endured trauma often experience an array of symptoms—they can be incredibly overwhelming and hard to contend with, so having safety in a support system is absolutely vital when processing and engaging with trauma in our lives.

Trauma psychotherapist and author of *The Body Remembers: The Psychophysiology of Trauma and Trauma Treatment,* Babette Rothschild, describes trauma symptoms as a disruption to the functioning of those afflicted by it, interfering with the ability to meet their daily needs and perform the most basic tasks. The body symptoms are characteristic of hyperarousal: accelerated heartbeat, cold sweating, rapid breathing, heart palpitations, hypervigilance, and hyper startle response (jumpiness). These symptoms lead to sleep disturbances, loss of appetite, sexual dysfunction, and difficulties in concentrating.[3]

Psychological symptoms can look like: shock and disbelief, anxiety and panic attacks, memory loss, lack of interest in things you have once enjoyed, depression, overwhelming sense of fear and dread, numbing emotionally, feeling guilt, anger, irritability, and mood swings. There may be the avoidance of anything reminding you of the trauma, or the incessant reliving/reexperiencing of what happened, as well as nightmares and flashbacks, which can be terrifying. It can lead people to isolate and withdraw, because the unpredictable experience can feel devastating.

Responses to a traumatic event can be different for everyone, as your experiences are unique to you. These symptoms and signs vary in severity and length of time based on someone's age, history, support system, personality, ways of coping, feelings of helplessness, and life stressors. That's a lot to take in, I know, but the more you understand how trauma may have impacted you or continues to be with you (before your loss, or because of your loss), the more you may be able to understand why your grief feels the way it does, too.

You may look at some of the symptoms above and have a lightbulb moment where you recognize this feels the same as the grief you've experienced. Many of the symptoms overlap and it makes sense, since loss is an immense life stressor that activates our survival mechanism in renegotiating how to...go on. We will talk more about this in a moment.

With that in mind, my hope is that this chapter brings you closer to understanding your traumatic experiences and the way that your body, mind, and nervous system have tried to metabolize those experiences—knowing this can be a guide for you on the trauma-informed path to healing.

Trauma, Grief, and Their Relationship with Our Nervous System

We can't talk about trauma (or loss) without bringing in the nervous system. It's our smoke detector when it comes to danger and stressors, always on alert for fire, and it can be so exhausting and challenging to live with this sense of high alert after enduring a loss. We need it, and yet, learning how to engage with it can be really tricky. What I want to stress most here is your learning how to identify what nervous system arousal looks like in a simple way, and also what to do with it once you feel activated by an event, memory, or trigger. All of the symptoms we discussed earlier come about when our nervous system has gone into survival mode after experiencing something outside of its own resources to cope with what has happened.

Psychiatrist and author Dr. Judith Lewis Herman tells us that "after a traumatic experience, the human system of self-preservation seems to go into permanent alert, as if the danger might return at any moment."[4] Enduring trauma can feel overwhelming, exhausting, and debilitating, especially if we don't know what it is that we are experiencing.

With trauma, there is a fear for our own survival, so a very old survival mechanism will kick in after a significant loss. Naturally when we are in the midst of grief and loss, our body will be experiencing a lot of stress.

When faced with a threat, our nervous system releases hormones (hello, adrenaline, epinephrine, and cortisol) that will help us to choose a way to mobilize for our own safety. They literally are there to save our lives, so I want to acknowledge the positive aspects of the way our nervous system does its job astoundingly well.

So, in understanding that our nervous system is here for the sole purpose of protecting us, we may be able to better see how fight, flight, or freeze is important when in grief, especially early grief, because your nervous system is going to thrust you into a stress survival response. As a quick refresher, here I want to go over what these stress responses are and how they may look after a loss that feels particularly traumatic for you.

As a quick recap: *Fight* is you fighting the threat in some way. *Flight* is your body's involuntary response that has you flee from the danger, which can be literally running away or mentally taking yourself somewhere else, and *freeze* is your body's temporary inability to fight *or* flee. This response can manifest as a physical freeze, where you temporarily can't seem to move or run away, or a mental/emotional freeze in which you're temporarily unable to respond to a threat in a self-protective way. This doesn't mean your body is not triggered or activated, it's just in a state of hyperarousal.

Each of these are our built-in defense mechanisms that are there to guard us against what we may perceive as death or severe danger. These symptoms aren't typically permanent, but may occur from time to time when upsetting emotions, memories, or events occur, and your brain thinks you are in danger.

Which of these FFF responses occur for you is based partly on how you typically respond to stress or unpredictable events. My client

Joseph, for example, noticed he was in a state of fight after losing his brother, wanting to immediately confront and punish those he felt were responsible for not helping his brother after an overdose. But other clients talk about their experience of feeling frozen in time after hearing the news and not being able to move or think straight. Or I had a client who flew three thousand miles away to Italy for three months because she felt she couldn't be near all of the reminders of losing her six-year-old son, Lucas, to leukemia. You may not physically flee what you perceive as danger or overwhelm, but your brain's way of dealing with a powerful stress response will propel you to protect yourself at all costs. Some things we cannot escape, and grief is one of those things.

When you feel yourself going into an FFF stress response (and provided there is no immediate danger around you), I want you to take a moment and practice this grounding exercise to help take your nervous system off high alert. Let's do it here together, and I invite you to come back to this exercise whenever you feel overwhelmed by a thought or emotion around your loss (or trauma) throughout this book and beyond.

Exercise for Re-Grounding

5 things you can see: your hands, the sky, a tree around you, the floor

4 things you can physically feel: your feet on the ground, the arm of the chair, your own body, the texture of your shirt

3 things you can hear: the birds chirping, traffic, a dog barking, the hum of the refrigerator, a heater or air conditioner buzzing, or even your own breathing

2 things you can smell: your own perfume or cologne, flowers, the outside air, something cooking

1 thing you can taste: the fresh air around you, a piece of gum, your coffee or tea, water

Supporting Our Activated Nervous System

Understatement of the year: Both grief and trauma are utterly over-whelming to us, in every way. You heard me say earlier that we have to remember that our nervous system plays a really big role in how we are able to contend with the effects of trauma, traumatic loss, and loss that *feels* traumatic to our system. Going through major stress can really upend us and toss us into sympathetic arousal (that FFF we just learned about). Sometimes, our stress response feels really over-whelming and we have to actively work on getting our nervous system back into parasympathetic mode. Let's talk more about other ways we can do that.

The short grounding exercise you see here is an example of ways to calm and regulate your nervous system. You may not be a "medita-tor," but there are more ways to meditate than sitting cross-legged on a pillow with your eyes closed. For some of you, closing your eyes may feel really scary, so trust that instinct. Here are some ideas that can be helpful when you are struggling to regulate your nervous system and stress response. You can try them all, or some, and see what works for you at different times.

- **Deep Breathing**: Box breathing can be helpful to ground our-selves. It looks like breathing in for four seconds, holding that breath for four seconds, exhaling for four seconds and holding it for four seconds before taking your next breath. Repeat this for three cycles.
- **Sitting, Moving, or Walking Meditation**: Focus on your breathing, as we have above, or simply notice yourself taking deeper inhalations, notice what's around you, notice the rhythm of your breath or your body against a surface, and stay as pres-ent as you can for as long as you can. If you are walking, make sure you are not rushing or walking with a sense of rushing. The

purpose here is to slow our system down enough to allow it to
get present and calm.

- **Journaling**: The very act of writing can help us to release pent-up
emotions. You can use this to write about what you're feeling in
the moment, write a letter to your loved one who is no longer
here expressing your feelings and thoughts, or write a letter to
your future self with all the ways you'd like to feel. However you
are able to use this, remember that the goal is relief.

These three activities can help to regulate your nervous system and
help to center and ground you when you're feeling activated. Here's
my caveat—have patience with yourself if it's hard to do any of these
at first. Stick with them, though, as over time, it will become easier,
as with any practice (especially if it's new to us). The goal in any kind
of trauma or grief work is not to push us into a place of being *more*
overwhelmed and activated. If we feel like a "whole can of worms"
has been opened in thinking or talking about our trauma or loss, it's
important then to safely close it back up and open it again only a little
at a time with the right support. There is no rush, there is no expectation that you will open and clean your emotional wounds in three
easy steps. That's unrealistic and dangerous. We are here to engage
and learn, but there are no healthy shortcuts. Remember this as we
move along in the book. Slow and steady. Safety first, always.

Looking Closer at What Can Make Loss Traumatizing

Now knowing all we do about trauma, you may have felt some of what
we talked about in your own grief experience. Grief and trauma can
get tangled at times, because there is certainly loss within a trauma
(loss of self, loss of safety, loss of control, etc.), and teasing the two
apart can become challenging. But the experience of a traumatizing

loss merits its own consideration and care. So, with that in mind, let's look at how loss could be experienced as traumatizing.

There is some disagreement in the mental health field when it comes to the overlap of grief and trauma as well as trauma's role in grief. When I was first studying this topic, we were taught (and I believed) that the only kind of traumatic loss was a loss that was sudden, unexpected, violent, or ambiguous. According to research on traumatic loss in the *European Journal of Psychotraumatology* (and, yes, *psychotraumatology* is a word!), "Traumatic loss involves the loss of loved ones in the context of potentially traumatizing circumstances and is a commonly reported traumatic event."[5] It's a very specific definition that manages to be both limiting and maddeningly vague. Over time I got the sense that, as a field, we were disinclined to consider the ways that loss, of so many kinds, could be truly traumatic for the person experiencing it.

To an extent, the caution is understandable: As therapists, researchers, and mental health professionals, we owe it to the well-being of our clients to be careful and at times even conservative with such big labels. However, the more we learn about both grief and trauma, the more obvious it becomes that they share common ground through our nervous systems, and it's my opinion that we rob ourselves of healing and understanding when we don't look at that bigger picture.

For decades, people studying and working with trauma have focused on what happened—the circumstances of the event itself—as the basis for identifying a trauma, as opposed to how the brain and nervous system reacted to what happened. The problem is that, ultimately, the nervous system is *not rational*. It's not meant to be. It's not going to sit and ponder if an event is life-changing enough or not. It's going to react to protect you.

The brain is a mysterious but simple organ, as we saw a little in the last chapter. According to Dr. Lisa Shulman, a professor of neurology at the University of Maryland and author of *Before and After Loss*, the brain doesn't have a way of deciphering one form of emotional trauma from another.

For example, your brain will not be able to tell the difference between a car accident you've been in, a devastating divorce, a family member's illness, or losing your cat. Regardless of the hierarchy we, or society more broadly, may assign to those events, the emotional trauma may all feel the same to your brain. As Dr. Shulman explains, "the human brain handles emotional trauma and stress using the same set of processes,"[6] so, from the standpoint of the brain, a traumatic loss is a loss that threatens your survival, safety, and well-being. Your brain is acting as if it is at risk for something very dangerous and life threatening. Your brain doesn't know the details of the situation, it's doing what a brain is programmed to do: protect itself for survival.

In many circumstances, that intense nervous system reaction doesn't stick around for too long. The loss may feel traumatizing for a while, but with time and support, it becomes less and less distressing. But there are times when that's not the case, and our nervous system gets stuck in overdrive, scanning again and again and again for danger, for the threat of more loss.

Why do some losses get "stuck" and others don't? Well, our history plays such a huge role. What's in your past will tell you how to perceive what happens in your present, and there are five key factors that can contribute to a higher likelihood that loss may more profoundly impact your nervous system:

Type of Loss

While it is not the only factor, the type of loss plays a large part in how we perceive the loss, especially if the loss was surprising or unexpected. Having a loss come out of left field can be utterly disorienting and traumatizing for many people. Common examples of traumatic loss are losses due to homicide, suicide, accidents, and natural disasters, ambiguous loss, and losses resulting from war and terror.

A History of Trauma and/or PTSD/CPTSD/Complex Grief

If we have experienced trauma or previous traumatic loss in our life, a new loss can send the nervous system's stress response into overdrive. Having a history of complex post-traumatic stress disorder can mimic the same thoughts and reactions as complex grief or prolonged grief.

A History of Immense Anxiety

If our baseline of anxiety or adrenaline prior to grief is very high and sometimes overwhelming, we may be more likely to feel traumatized by our loss experience. Anxiety is a condition that already elicits fear, worry, and physical manifestations of that fear and worry, so add in a major or significant loss, and this will be heightened. The higher the levels of anxiety and adrenaline before a loss, the more anxiety-provoking and flooding the loss can feel to a person, as grief will elevate the adrenaline in your body. If it's already high, your nervous system can become overwhelmed and cause adrenal glands to burn out with the release of the stress hormone cortisol (which will already naturally be higher because of your higher baseline of anxiety). Without inner resources to cope with the increased stress response, what someone is perceiving can feel threatening to them, and a trauma reaction may follow.

Having Weak Coping Skills

Some people are more sensitive and reactive to stress. Having or developing strong coping skills is vital for being able to manage our emotions, physical health, and stress response after loss, and it can be done with practice, the right tools, and guidance. However, if this is something we struggle with, we may become overwhelmed and lack the ability to find, utilize, or keep resources close at hand for when we become flooded with our grief experience. This can, in turn, make a loss experience feel more traumatizing.

The Attachment History with Whom or What Has Been Lost

What was the attachment like? Was it safe? Were they a secure, loving connection, or was there anxiety or abuse surrounding the relationship? Was the person we lost someone we depended on for our physical, mental, or emotional well-being and survival? Did we have a rift and not expect them to die before we came back together? Did we caretake and now have lost our purpose? This can play a part in how your nervous system responds to the loss, which could make it feel more complicated or traumatizing.

As I say in my own work: We cannot give an objective judgment on what is a subjective experience. Who am I to tell someone their loss was not traumatic for them? How can I contradict the experience of someone whose entire nervous system is obviously trying to reconcile what feels like danger and what does not to them?

Instead of lingering over long questions of whether something is or is not, in fact, trauma, what I aim to do is help my clients to regulate their nervous system as best I can, teach them to do the same as needed, and validate their experience. I'd like to do the same thing for you here. My goal is that, together, we can take the sting out just enough that you can begin to process the emotions and full experience of your loss without the fear of not surviving it. Taking the sting out begins with grounding ourselves and learning about what may come up for us. This way, if/when it does, we will be more prepared to support ourselves if things begin to feel overwhelming. Let's start with understanding just a little more about our nervous system's built-in protection mechanism.

When We Don't Feel Safe After Loss

Loss rearranges our world, both inner and outer, and how we look at it and how we understand and experience it can help to determine how we move forward. Some people can't just feel the feelings or talk it out after a significant loss. For some people, trying to talk about loss may bring it up to the surface and overwhelm the nervous system with emotions and sensations that may feel incredibly dangerous. They may be some of the symptoms we spoke of earlier or it could be a new experience for you to feel these feelings that are coming up, and it's overwhelming.

Maybe your loss kicked up memories of another painful loss that you never processed and now you feel flooded with emotions and physical sensations that you don't have the inner resources to calm or ground. Or maybe the attachment to whomever you lost brought up a history of painful memories or trauma and abuse that it can feel like you're reliving. Maybe you can't function the way you used to after your loss, because you are afraid you will be hurt or harmed in a similar fashion. These are trauma responses that come up when a loss leads to your nervous system feeling like it needs to protect itself from major danger. And it can feel downright debilitating.

Because of the prevalence of clients telling me they are having a harder time coping with the feelings and sensations of their loss, to the point of feeling like they are emotionally, psychologically, even physically upended, it's important to me to help normalize your experience here if you are experiencing an acute, fear-based response to loss. For example, you may be afraid to drive for some time if you lost someone you loved to a drunk driver. As one client who endured such a loss rightfully asked, "If, around any turn, we can lose someone close to us without warning, how can we say life is safe?" Short answer? We can't, but we do our best as humans to make our lives as safe as possible, just in case.

Truth is, though, we are no longer living in normal times (if we ever were). Since COVID-19, the world has felt unpredictable and unsafe for many communities around the globe and there is a heightened sense of being on guard for danger around any bend. We have to acknowledge this, and that the ways we used to tend to our wounds may need a little more attention and care than they did before.

When to Seek Support

The signs and symptoms of trauma we spoke of earlier may persist over time, which can lead to "complicated grief" (or prolonged grief disorder, which I will touch upon in chapter 8). Although I do not like tossing labels out there, if significant time has passed after a loss but you still aren't able to experience less distress, and painful, intrusive symptoms persist, I do encourage you to reach out for support. It doesn't have to be a therapist, but having a support system and someone to help you find a way to relieve your symptoms is important for your overall well-being. I believe in trauma-informed care; there is a three-pronged approach needed: giving attention and support to the mind, the body, and the nervous system as a way to work toward impactful and long-term healing.

"Trauma-Informed" Care—What Does It Mean?

The benefit of seeing grief's interplay with trauma is that it opens a new, body-first way of healing and integrating our experiences, as well as finding a way to safety. After all, both grief and trauma manifest in the body in ways we haven't been taught to pay any attention to until quite recently. The interconnectedness of mind and body is often the missing variable in healing and integrating experiences like grief and trauma. In fact, our bodies talk to us all the time, and sensations are their language. Many of the sensations that we experience within grief are often the same for trauma.

In Bessel A. van der Kolk's *The Body Keeps the Score: Brain, Mind, and Body in the Healing of Trauma*, he asserts, "Traumatized people chronically feel unsafe inside their bodies: The past is alive in the form of gnawing interior discomfort. Their bodies are constantly bombarded by visceral warning signs, and, in an attempt to control these processes, they often become expert at ignoring their gut feelings and in numbing awareness of what is playing out inside. They learn to hide from themselves."[7]

So, healing from trauma within grief and loss all comes down to first feeling safe within our bodies, specifically learning how to regulate our nervous system, so over time, we may feel less on high alert. It will not take away your loss or make your emotions feel less painful, but it can make it possible for you to feel and process emotions in a safer way. After all, how can we find ways of healing all the while feeling stuck in a loop of feeling scared and on guard, which is how trauma can have us constantly feeling? We are absolutely able to heal and adapt and thrive again after trauma or traumatic loss, so long as we are able to look at, engage with, and process it in a way that safely includes the full self (body, mind, and nervous system) in the healing.

We can handle a lot as humans, but when enough loss accumulates in the body, the pressure of a fresh, new loss can burst open the dam, flooding the mind, heart, and body with emotions and sensations we have (sometimes unknowingly) been repressing. When that happens, we must slow down, be with, and hold all of what is coming to the surface. It's also an important opportunity to witness and ultimately begin to heal old wounds slowly, gently, and one tiny step at a time.

Having trauma-informed care in your healing process can be a game changer, in that however you are supported, whether by

therapist, coach, support group, or healer, they will have a deep understanding of the impact of trauma and how it can interfere with your
ability to cope. With that in mind, physical, emotional, and psychological safety is always the priority. That means that no one who is
trauma-informed should ever push or pressure you for details (like,
ever) or ask you to share anything vulnerable without you first being
safe and secure in your mind and body. I hope you're almost exhausted
by my talking about safety so far, because I will know for sure I've gotten my point across!

After trauma or traumatic loss (or loss that feels traumatizing), the
way someone may function is changed. I had a client who wasn't able
to cross the street for almost a year after her little dog ran out and was
hit by a car, dying shortly after. This affected her sense of safety and
predictability in the world, and her nervous system was always scanning for rogue cars that may threaten to hit her, too. It made sense
that she was so scared and that triggers were everywhere for her. She
kept telling me that she'd gone crazy. I kept telling her she'd endured
a major loss and trauma in watching her dog get hit by a car. For a
long time, it was most important for our work to focus on her sense
of safety and resourcing (simply creating/gathering/using inner and
outer resources to feel safer and calmer when activated). How can
we access emotions and new understanding when we are in a state of
panic?

After some time, we were able to talk about how this experience
of losing her dog led her back to a time when her mom flushed her
beloved goldfish, Neptune, down the toilet and told her it was because
he wasn't happy being her fish, so he died. Wow, right? So, she felt like
she was a failure as a pet owner from childhood, that it was inevitable
that her dog might die, and she'd always wind up losing a pet. This is
where the work began—when she was safe enough to look closer at
her traumatic experience with her dog and how it tied back to something old and wounded within her that she was never able to process.

Not everyone has a history of trauma, of course, but creating a sense of safety is the top priority when we have any experience that has catapulted us into a place where everything feels threatening, scary, and uncertain. When we feel safe enough, older, fragile moments in our lives can open up with us that have longed to be seen and witnessed. That's the power in the healing process, as scary as it can feel at times.

And that's why I insist (over and over) on seeking support that is trauma-informed. I believe that time and the right, safe connection and unique-to-you modality can be pivotal in moving through trauma and grief (please see the body-centered healing modalities mentioned in chapter 4).

Understanding how trauma may be intertwined within your loss may give you a sense of new direction in how you respond to your loss, if, when, and how you get support in this process. I hope if you are navigating this path right now, you allow yourself the grace to not go through this alone. You weren't meant to, and there is the right support and guidance out there if you are struggling with the traumatic experience of a loss.

Containing Strategy—for When It Feels Like Too Much

As we close out this chapter with a lot of information to take in, I want to introduce you to an additional exercise that you can use however you need to move forward when you are feeling really overwhelmed in thinking about your loss. This is another way we can support our nervous system, like we discussed earlier in the chapter.

Talking about, and even thinking about our grief or trauma can be very activating. Both inherently threaten your sense of self, safety, and control, but it doesn't mean it will always be this way or that they will always take over and overwhelm you without your having any control.

Babette Rothschild, the trauma therapist whom we spoke of earlier when discussing symptoms, has an amazing YouTube video that talks about the importance of going slow when engaging trauma. I believe the same applies to engaging with our grief. In her well-known "Shaking the Coke Bottle" video, Rothschild tells us that the best and only way to engage someone who is shaken up and traumatized is gradually. To look at it all just a little at a time and to remain safe and contained, or "putting on the brakes," as Rothschild says.[8]

The exercise below comes from a type of therapeutic modality called EMDR (eye movement desensitization and reprocessing) often used by people who have experienced trauma, although it's helpful for many different distressing emotional experiences. It's a way to "put on the brakes," as Rothschild would say, and to gradually approach your trauma or traumatic loss, so as to not inundate yourself with the symptoms or feelings of being flooded.

This is a strategy that I encourage you to put in your toolbox for times that feel like "too much" is being asked of you or you're feeling really overwhelmed by a barrage of emotions. This exercise, adapted here with the permission of my colleague Rebecca Kase, LCSW, will ask you to use imagery to create a safe place for yourself to put overwhelming emotions or sensations away until you feel more able to process or engage with them.

I'd like for us to develop a container image now. This is a tool that you use to put disturbing stuff away. The idea is that you're putting it away so it won't disturb you right now, but you will come back to it and attend to it (or work on it) at a later time.

So, with your eyes open or closed (whatever feels safer), let your mind come up with an image of a container that can hold disturbing thoughts, emotions, and images in your mind. Just let something come to mind that is strong enough to hold anything painful. It can be surprising or unusual; whatever comes to your mind is good.

Take a moment to really be there next to this container.

Notice what color it is...

Notice how large it is...

Notice what material it is made of...

Notice how it both opens and closes...

Let's practice using this container to put something away that is on your mind right now.

What thought is bothering you in this moment that might feel good to put into this container until later, even until tomorrow or until you speak with someone with whom you can share it?

Gather all of the most disturbing parts of the issue—the images, thoughts, emotions, body sensations—and gradually put them each into the container. You can do it quickly or it might take you awhile. Take as long as you need to.

Now, close the container and put it away.

Where would be a good place to put this container for the time being? Is there anything else that needs to be done to store this container?

Once the container is fully stowed away, take a deep breath in and let it out with a sigh.

You don't have to tend to the upsetting material right now. It's safely within this container for when you are ready to take it out later on.

Using a Trauma-Informed Lens as You Move Through the Rest of This Book

As we have come to realize, grieving and doing grief work is hard, and it's harder still if you experience intrusive, relentless thoughts and traumatic reactions around your loss. Understanding how trauma overlaps with grief can help you understand why your loss may feel different or more intense at times, or why triggers come often and ferociously. Most importantly, it can help you know what you need to feel safe through the overwhelm, likely still struggling, but not so flooded that you can't take another step.

If at any other point in this book, you are triggered or any memories, traumatic symptoms, or overwhelming emotions feel threatening to your well-being, I want you to remember our earlier grounding exercise, the other supportive nervous system activities, or bring out that container, place whatever disturbing material is front and center in there, and save it for when you feel safer or more grounded. Remember, you don't have to take it all out at once, and you can choose whatever you feel most comfortable bringing out of the container at first. There is no pressure to process or feel everything at once. I prefer you feel safe, steady, and less inundated with the grief and trauma experience and checking in with your nervous system as needed.

You are the captain of your ship, and I want you to keep tabs on how you're feeling, so you don't push yourself harder than you need to. You can do the hard work of healing, one tiny step at a time, *and* you can put the hard stuff away for a little while to rest. Find support, and only do what you can tolerate in a given moment. You're already going through so much, this is the time to be gentle, stay present, notice your surroundings, and keep your feet on the floor.

CHAPTER 6

Self-Compassion and Grieving to Our Own Rhythm

"Tender self-compassion allows us to accept the discomfort of an unwanted task and to be non-judgmental about our desire to put it off. Fierce self-compassion then propels us to take action so that we do what's needed."

—Kristin Neff, *Fierce Self-Compassion: How Women Can Harness Kindness to Speak Up, Claim Their Power, and Thrive*

Gina, how long am I allowed to grieve?

Without fail, at some point during our work together, each and every one of my clients sits on my couch and asks me this question. And each time it breaks my heart, because it signals to me that someone in their life has decided that time's up.

In many ways, grief is the most acceptable and palatable of mental health burdens, eliciting outpourings of sympathy and care. Still, society is quick to tell us when we've grieved long enough. I mean, we have plenty of sympathy cards in the supermarket, but we don't have "anxiety" or "depression" cards (though we should). We have special bouquets and whole websites dedicated to sympathy gift ideas, but very few "I'm sorry your world still feels like it's fallen apart and won't ever be the same again even though it's been three years" statuettes.

If you're lucky, you have a few days or a week of bereavement leave before needing to get back to work, and well, your neighbors only have so many casserole dishes. Friends' lives keep going and people ebb and flow into the weird arena of "Are you feeling better yet?" and before you know it, the same people who sent Edible Arrangements and texted every day for a month are the first to tell you that you need to be back to "normal" (whatever that is).

It's no wonder people walk around dazed and confused about their grief process.

I'd love nothing more than to get on a megaphone and help the people in your life who just don't get it, trust me. That may be a future project. But for now, I can talk with you. And I want to start by telling you that wherever you are in your journey, however you're coping (or not), however long it is taking, it is perfectly okay. In fact, before we get any further, let me set the record straight. There are only six grief rules:

- ✓ It lasts for as long as it lasts.
- ✓ You don't need good reasons to prioritize your feelings and needs.
- ✓ You can grieve in your own way without justifying it.
- ✓ You deserve support for as long as you need and/or want it.
- ✓ You don't owe anyone anything (my personal favorite).
- ✓ There are no expectations that you need to live up to in your grief.

Metabolizing a loss takes time, endurance, and yes, patience. We all move through our grief differently as our minds and bodies work overtime to stay afloat. We fear stalling out for too long and we cycle through ways of making sense of the world, attempting to regain a sense of control over ourselves and our lives—stepping into tendencies that I call the Grief Rhythms. In this chapter, we're going to look at these rhythms more closely, getting friendly with how we cope, giving ourselves permission to grieve at our own pace, and learning to support ourselves even when the world says to move on.

The Fear of Feeling Stuck

Everywhere we look, we see the idea that grieving is a journey of constant forward movement. Take, for example, the TV show *This Is Us*, where every episode should come with its own box of tissues and a trigger warning. No matter what tragedy befalls the Pearson family, by next week's episode there is peace, resolution, or at least, enlightenment. If only real-life grief fit so neatly into a self-contained unit with a beginning, middle, and end.

Instead, grief grips both when we expect it and after we're sure we've "healed" from it. For so many people, it can be a long and messy and horribly painful road. Not surprisingly, fear of grieving is a thing. And it makes sense that it's a thing, because society still wants us to fit our grief into some version of an episode—perhaps six months, perhaps a year, at which point we're supposed to be "better" and ready to "move on." It can be hard to take in the reality that the grief journey has no definitive finish line, or if we can take that in, it only feels more overwhelming to imagine that we'll suffer in varying levels of intensity for an indeterminate amount of time.

So as we're traversing this overwhelming and amorphous journey, we're inevitably confronted by the societal stigma around being, or appearing to be, "stuck" or "wallowing" when we are just grieving authentically and honestly. The whole *"You're still grieving?"* question gets old, right? The societal stigma, coupled with the knowledge that we're emotionally ill-equipped to cope with loss, and it's no wonder people fear grief. It's as though your friend invited you on a trip, but neglected to inform you that the hotel room is one thousand dollars a night and you can't afford it, but you're too embarrassed to tell them you can't afford it and there's nowhere else to go, so now you're just stuck in this place where you feel hopeless, choiceless, and disempowered. This is a simple example of the triple whammy of shame/terror/ stuckness. My people pleasers here will definitely get it.

Oh, and let's not forget, grief *hurts*. Desperate to escape the pain of our losses, many of us resort to moving...somewhere, really *anywhere* that feels less like we're drowning in emotions we don't know what to do with. While this reaction to grief is entirely understandable and there is no "right" way to grieve, it's important to also consider that at times, what may feel or look like being "stuck" is in fact a form of healing.

Remember back in chapter 3 when I told you that this is a time in your life where you need safety, time, and space to feel what you feel? Here I am again to remind you of that. Just as the human body needs a certain amount of rest to heal a broken bone, your body, mind, heart, and soul may require a certain amount of inertia to integrate the loss you've suffered. Allowing yourself to be where you are in your grieving journey, whatever that may look and feel like, is the only way to allow your grief the time and space it needs to evolve.

I know that it's hard to pause and feel, especially when it feels endless. It may feel like way too much. But while only you know how much you can tolerate on a given day or in a given moment, this is not a time in your life to stay distracted indefinitely or keep spinning on the hamster wheel. This is a time when slowness and tenderness and attention to your heart and body isn't just part of the work. It's *the* work.

Why Grief Isn't Linear and the "Myth" of Letting Go

We are all guilty of wanting structure to the chaos, and a course of action when things feel out of control. Part of the reason the five stages of grief by Elisabeth Kübler-Ross has held strong as a guidepost for so many people is because it offers a sequenced *plan*. And as I said earlier in the book, despite it being created specifically for those actively in the dying process, it became a stronghold for those left behind, too, because it's obvious that people need a way to engage with and process what can be a truly upending life experience.

With the utmost respect to Kübler-Ross, grief is not a neat sequence of stages. Because of its unpredictability, and because it hits us all in different ways and in different times, grief just cannot be seen as linear. We cycle through ways of feeling and experiencing, buffering, processing, integrating, and doing it all over again. So, please do not be alarmed if you find yourself cycling through the tears, anger, intellectualizing, feeling peace, or any other experiences and then it circles back—sometimes within a day, sometimes within moments! This is common. You aren't weird, and yet, it's a weird, sometimes super unnerving experience. This is also why there really isn't a "letting go" phase. Grief just doesn't work that way. We don't just wake up one morning, sit up in bed with outstretched arms, notice the sound of birds, and think to ourselves, *Well, I am glad that's over!* and then never feel the pang of our yearning to go back or feel the sting that comes on anniversaries, or have our breath taken away when a memory flies into our mind out of the blue. No. We are affected. We always will be, just to different extents along the way that hold their own meaning and rhythm.

Grieving Rhythms

Given that so many of us are so ill-prepared for the grief state we are thrust into, I find that it can help to have any opportunity to recognize our inner callings and needs. A way I like to look deeper at these tendencies is to see them as rhythms. Rhythms that change each day with different circumstances or reminders, emotions that spring up, or just wanting to be more connected to the grief process. Each Grief Rhythm exemplifies clusters of traits and habits you may exhibit at different points in the grief process. What I want to emphasize is that each rhythm is a protector, not to be put under scrutiny. Whether you're inclined to read everything you can get your hands on, or run until you can't anymore, or laser focus on the day-to-day problems in front of you, all of the rhythms are your mind's way of shielding you from the pain and overwhelm.

As you look at some of the ways that grief can manifest for you, understand that there is no good or bad here, no right or wrong. I mean it! No judging! Each of these rhythms is normal, and common. I've seen every single one of them play out during thousands of hours in the therapy room with my clients (and even for myself!). Think of these rhythms as reference points, trail markers for your experience, that can be even funny to see in action sometimes. They can also help you and others, including a therapist like me, determine a more specific healing path when you're struggling to understand what's happening inside you. Remember, it's not about fitting into neat little grief boxes; it's about naming and understanding all the ways that we can all both engage with and avoid our grief at times.

You may see yourself in one of these rhythms, or a few, or several, or maybe none of them. You may also flow in and out of some of these during the course of a day. It's not cut-and-dried—we are ever-shifting humans after all. Whatever your rhythm, know that it's perfectly normal. I like to see them as dependable friends that help us cope with our painful losses.

However you choose to view your rhythm, remember that you are not grieving wrong; you never could.

Our Inner Grief Rhythms

The Survivor—The Survivor is a rhythm based solely on...you guessed it, *survival*. If this is you, your primary need is the continuity of what is right in front of you. Whether it's pragmatic planning, taking care of kids, being a caregiver to someone else, a job that needs your attention, or simply making sure you're taking good care of your own physical and mental well-being. Some may begin the grieving experience in this rhythm and that's *very normal*. Especially if you're in shock, such as if you're a caretaker, parent, or have more pragmatic, urgent needs at hand like housing or income. This rhythm may also show up in the aftermath of a traumatic loss, where the intensity of emotion is so overwhelming that our brain can only focus on its survival (which is a helpful protective mechanism).

At its best, the Survivor Rhythm can help keep us emotionally safe and focused on urgent matters. It's ideal for the triage of those early days and months, when logistics have to take center stage and we're caught navigating an overwhelming amount of change. The Survivor mode is what makes you take out the trash, show up on time for work, and occasionally microwave a Trader Joe's burrito.

Over time, though, it can undermine our emotional need to feel and get the overwhelming emotions out of our body. It may be a gateway to the Compartmentalizer Rhythm, where we put some emotions in boxes and push some other intense emotions down to prioritize surviving. It also can prevent you from getting the comfort and consolation you need, because the people around you witness you "keep going," and mistake that for a signal that you're okay.

Being as honest as you can with safe and trusted people in your life about your feelings is key to being able to move through this rhythm when the time is right for you, while also having close people remind you that it's okay to release a little, and perhaps will offer that hand!

The Intellectualizer—This is the rhythm of information gatherers! In this mode, you may be someone who can identify and talk about feeling emotions but rarely seem to actually *feel* them. Knowing what we feel, and *experiencing* the emotion fully in our body, are two different animals, and for some people, this can be confusing and frustrating.

For example, when we intellectualize our emotions, we can likely name the anxiety or exhaustion when it comes up, but we don't notice or potentially shut down the sensations of sadness, anger, fear, pain, or physical symptoms like headaches or indigestion or insomnia that can accompany them.

The Intellectualizer likes to know what's going on and feels safest when it can observe itself from a distance. The Intellect often prefers books and empirical, evidence-based practices to help us understand, thinking that, if we know enough, we won't feel as overrun by our own grief. To an extent, understanding what we are experiencing can help us lessen that fear of the unknown, which turns down the volume on our "what's happening to me?!" panic, and allows for emotions to come forward. Too often, though, we use our knowledge to hide out in our minds. Rather than facilitating and normalizing our feelings, we wield our Intellect to keep them at bay. In time you might get so used to being in this rhythm (just like I did) that when the emotions do finally come forward, they take you by surprise, as you may believe you have already experienced the grief in its fullness.

Understanding that grief cycles can turn up in different ways at different times can help us remember to find a balance between our *understanding* of what's going on within us, and our *felt experience* (a bodily awareness) of the emotions and sensations associated with it.

The Diver—The Diver is comfortable with feelings, and as a result, may feel your way into the grieving process more easily than the Intellectualizer. If this sounds like you, you find the most comfort in sharing and connecting, and you actively look for those opportunities both online and in real life. People with this tendency actively seek therapy, support groups, and other comforting connections to feel less alone in their grief. The Diver wants to go all in, tell the world, buy every book on grief, and feel all the feelings that come up as soon as they come up all at once right now this exact second.

It's a super open rhythm, because it allows whatever comes up to come up! But in other ways, this rhythm can be overwhelming. Desperate to feel the feels and feel better, you may exhaust yourself emotionally, overload on all things "grief and loss," and neglect to listen to your body's signals that it's at capacity. You may also dive into the emotions headfirst without caring who your audience might be, and experience the hurt that comes with not being seen, met, or heard in your experience. If this is you, remember, grief isn't a race of feeling all you need to in one fell swoop. Having a break, getting some rest, setting boundaries, and taking care of yourself may not always be at the top of the priority list, but it's essential to your healing. Bring your attention to how deeply you're diving in, and to your pace. It's okay to take your time and meet the grief experience with patience and tender acceptance.

The Mover—The Mover Rhythm is just about that: *moving*. If this rhythm feels like you, you may find yourself wanting or needing to simply always be on the go. This can be cycling or hiking every day, going on long runs alone, attending exercise classes, working longer hours, running endless errands, staying out of your house, or generally anything that keeps you busy! The Mover Rhythm moves sometimes out of a need to run away from the reality of a loss, or simply as a way to process it while in movement.

People in this rhythm are uniquely game to literally feel grief, experiencing and processing its feelings through the body's movement. This can be a confusing rhythm to the outside world, who may assume you're avoiding your grief by quite literally trying to outrun it, but that isn't always the case. If you're a Mover, it may be that the need to "talk" about it feels less important in the moment, but the grief is a tab in the background, always running and processing new information even if it's not obvious to outsiders.

To know if you're truly a Mover or if you're in avoidance mode, simply notice if the loss is on your mind and how it is allowed to be present while you are in movement (or are working, running errands, or out with friends). For those who are Movers, you are not actively, consciously avoiding the loss experience, but rather internalizing, buffering, processing, feeling, and integrating while also avoiding the intense emotions and sensations that can arise in any given moment.

The Compartmentalizer—The Compartmentalizer Rhythm sits at the control board of our feelings, ready to turn on autopilot at any moment to get through a social situation or to take care of practical things without emotion getting in the way. For example, being a therapist during my own personal loss was hard, but in my work, it's imperative to be able to put my own "stuff" away and focus on the person and situation in front of me. It doesn't mean I ignore my own feelings or shove them down indefinitely; it just means that for right now, or for a determinate amount of time, my feelings must be put aside.

Compartmentalizers are experts at putting feelings into categories and boxes, to be examined at a later date. This is a vital skill when we don't have the luxury of immediately grieving because of other urgent obligations. Compartmentalizing can also be a protective mechanism to defend us against the too-muchness of our grief (like most of these rhythms), but it is not negative. Sometimes we do have to put some emotions aside to tackle something else at the moment.

For Compartmentalizers, our environment plays the largest role in how we allow in and express our emotions and thoughts around our loss. For example, how safe do we feel to express ourselves and/or do we have time, space, and people who will be able to hold our grief along with us? If you're at work and can't cry or express feelings during a meeting, can you put it aside until after work or until you can go to the bathroom and release the tears? However, if you compartmentalize too consistently for too long, more and more emotions get shoved to the back of the closet and it may feel harder to pull them out the longer they've been back there.

*   *   *

The Ruminator—Ruminators tend to spend a lot of time replaying all the things they wish went differently. Imagining a different ending to that loss. Cycling with guilt scenarios over and over. The Ruminator Rhythm within us can be subtle at first. People in this rhythm will quietly think things over...and over and over and over. After initially feeling perhaps a sense of shock at the loss, the Ruminator within us will sit down with a magnifying glass to go over every detail of the loss, particularly what *wasn't* done or said. As a result, Ruminators can battle immense guilt, shame, regret, and responsibility for the details surrounding their loss.

Though it's a bit more counterintuitive, just like the other rhythms, Rumination is a self-protective rhythm, bringing a sense of safety to an otherwise unsafe-feeling experience by making us believe we have had more control than we have had over our loss. Yup, that's right: Painful as it can feel sometimes, our brains would rather shame us for the moments we did or might have had a choice, rather than accept that we did not have a choice or any control over what happened.

While it's absolutely normal to think back over our relationship, we have to be careful not to park in this tendency for too long. Even if we wish it so, there was most likely truly nothing we could have done to have changed the outcome of our loss either in the moment or in the future and, if this is you, I want you to be able to let yourself off the hook for not knowing or being able to change anything. It may not be easy to let the narrative go, but tender reframing with a trusted person can help it loosen the grip on our story over time.

The Emotional/Spiritual Bypasser (ESB)—The ESB Rhythm will use clichés, quotes, religious and spiritual texts, or adages to comfort themselves and sidestep the agony of grief. This rhythm has a zero-tolerance policy for the painful aspects of loss so, instead, ESBs will convince themselves only to look on the bright side. After all, if nothing "bad" happened, if it all works out in the end, then there's nothing to be sad or angry about . . . right? If you find yourself saying it was "meant to be" or "this is a lesson that I needed to expand my consciousness," this might be your go-to rhythm.

In the short term, bypassing our emotions can offer relief during an intense grieving moment. But more often than not, it's like putting a Band-Aid over the kind of gaping wound that needs stitches. When we lean on spiritual clichés, we don't leave space for ourselves to feel anything but those "good vibes only." As a caveat, I want to be clear that emotional and spiritual bypassing is *not* the same as having faith, and someone's true expression of faith is not bypassing. It's the difference between someone who uses faith for comfort and guidance to get through the painful times, as opposed to using spirituality or positive thinking to circumvent them altogether. This rhythm is meant for those who believe in "positive vibes only," and have trouble allowing the authentic emotions of their loss to be front and center.

The Quality Controller—I put this rhythm last, because this rhythm will want to oversee all the other rhythms and make sure they are doing them "right"! It's the rhythm that wants to make sure it is reading the right books, listening to the right podcasts, sharing in a way the rhythm deems "appropriate," but who really knows what that is. This rhythm wants to talk about their loss, but not talk "too much" about it, to make sure we read the room when we are around others, and also do whatever we can do to keep the grief boat moving in the "right" direction.

The Quality Controller Rhythm wants to protect you from the needless dragging out of your pain and is on high alert that you aren't abandoned in the process. Despite the knowledge it gains over its own experience, this rhythm can really keep us a little too buttoned up in what may be at times an otherwise supremely messy full-body experience. In trying not to have things drag out, Quality Controllers inadvertently prolong their journeys, playing it too safe or too well behaved, and taking other people's feelings too much into account. This can be a very likable tendency to others on the outside, but I want us to make sure we are prioritizing our own needs and feelings above proving ourselves to others, okay?

Let's Check In: Seeing Your Rhythms

Do any of these grieving rhythms resonate? Do you feel "called out"? Do you recognize the ways you either hide, avoid, or engage and process your grief in a way you didn't know about before? If you felt these rhythms could easily blend together, you'd be right. It's easy for them to overlap or blend either in the early parts of our grief experience or as time moves forward.

This is really about self-learning and also giving ourselves the permission to have the inner journey we need to have after loss. If you feel comfortable, keep an eye on your Grief Rhythms and see if they give you any more insight and even comfort in knowing however your grief arises is common and perfectly normal.

In my own journey, I swam back and forth between hard-core Intellectualizer and Compartmentalizer, sprinkled with the Mover. At some point, I was even doing some major Quality Control, popping in to make sure that once I realized I wasn't grieving, I got started and I got started "right." Once I realized what I was doing, I had a good laugh at myself, but then I realized that going forward, I was dancing along to every one of these Grief Rhythms. Each of them brought me closer to understanding my coping mechanisms and tendencies, which in turn helped me to understand what I needed next. After all, each rhythm is there to protect us, offering something it thought would give us space and safety, or ensure our survival, pointing us directly toward the core of our need. For example, maybe we need to slow down and connect to our emotions if we intellectualize. Maybe we need to create space and time to grieve if we find ourselves pushing it away and compartmentalizing. Maybe we need to cut ourselves some slack and just allow whatever comes up to come up and know that whatever it is, it is RIGHT (thanks, Quality Controller). Regardless of what rhythms show up for you, or how often you cycle between them, there is one core need that all of the rhythms point to, and that's a need for self-compassion.

The Importance of Self-Compassion While Grieving

I witness a surprising amount of self-blame when it comes to grief. So many of my clients think they should have come to therapy already half-healed and ready to just package up the messiness sticking out of their corners and call it a day. And there I am, the human-shaped stop sign asking them to slow their roll, because grief has no finish line to race to, nor can we beat the grief out of ourselves by insulting, berating, or bullying ourselves to be "better" (whatever that even means). And that's where self-compassion comes in.

The Grief Rhythms are where our minds default for self-protection. Like we've talked about, our brains are going to try and avoid or minimize the pain of our loss, so we bypass, run, push it down, intellectualize—whatever we can do to cut the pain down to a manageable size or, better yet, evade it altogether. A gentle and healthy way we can interrupt these cycles and avoid the "stuckness" is to apply self-compassion. To listen to what the rhythm is signaling you need, and to try to meet that need with tenderness and understanding.

According to Dr. Kristin Neff, bestselling author, researcher, and leading expert on self-compassion, "Self-compassion involves acting the same way towards yourself when you are having a difficult time, fail, or notice something you don't like about yourself."[1] Or, as I like to tell my clients, drop the knife at your own throat, please, and I ask them to instead inquire on how they can be kind and tender with themselves.

I know, I know, "just be nice to yourself" can sound very Pollyanna when you're in the midst of intense suffering. It's like that very sneaky key ingredient, the piece of healing that you can't be successful without, like something your grandmother might put in a family recipe but never tell you.

"How can I comfort and care for myself in this moment when I feel so all over the place?" a client may ask, to which they have already answered—to be in this very moment, just tending gently to whatever your heart (or body) may need. Sometimes it's a comforting word, sometimes it's a glass of water, but being present and caring toward ourselves in this fragile time is where I want us to go. Without actively bringing in self-compassion, we run the risk of chastising ourselves and our grief process—saying things like, "Why is this taking so long?" or "What's wrong with me that I am still affected by this after so many years?" Trust me, the brain can be mean sometimes. Self-compassion simply adds a softness and a permission to be, feel, and experience whatever and however we are in any given moment without the harsh narrative of judgment.

For example, as a Ruminator, instead of the could'ves and should'ves, can you imagine a scenario where you did your best and are still doing your best? If you notice you're trying to bypass, ESBs, allow yourself to get quiet and curious about what needs to be seen and felt. Or how about Survivors giving yourself props for just getting out of bed on your worst days?

Rarely do we talk to ourselves as compassionately as we would speak to someone we deeply care for, am I right? But the question is, *Why not?* Grief, as we know all too well, can be isolating and scary, and we can sometimes further alienate ourselves when we need comfort the most with our own judgment. Contrary to popular belief, the antidote to feeling weak, impatient, and frustrated with ourselves isn't to beat ourselves up or berate ourselves for where we are, or even withhold our deepest needs. Rather, it's granting ourselves more compassion, kindness, and curiosity.

Dr. Neff goes on to teach us that "self-compassion involves acting the same way towards yourself when you are having a difficult time, fail, or notice something you don't like about yourself. Instead of just ignoring your pain with a 'stiff upper lip' mentality, you stop to tell yourself 'this is really difficult right now, how can I comfort and care for myself in this moment?'" It will not take away the pain of loss, but having self-compassion when we are in this dark abyss of grief can powerfully shift our perception of our experience just enough to breathe easier at a minimum. Self-compassion helps us to prevent piling on to our already too heavy emotional burden. We don't need to compound the pain of loss with the pain of self-disparagement. If and when you find yourself being more self-critical at any given time on your grief journey, I invite you to come to a place of softness and inner reflection. Below are questions that I hope serve as a reminder to simply keep coming back to the tenderness that grief calls for, even if it takes time to get used to. This time calls for kindness from self, above all.

Grief Self-Compassion Reflection

As you give some thought to these questions, make a note of where you could be more loving and compassionate, as well as where your heart is already acting toward what is good and nurturing for yourself. Please try to reflect without judgment or criticism—that defeats the purpose! This reflection is for you to look honestly at how you treat yourself when you're feeling vulnerable and fragile.

- Have you been patient with your grieving process overall?
- Have you judged, punished, or pressured yourself for not moving at the pace you believe you should be moving on your grief journey?
- Are you berating yourself for all the things you believe you did "wrong"?
- Do you speak to yourself with patience and love when you're at your most fragile?

- Do you meet your pain with care and curiosity?
- Will you allow yourself to have help from others when you need it most?
- Are you able to give yourself credit for the tiny steps you take toward healing?
- Do you treat yourself like an adversary or a dear friend when you're feeling your weakest?

Don't panic if the painful feelings don't move the way you think they should or on the timeline you feel they should. It's normal and far more frequent than you may think for grief to take years (yes, years plural, sorry!) to fully process in our minds and hearts. This doesn't mean that there will not be relief from the intensity along the way, but grief stays with us.

If you are struggling with judging your grief experience or ruminating over what you couldn't change, if you are avoiding the feelings or ignoring the physical calls for attention, if you're trying to keep busy, or if you are putting the emotions into tightly locked boxes or focusing only on the good vibes in your life, I encourage you to be gentle with yourself. Slowly allow in the idea that you are allowed to experience your grief in all sorts of different ways at different times. There is no one way or right way to grieve, you know? How could there be—after all, no one experiences the same exact loss. We all have unique relationships and relationship dynamics with who or what we have lost. No two people could grieve in exactly the same way, because no two people have experienced exactly the same loss. Your job isn't to conform to some imaginary timeline, to progress through your grief like it's a couch-to-5K, or to follow anyone else's schedule or set of expectations. You will find yourself experiencing so many different things emotionally and physically, all the while your mind is ping-ponging back and forth over all the things you might have done differently, or how to look at your life now with such a huge void.

Your job is as challenging as it is simple: to bear witness to the feelings, perceptions, physical sensations, and rhythms you fall into. Allowing yourself to be with what is true for you now, in this very moment—that is more than enough. You are not stuck. You're showing up. And that's more than enough.

CHAPTER 7

Retracing Our Steps, Redefining Ourselves

"...sooner or later she had to give up the hope for a better past."

—Irvin D. Yalom, *Staring at the Sun: Overcoming the Terror of Death*

After my mom died, I wanted so badly to be able to talk about her in superlatives only—to express how *amazing* she was, how *totally* loved I'd felt, how *incredibly* supportive she'd been. All of that was true, but I hesitated to say those things too often because there were other truths that were at play within our relationship. The fact was, she and I were very different people (she thought I was "weird" for my out-of-the-box spiritual beliefs, for starters). We loved each other fiercely, but we also struggled to understand each other at times. We lived the width and breadth of a mother-daughter relationship, and that included petty arguments from time to time. With her suddenly gone, that confusing blend of truths felt challenging to reconcile, and I found myself replaying so many of our moments together, wishing I'd responded to them this way or that way, always somehow "better" than I had. Sometimes, my guilt felt like it might pare me from the inside out. It had become part of me and how I defined myself.

I remember being on the train ride home just after her death, incessantly replaying a moment during her illness when she'd needed help.

It was an early morning after ten days of watching her body begin to shut down. I'd heard her calling from upstairs that she wanted to get up—but I struggled to get up myself, too weighed down by fatigue to react much faster than a snail. Of course, I did go to her, but had I been a little more rested, I'd have jumped up without pause. As I sat there on the train watching the world whizz by my window, I just kept wishing I'd gotten to her bedside sooner. She'd been fine once I'd arrived, but over and over in my mind, self-recrimination kept repeating—why hadn't I moved quicker? What was wrong with me? I should have jumped out of bed to get to her... those thoughts still grip me from time to time and sting like a paper cut on my heart.

As the days lengthened into weeks and then months, countless moments, many from my younger years, played and replayed in my mind, as if stuck on loop. Moments that, before her death, had felt like standard parts of our relationship became catalysts for further guilt and regret. So many seemingly tiny moments began to take on more importance than they perhaps deserved. More than anything, I yearned to relive those slices of time, to do them differently.

I was doing what most people do when they lose a loved one—retracing the steps of our relationship, trying to make peace with how I'd shown up as a daughter and how she'd been as my mother. It's one of those things we do when we're grieving; we imagine saying the words we never did, speaking our truth more fully than we ever dared to, doing the things we meant to do but somehow never could.

It's natural to replay our losses. We watch them, we wonder, we agonize over how things could have been different. As normal as this part of the grieving process is, it's not a place we should let ourselves stay in for too long. Endlessly scrutinizing how we showed up can begin to warp how we define and relate to ourselves, and if we let them linger for too long, guilt, regret, and other unresolved feelings can become embedded in our identity. Since the way we feel about ourselves impacts so much in our lives, it's important to notice and unearth our tendency of going from ruminating to self-flagellation, and when necessary, face the unacknowledged pain hidden inside them. Looking at our losses with a more compassionate, neutral lens is vital to help us not define ourselves by our actions (or lack thereof) when we were simply doing the best we could at the time.

Why Do We Retrace Steps?

Looking back on moments with my mom, I inevitably resorted to turning on myself, reinventing our history together. *If I'd only been more loving that day... and more patient when she'd call to check on me... and rolled my eyes less often when she (once again) sent me home with meatballs.* (She was the quintessential Italian mother, happiest at her table, surrounded by friends and family.) *If only, if only, if only...* As the days added up, the list grew. The truth, of course, was that showing up as someone other than myself would have diminished our relationship, rather than strengthened it. Adversity and conflict aren't always fun, but they can be important, even necessary and constructive, parts of a healthy, loving relationship.

Another truth was that I couldn't relive those moments, or any moments with her. It hurt so much because I still really needed her. I'd known she was sick for a long while, but I still didn't feel anywhere near ready to lose her. I craved her validation and wanted so badly to hear her say that she was proud of me and everything I'd accomplished. I yearned to feel connected to her, to know that she was gone, but not entirely.

These longings to resolve past challenges and conflicts and meet our own need for validation and connection are some of the many reasons we retrace steps when we're grieving; we're searching for ways to understand our relationship with the person, and perhaps to forgive the imperfect ways we—and they—showed up in that relationship. I call this the Death Digression, that place where we get stuck feeling guilt or regret about things we think we did or said "wrong." It's like when you have a fight with someone close to you and can't stop thinking about one thing you said, or they said. For a period of time, that single sentence, uttered once, stops you from looking at the entirety of your relationship with that person. In the Death Digression, we may lose sight of the whole relationship, because we get hyperfocused on what could or should have been. Like many grievers, I found myself periodically getting stuck in that obsessive place, if only to sustain our connection to each other.

I felt so desperate to feel connected to her, in fact, that I decided to turn it into a routine. In the days and weeks after she died, I would put in my earphones and walk the streets of the Upper West Side, saying frantically, *"Thanks for being such a good mom, and oh, I still need you, and also, will you help to find a new apartment, and oh just in case, thank you again so much for being such a great mom, but I still do really need you!"* I soon lovingly (and jokingly) began referring to this experience as my interstellar mother-daughter time.

Through those walks I began to contend with my inability to see past my own needs in my relationship with her at times, including during her final months. Slowly but surely, our interstellar time helped me to forgive myself for being myself—which is to say human, and therefore imperfect. During our many mother-daughter interstellar sessions, I slowly began to let go of my need to guilt or blame myself for not being "enough" of this or being "too much" of that. Instead, I was able to let myself feel the pain of losing her. Then, little by little, I was able to fall in love all over again with a mother-daughter relationship that had been flawed in some ways, yes, but also incredibly meaningful. Her voice, her hugs, her words, and her phone calls had always been so powerfully present in me and my life. Our imperfections, however imperfect, had all been intrinsic to the deep and abiding love we'd always felt for each other. We were who we were, and that, in fact, was part of the depth and breadth of our intense connection to each other.

To this day, whenever I'm feeling lonely or like I need her input or nurturing, I put in my AirPods and head outside for a walk to co-create the next episode of our interstellar mother-daughter time. Weird? Maybe, but it's helped me to feel like our relationship is continuing to evolve. If you feel inclined to try it, I highly recommend it. If it feels uncomfortable at first, keep trying it out from time to time to see if it feels useful to you. (Tip: If you're walking in a populated area, bring sunglasses in case tears begin to flow and you'd prefer some privacy.)

Retracing the Steps of Non-Caregiver Attachments

Because this kind of rumination and retracing is particularly fraught after the loss of an attachment figure (a parent, grandparent, or another childhood caregiver), I'm going to speak primarily to those losses in this chapter. That said, the process of replaying moments and blaming ourselves for our "failures" can apply equally to other kinds of losses, from breakups and divorce to friendships ending, lost jobs, and more. *If I'd only done/said this or that . . . If I'd only realized this or that sooner . . .* or *What the hell happened?!* . . . It can be so easy to resort to this way of thinking whenever we've lost something or someone we've loved and/or relied on—especially if that loss is an ambiguous one. The lessons we learn from loss can be powerful, positive forces in our lives, but please be mindful that your self-questioning is in line with your highest good, and not a form of self-punishment.

When Grieving Means Facing Primal Attachment Wounds

The only daughter in her family, Patricia had noticed from an early age how much more attention her brothers received from her father. Yearning for similar recognition, she went out of her way to do what her brothers did, hoping desperately to gain his approval. No matter how hard she tried, though, she never succeeded, a fact that eventually convinced her that she was somehow to blame for his disinterest.

When Patricia's mother passed away, their relationship seemed to shift. For the first time, her father began asking her for help. Feeling like this was her chance to grow closer to him—and to feel worthy of his love and attention—she gladly stepped in to fill the void. One day, he asked her to check on his investment portfolio, since, he said, she was the "smart one." It was the first time he'd ever praised her, and for her that one comment felt like the approval and validation she'd always craved. Soon afterward, however, his attention and praise abruptly ended. Instead of reaching out to her, he began calling her brothers for help. Knowing that he seemed to enjoy communicating with friends via email, she began sending him an occasional note, but never got a reply. In fact, he never even acknowledged receiving her emails, although he did tell one of her brothers about them. Just like that, the window of opportunity he'd seemed to have opened in their relationship had slammed shut as abruptly as it had appeared. The rejection and shame of being the "unworthy child" became even more deeply embedded inside her.

In the years since, Patricia has repeatedly replayed that moment when her father referred to her as the "smart one," retracing the steps of their interaction, her reaction, and what she'd done "wrong" that had made him start relying on her brothers again, rather than her. They were questions she could never answer, and when her father died just a year after her mother, she was assaulted by the reality that there were no more opportunities to connect with him. No more opportunities to understand, or to receive the recognition she craved. That door was closed for good.

In cases like Patricia's, when an absence in a critical relationship is left unfulfilled, retracing our steps often amplifies pain that can't be easily resolved or addressed, largely because the wounds it leaves are so intricately woven into our identity. Even before we realize it's happened, the pain left by these primal bonds becomes part of our answers to critical questions like *Who am I?* and *Am I even worthy of love?*

These deep dents in our identity can feel especially indelible when a lack of safety, love, and connection existed within one or more of our caretaker relationships. Looking at these core attachment wounds is essential to our evolution and healing because they impact us so profoundly. Core attachment wounds are an emotional wound formed from inconsistent safety and love within childhood. Whether we like it or not, we all crave validation from our parents; it's one of our basic human needs. When that validation isn't given, the multilayered loss that void leaves behind forces people into grieving, whether consciously or unconsciously. Oftentimes, like we talked about in chapter 2, that grief over the parent-child relationship that "should have been" begins long before the parent has even died, in the form of ambiguous grief.

Like so many clients, while retracing the steps of her relationship with her father, Patricia came face-to-face with her core attachment wounds. By depriving her of his love and attention, her father had created this growing feeling inside her like, *If my own father wasn't interested in me, then I must not be worthy of the love I want.* Rather than considering what was lacking in him, she turned on herself. It's a heartbreaking but incredibly common pattern that stems from experiencing neglect or abuse starting at an early age. Unless and until that pain is aired and healed, grief and the shame it's burying stay lodged inside us, and we remain in a cycle of retracing our steps, wondering if "things" might have been different if we'd not said this or if we had done that or just been "better."

As Patricia slowly began to peel away the layers of her grief over her father and everything he hadn't given her, she realized that she'd internalized many of the negative things he'd said to her. She ingested the idea that she was "less than" because she wasn't similar enough to her brothers. She believed that she wasn't interesting because he hadn't been interested. With her father now gone, she needed to find her way out of this dark web of misguided and misleading beliefs around who she was, what she deserved, and who would define her worth from that point onward.

We can and need to continue to do the healing work that comes with painful ruptures in relationships—with or without the attachment figure present. Relationships can continue to evolve (or devolve) even without one of the people physically present. It's hard, but worthy inner work.

Peeling Away Deeper Layers

What can I say? Loss breaks our relationships wide-open, exposing the sedimentary layers of emotional wounds that we all bear from those we love. The impossibility of the new—new experiences, new memories, new conversations, new behaviors—forces us to confront what was, without the rosy tint of hope that there can be something different in the future. As painful as those realizations are, the most profound healing happens in seeing the layers we wish we could avoid—all the other tender, painful places within our hearts that we weren't expecting to have to see or feel, let alone explore, until grief kicked it all up,

In cases like Patricia's, this means facing, and ultimately nurturing, the inner child who still needs the love and care they never got. Looking deeper at unhealed parts of ourselves can be painful. A client once told me that she realized after losing her dad that she actually never had a reliable man in her life who followed through for her or made her a priority, and this opened a lot of issues around her sense of worth. The layers of unresolved hurt and new realizations can be a painful sidekick at times when we already feel so bulldozed by our loss.

As much as we may want to avoid these unhealed parts of ourselves (if only because "inner child work" has become a bad pop psychology catchphrase), so many of these deeper wounds do ultimately lead us back to our younger selves. These younger selves are the parts of us who weren't met, seen, valued, loved, or nurtured in the way they needed by their caregivers. Especially when those caregivers are no longer here to be part of the repair, we have to learn to step in on our own behalf. Even when this work feels irrelevant or grating, try to stay open to the idea that your inner child really may be craving a new or different kind of attention. As I have seen in my work, heeding that call from within really does transform people's lives in amazing ways.

After Patricia's father died, some of her healing came from writing letters to her father where she expressed what she wanted to say. She also wrote letters to him from her younger self explaining what that little girl had needed from him. That can be very therapeutic, reclaiming those parts of ourselves, speaking our truth, even when the person they're intended for is deceased, or unable or unwilling to listen. The question then becomes, how do you live life on your terms and what does that feel like? Patricia's entire identity as a young girl had been shaped by her ongoing campaign to appease her father. As she wades through the layers of her grief, reacquainting herself with the inner child who still needs so much love, she's inevitably faced with the question—Who might little Patricia have been if she'd been loved unconditionally by her father? Did she really love ice hockey as much as her father and brothers? What interests and friends might she have gravitated toward if she hadn't been yearning for her father's attention? Since all of these early choices have shaped the woman she's become, she's not only mourning the father and childhood she never had, she's faced with an incredibly confusing question—*Who am I, really?* She can't undo her history with her father—that's a part of her now—but she also can't continue denying the parts of herself she shunned for her father's benefit. But what even are those buried pieces of her and how can she get to them?

When we go spelunking around in our childhood wounds, people inevitably encounter the scars inflicted by their shame—*Do I, or my feelings, even matter? Does anyone actually care about me? How can I face all this pain while nursing this overriding sense of worthlessness?* See all the old, wounded, insecure stories that grief can churn up in its wake? No wonder we'd rather stick our heads in the sand. Partly because there's so much deeply embedded pain to unearth, this work requires tremendous courage and dedication. At times, it feels exhausting trying to notice and understand all the ways that a parent's neglect/abandonment/mistreatment has affected you and your life, largely because the impact is so complex and all-encompassing.

This work can also feel heartbreakingly lonely if you are someone who has only ever had yourself to rely on. After all, the entire reason you even need to do this work is because a critical figure in your life abandoned you, if not physically, then certainly emotionally, which is equally true in cases involving abuse and trauma. It's kind of like, *Wait, so I've been alone all my life, yearning for SOMEONE ELSE'S love, and now I'm supposed to focus on receiving that love from MYSELF??? How depressing is that!?!* For many people, it's crushing to realize that no one is going to pop out of the woodwork and shower them with the love, attention, and validation that's already decades overdue. No matter what positive, loving relationships you have in your life now, or how you feel toward your caregivers, you may always continue to mourn real-life validation from your parents with varying levels of intensity. Grieving that loss and its endless ripple effects can be worse than grieving the death of a person. And I am so truly sorry for that. You deserved better then, and you deserve better now.

Yet the popular adage that we have to break down to break through remains true, so while the severed shards of this kind of multilayered grief do feel cutting, this often slow and harrowing process of dissolving the person you felt others expected you to be is necessary to become who you really are. When it's handled with care and respect, which it absolutely must be, it can become an important passageway toward deep and authentic healing.

Let's Check In

Truth is, no one's childhood is perfect—and sometimes, they can feel pretty turbulent. Looking back can bring up a lot of emotions or sensations—maybe even positive memories, too. I want you to take a moment and close your eyes and think back on your younger self.

I don't want you to do anything more than become aware of what came up for you right at this moment. Looking back doesn't have to involve blame or shame or taking any action toward someone. It can just mean we become more aware of the stories we've inherited, the stories we tell ourselves, what still feels raw and unresolved, and whether we are ready to take a step closer to understanding that hurt.

If something felt obviously painful or missing, I'd like for you to tenderly think of ways to give yourself what you felt was missing for you, or begin to think about ways you can provide yourself with what you wish you'd had growing up, especially emotionally.

If or when you feel up to it, I'd like to have you write a letter to that younger version of yourself from where you are today. What would you say to your younger self? What could you offer them going forward? Maybe a promise to check in, to listen to your heart and intuition? Respect your own needs and boundaries going forward. Giving attention and love to our younger selves is all they ever needed . . . and it's never too late.

Getting Stuck at What Might Have Been

Like many parents, Aziz's father had always harbored a mental map of who his son would be and what kind of life he would pursue as an adult. Aziz would go into law, his father always imagined, and become wealthy. That would allow him to overcome the financial struggles his father had experienced as a hardworking middle manager. Once Aziz was on his own, however, he realized that he wanted to become a musician instead. His father was furious, continually shaming and minimizing his son. To his father, Aziz becoming a musician was a living, breathing expression of ingratitude for all his father had done for him. Although some of Aziz's family members supported his dream in private, none of them ever spoke up to defend him in the presence of his commanding, overbearing father.

Once his father died, Aziz found himself consumed by regret. His career wasn't the only area in which he'd "betrayed" his father's vision of who he was meant to be. After many years of denying, including to himself, that he was attracted to men and women, he had finally begun to come out in his twenties. But he'd never told his parents. As he and I began to work through his fractured relationship with his father, Aziz was overtaken by regret that he'd never told his father that he was bisexual. For a long time he remained convinced that he and his father would have been able to bond—if only Aziz had spoken his truth.

This often happens in the Death Digression: We get so stuck in our guilt or regret that we almost rewrite history, convincing ourselves that whatever went "wrong" was somehow our fault, or could have been corrected if only we'd done X or Y. Often this is a way of avoiding facing the deeper layers of our grief. We don't feel ready to face the more painful truths that lie in wait, so we blame ourselves instead. However excruciating that blame, regret, even remorse may be, it can feel easier than confronting the darker truths we sense are buried beneath.

What often happens in these cases is that people tend to repeat the patterns they're most desperate to heal from. For instance, someone who has had an emotionally and/or physically abusive parent may inadvertently choose similarly abusive partners. Or they may become the unofficial subordinate in their friendships and relationships, always giving love, care, and attention to people who don't give any of it back. The simple fact is, if you don't have a model for a healthy relationship, you will resort to what you know. The pain of the familiar is always easier than the pain of the unknown.

Re-creating these relationship dynamics compounds our grief, because it confirms both people's worst fears and what they have been taught to believe—that they don't matter, certainly not to the extent that other people do. This is shame in its purest form. It hurts deeply, but paradoxically it's not as scary as daring to invest in their intrinsic worthiness. If you continue believing you're unworthy, after all, you have an ironclad reason not to take risks, to avoid situations where you might endure more hurt. When we're guided by shame, we would rather accept the pain we know, rather than risk the pain of a failure, especially one that could confirm our utter worthlessness once and for all. Paradoxically, investing in shame from the get-go almost seems like the saner, safer choice.

Now, am I saying all of this is conscious? That we wake up in the morning and think, *You know what? Texting the person who has been super emotionally unavailable seems like the best, healthiest choice for me today. Let's do it!* No! Not at all. But brains are strange and magical protectors, and you might be surprised how often your shame is running the show. Because that is the terrible, suffocating thing about shame—once it's firmly in place, it distorts how we perceive literally everything, every-one, and every experience in our lives and, most importantly, how we view and treat ourselves. Shame, when accompanying grief, becomes a weighty darkness planted inside us, devouring all potential for light, love, connection, intimacy, and any sense of security around being seen and heard.

Like I said earlier, for those carrying shame and guilt along with their grief, so often the most profound healing happens in the dark, deep layers we wish didn't even exist, like when a client thinks they are coming in to process a loss and they begin to examine and pro-cess the relationship as a whole and their experiences around different types of loss they never even realized was loss. When it comes to grief, healing can involve looking at our entire lives from a bird's-eye view and watching the ripple effects of our losses and wounds. We are the sum of all of our parts and experiences, after all.

Memories Through Grief-Colored Glasses

Almost everyone has heard the adage "Do not speak ill of the dead." It's as though the second someone dies, *boom*, clean slate. We shine a light only on their most desirable, praiseworthy qualities to avoid scarring their image. Unfortunately, this not only creates a chronically inaccurate record of history, it deprives us of the chance to grieve honestly and authentically.

As we know by now, naming our feelings and relationship dynamics is a vital part of processing our losses. Yet clients often tell me that they just don't feel comfortable sharing the parts of their loved one that weren't so shiny. Trying not to "speak ill of the dead," sometimes they speak this in a whisper as if the deceased person might hear them, which I am always amused by . . . I'm pretty sure a whisper reaches the other side, too, but I digress!

So why is it that when we lose someone or even something, we automatically give so much more weight and value to them or it? Why does death demand that we revere only the best within someone? And what happens when we know it wasn't all quite so shiny?

While it's true that loss can, sometimes, help us appreciate someone differently—noticing after your divorce, for example, the way that you realized how amazing your group of friends is, or how your first real job with the terrible boss gave you valuable lessons to carry forward. It may not be at the forefront of our hearts and minds while in the midst of deep pain, but it can come up from time to time, that sense of looking back on it differently or with a changed perspective.

But, we cannot simply paint over parts of someone that may have hurt us. Burying the truth of a person who has died, or is simply no longer in our lives, forces us to bury parts of our relationship with them, and by extension, parts of ourselves. That only adds grief onto grief, and potentially piles trauma on top of grief.

If it feels authentic to do so, by all means honor the good things about someone who has died! Acknowledging the bad doesn't negate the good. And, as you feel ready, I encourage you to confront the tough stuff that any loving relationship inevitably harbors. Naming that your best friend was amazing and so supportive during your breakup with your ex, while also acknowledging that she can be mean, dismissive, and gaslighting when you are feeling vulnerable and fragile; or how your mom always knew exactly how to coax an orchid to life but never made it to a single one of your school plays; or feeling gratitude to your dad for introducing you to a lifelong love of music, while still feeling the sting of his critique after every piano lesson—none of these takes away the relationship you had with those people. There's no shame or dishonor in honesty.

Working through loss means allowing yourself to acknowledge the truth of the loss you've experienced, which includes who they (actually) were as well as your relationship with them and how it's impacted you and your life.

Embracing Imperfection

When I got stuck in my own Death Digression, replaying moments when I "should" have reacted differently to my mom, I was also avoiding facing the realities of our loving but never-perfect relationship. Working with Aziz, Patricia, and other clients who get stuck in this place of regret and guilt, I eventually ask them to consider the idea that the conversation they wish they'd had or the action they wish they'd taken might *not* have turned out the way they think. What if coming out to his father had weakened, rather than strengthened, Aziz's relationship with his dad? What if me being a different kind of kid had caused me and my mom to grow apart, rather than closer together? They're unanswerable questions, but should be considered when we get lost blaming and shaming ourselves for scenarios and outcomes that can only ever exist inside our imagination.

We constantly see, like, and share sayings and social media posts about self-acceptance and self-love, but truly accepting and loving yourself, especially in the absence of essential love like that of a parent or caregiver, is deep, sometimes excruciating, work. There's no shortcut or express route to healing from those primal wounds. We all have to wade through the dark, murky waters of the many moments that inevitably replay in our minds, as well as fear, shame, anger/rage, regret, and sadness, among other emotions. It can be a labor-intensive, stop-and-start process that must take its own path, on its own timeline. It asks you to be present with your experience, which is so important, because everything we have learned so far helps. And we need to give ourselves the permission to feel, notice, and honor the needs we have, emotionally, psychologically, physically, and even spiritually. From this place, you can then begin to see and feel all the joy and light you deserve to experience in this moment and many others.

Our relationships change us, before loss and after. Ruminating and shaming ourselves—clinging to what-if scenarios, or trying to recast the relationships as all #goodvibesonly—will keep us stuck in our pain. Retracing our steps to learn more about ourselves, the relationship, the relationship dynamics, and our own inner experiences can give us a way forward. In turn, you get to form a new relationship with yourself. As Alice Miller said in *The Drama of the Gifted Child: The Search for the True Self*, "In order to become whole we must try, in a long process, to discover our own personal truth, a truth that may cause pain before giving us a new sphere of freedom." Seeing ourselves and our lives in a truer light is the path to healing, slowly, but surely.

CHAPTER 8

The Weight of Grief:
When It's All Just Too Much

"No one ever told me that grief felt so like fear."
—C. S. Lewis, *A Grief Observed*

Up to this point we've been getting more and more intimate with our grief experience. We've journeyed through the portal of the griefall and have come face-to-face with some huge and overwhelming feelings, as well as the physical and nervous system responses that may have come up in response to your loss. We've learned about flowing with our Grief Rhythms, and just how important it is to extend ourselves compassion when we feel "stuck." By now, you also know that your grief is a process without a timeline or clear direction. That thought alone may feel like *a lot*. Or, at least, a lot more than you'd like. You may still feel like you're stranded in this foreign place, looking around to try to get your bearings, and I am sure you'd rather hightail it back to your life pre-loss as fast as you can. I don't blame you for a minute. It's a lot for one person to contend with, and you may feel yourself completely underwater in your grief experience. So let's talk about it. Let's dive in, together.

Sometimes, loss hits harder and longer than we may have anticipated or feel we can bear. Sometimes, our grief experience is downright crippling, and when that happens it's completely normal to feel depressed, anxious, or like you can't imagine your future (or don't want to) in light of your loss. And yet that feeling that you can't anymore—that you've lost the will to go on—it can be a scary moment.

Suicidal ideation is a part of grief that we rarely talk about, and it affects a lot more people than you might imagine. It doesn't mean that I, as a therapist, gloss over it and assume it's just going to pass. The desire not to go on needs to be witnessed and tended to, first as a human, and then clinically, if needed. We cannot hide away in shame our deepest, most desperate achings.

When we suppress and shove down our emotional truths, even the most "shameful" ones, they become bigger and knock louder to come out. They can become the secret knowledge we carry as rocks in our pockets. But you don't have to hide these thoughts and feelings alone in the dark.

Let's Check In

I want to remind you here to be mindful and gentle, as we are in what can feel like really tough territory, emotionally speaking. I want you to go at your own pace, which means to slow down, stop, or even call a hotline if you feel you need more care, safety, or time to process your experience. As Coach Taylor would always say on *Friday Night Lights*, "Clear eyes, full hearts, can't lose." Not to mention, going in it *together.*

When the Future Vanishes Before Us

I vividly remember running a grief support group for older adults, where several of the group members spoke regularly of their desire not to go on since losing their spouse. It's a tricky moment as a therapist. How much do I inquire further? Do I jump into action and assess how likely they are to go through with it or do I pay quiet, close attention while outwardly encouraging them to express their deepest feelings and walk alongside their broken hearts without turning to a safety plan immediately unless there is a reason to do so?

In my personal life, I'd been anxious hearing such statements. I'll never forget watching my father pace the house after my mom died and, out of nowhere, announce that he wasn't afraid to die anymore, because then he'd see my mother again. Or how sobering it felt hearing my dad's dear friend Ray tell me immediately after burying his wife that he "had no future." He described in such vivid detail the feeling of being in a locked room with no doors or windows. Everyone begged him to come out, but he couldn't. More importantly, he wasn't sure he wanted to.

In the moment, hearing these longings—whether in ourselves or from a grieving friend or loved one—can be frightening. Very few of us are comfortable with the idea of suicide, and perhaps logically so. It's terrifying enough to imagine that a loved one could disappear at any moment, and scarier still to think that it's not chance but choice that could bring such terrible loss. Societally, death by suicide is so vilified and taboo that most of us fear speaking up lest we get hushed up and sent to the ER for evaluation.

But here's the thing: The feeling of not wanting to go on after a significant loss is absolutely *okay*. Feeling like the meaning just got pulled from your life, so why bother forging ahead? Uncertain how you can bear the idea of tomorrow, much less a year or a whole lifetime without your loved one? Your best friend? This is normal. Hang out with enough grieving people, and you'll start to notice just how common it is to interact a little differently with death.

We can't stop people from speaking their deepest thoughts simply because it scares us. Not as therapists, anyhow. Grief is about endings and loss, after all, and so allowing the support group members to explore their relationship and proximity to their own "ending" wasn't cause for alarm; it was a necessary part of the healing process. Feeling unafraid of dying, even longing to die, was how some of their grief was showing up at that moment. Pathologizing their experience so soon after such a significant loss would be more for my benefit than theirs, and thanks to years of training, I wasn't afraid of their despair, even if I did keep a close eye on it.

Like we talked about in chapter 2, every loss we suffer comes with ripple effects, and each can feel like a new burden to carry all on its own. A burden that no one can really understand, because the meaning of each "loss within the loss" is unique to us. But, all the ways in which we lose can add up, and that burden can feel like just too much. For example, in losing a loved one, we may also lose the person we thought we'd be, or the person we thought would always be there. We lose the kid we will never get to raise and the mother we thought we'd get to be. We lose the things we hope for, long for, and are terrified to not have, and those ripple effect losses can make it feel as though we have very little or nothing left to hold on to. When what we think, hope, and wish will be vanishes before us, grief healing work asks us to redefine what the future will look like, and in turn, rebuild ourselves along the way.

Over the course of several weeks, the dialogue in our group shifted and they began to talk about making plans for family outings, trips, and birthday parties; this was their grief process and there needed to be room for it all. A short time later, my dad joined a bereavement group, where he met other people navigating similarly intense grief. They gave one another the space to explore the depth of the pain together, without judgment or restriction. Grief needs tender witnessing. Over time they became an inseparable group of friends who supported each other (and by default me, too) through the twists and turns of grief. No one ran from my father's overwhelming feelings. No one backed away or stigmatized him for his apathy toward life after my mom died, because they each had felt this way at some point on the path, too. They realized this grief-related depression was par for the course, along with the anxiety of what the road ahead would even look like.

The connection and knowingness, the acknowledgment without hurrying to pathologize, can be one of the most healing threads when we are feeling lost and alone.

When to Seek Immediate Help

If you feel like living after your loss is too much to bear, please know you don't have to suffer alone. It is common and even normal to not want to go on after your loss, but it's another to *plan* to not go on.

If you or someone you know is experiencing intrusive suicidal thoughts and feelings, reach out immediately to their medical professional or therapist, or call the Suicide and Crisis Lifeline at 988. These support services are confidential, free, and available twenty-four hours a day.

All-Encompassing Grief

People react to loss in all sorts of ways. There's no part of your life that goes untouched by it. So what happens when it's all too much? Some people back away from the grief experience by creating a busy schedule or moving around a lot. Other people may numb out on substances, shut down totally, compartmentalize the more uncomfortable feelings, or it may feel so overwhelming that some have the feeling of stuckness. I have also had some people in my practice who have just wanted to get through the hard feelings as quickly as possible and try to rush to the very nonexistent "finish line," as the thought of staying in the full grief experience for another moment felt like complete and utter torture to them. I get it.

This is hard. Grief affects so many aspects of our lives, and we are left to reorient ourselves and try to fit back into life, work, relationships, routines, rituals, and our identity that each have shifted and don't quite fit the same. How could that *not* feel like too much? When it does feel like too much, it's so hard to imagine that anything can shift for the better. While I will never ask you to love and light yourself into any inauthentic feelings, I want to tell you that sometimes these painful rock-bottom-like feelings can allow us to make big changes, sometimes very necessary changes.

Questioning life and the point of it can be an important part of the grieving process. Purpose, meaning, love—so much has been seemingly stripped away. There can be a reevaluation of one's life and circumstances, which can lead to a greater sense of presence and the acknowledgment of what works in our lives and what really doesn't serve us anymore. With that in mind, I want to tell you about my client Hiroko ...

The Grief Overload: Ctrl Alt Delete as Needed

Hiroko was 6,739 miles from home when she got the news in 2020 that her mother had died after a long battle with cancer. With the coronavirus pandemic still at its initial peak, flying back to Tokyo wasn't an option. Hiroko was forced to stay in New York while her mother was being buried. During our initial consult phone call, Hiroko spoke to me through tears, often pausing to cry harder. I wanted to reach through the phone and hug her—there is something so cruel about being far away from our loved ones when they die, and being unable to get there, whatever the reason.

Hiroko was a reserved, sharply intelligent young woman who had come to New York after finishing graduate school in London. She had met her boyfriend, Charlie, when they were both studying abroad, and decided to join him in New York shortly after. She told me that they'd planned to get married in Japan in the next two years, and then settle back in New York City, where Charlie was raised. "He's a good boyfriend, I think, but it can be too much to cry to him every day. I am still trying to find a way back to Tokyo, but it will be after the fact. My sister has been helping with my father and grandmother, but I feel guilty for being so far away. My family always had a problem with me choosing to be in New York. They wish I chose to go back home after uni, but my mother always knew I wanted to live in the US." Hiroko's affect was flat for most of our first Zoom session, except for her furrowed brow.

Hiroko was understandably overwhelmed, and trying to contain her emotions for the sake of everyone around her, which left too little space for her grief. "Last night, I was looking at a photo my sister sent of my mother, and I was really sad to see it, but then all of a sudden I was really angry—so angry. I don't know why or how that happened. I felt really crazy and even Charlie said I was sounding crazy from the living room. He says losing my mother has made me crazy."

"It sounds to me like you're properly grieving, Hiroko. That's not at all *crazy*. That's loving and hurting and processing and feeling and trying to wrap your head around something that is nonsensical." As a therapist and a griever, I also endorse, even encourage, bed-hitting, as well as pillow-pounding and more healthy, harm-free ways to release big emotions like anger. It's so important to get that kind of intensity and pent-up aggression out of the body. When I told her so, Hiroko laughed and said it had felt good to get those feelings out, but then she needed a nap. I told her I always endorse naps when needed, and in the moments she needed to rest and "zone out," that was okay. It can sometimes all just be too much.

However, a few weeks later, Hiroko said she was feeling worse. Not being near her family was making her question everything. To add to her pain, Charlie was now also questioning her ability to one day be a mother if she "couldn't handle hard life events." She understandably felt devastated by his harsh judgments, and I was secretly pretty miffed by his cold words to Hiroko. To be clear, this is also a shining example of just how profoundly grief-illiterate our society is that some people would equate grieving the death of a mother to a woman's ability to mother her own child a few years down the road!?! Yikes.

The Fear of Moving Forward

Hiroko felt increasingly heavy guilt about not being in Japan for her mother's wake, as well as a deep yearning to be with her family. She wanted to live her life in New York and not put it all on hold, but didn't want to "move on," which she felt would equate to forgetting her mother. She was walking a high wire of two desires, needs, and identities, and for now, neither of them could merge. And, in my view, they didn't have to just yet. For right now, we had the grief in front of us to tend to.

Still, Hiroko was internalizing all Charlie had been telling her— to "move on and get on with it." Inevitably, that led to Hiroko's fears about leaving her mother behind as she "moved on" and continued living, waving goodbye, never to think of her again. Yeah, it just doesn't work that way. *Sorry, Charlie.*

As she began to get in touch with her grief and her life outside of her loss, Hiroko was realizing how unbearably alone and lost she'd been feeling. She didn't yet have many friends in New York and spent the majority of her time with Charlie and his friends. He told her that he felt better when she was being social like "her old self." Unsurprisingly, she reported feeling more and more depressed, as she was hiding so much of her grief within, afraid to let it out, because it made Charlie so uncomfortable. When we feel utterly alone in the world, and disconnected from ourselves and an authentically supportive community, motivation to "go on" feels far beyond the veil of deep sadness.

"What is the point of life if people we love just die and we are supposed to keep living?!" Hiroko asked almost every week for several months. *It was all too much,* she'd tell me. And I understood. One day Hiroko came to the session and talked about a tarot reading she had gotten from a friend the night before, because she thought it would help her feel more connected to her spirit. She told me she'd gotten the Tower card repeatedly. Since I knew a bit about tarot, that card didn't feel too far off from what she was going through: a clean slate. New beginnings. The end of what wasn't working for her. Of course, most people see the Tower as a harbinger of destruction or doom, and Hiroko certainly did. She was in a state of panic. I wondered, along with Hiroko, what she was hoping to get out of this reading—to which she said, "Hope."

Instead of hope, the reading only made Hiroko more anxious, confused, and despondent. She had talked often about feeling stuck in this place where her grief didn't feel real and yet it weighed heavier and heavier on her. She knew her mother had died, but not being able to get home to her family felt torturous. She wondered aloud if the Tower card was a sign that something else important in her life was ending, and that she should be questioning it all.

The irony was, of course, that Hiroko's life as she knew it *was* ending. That's what grief plunges us into—a state of irreversible change and upheaval that we are left to navigate when we feel least willing and able to. It didn't surprise me that pulling the Tower card rattled her as much as it did—seriously, who wouldn't be a little shaken by a card that represents catastrophic change when everything already feels so unstable?

I took Hiroko's admission of depression very seriously. It was something we touched on each week, sometimes even between sessions, in terms of how to get through the heavy, murky waters of grief and what resources (with options such as additional sessions with homework, body work, and/or medication) might be needed to do so.

For many years, the *DSM* (*Diagnostic and Statistical Manual of Mental Disorders*) has listed grief as an *exception* to the diagnosis of major depression, but it's still important to take anyone who is experiencing a relentless and persistent depressed mood seriously when it feels like too much for too long. Symptoms of depression can be similar to those of grief, though they are not the same thing, as with grief, there is an identifiable loss in someone's life and the focus of the emotional experience is on this loss. Grief also comes more in waves of experience, and clinical depression is persistent without much, if any, relief without a mental health intervention. If you are struggling in a similar way, I recommend reaching out to a mental health professional to help you pursue more clarity, as well as treatment options if they are necessary. At the risk of sounding cliché, there is so much strength in reaching out for help in whatever way might work for you.

Because a significant stressor in our lives can lead to the development of depression and/or anxiety for some people, it's important in therapy to pay close attention to intrusive symptoms or feeling as if you cannot complete life tasks over an extended period of time. It's different for everyone, but there is no shame in seeking the proper supportive treatment, whatever that might be, to help you through this difficult time.

Naturally, every client is unique; therefore, bringing in the need for a variety of approaches in the therapeutic paths we take. Interventions run the gamut based on very individualized needs of each client. In Hiroko's case, after exploring the options available to us during COVID, she chose to seek relief from the intensity of her symptoms with additional weekly therapy sessions with me, as well as consulting a psychiatrist I referred her to who helped her decide on whether a medication might help alleviate her anxiety. It did. This made her feel more in control of her mental health and she reported feeling more ease and motivation throughout her day to participate in social activities. I began to notice that Hiroko was able to talk about her grief and her future at the same time.

Almost a year into our work together, Hiroko was able to return to Tokyo to be with family. Being home was deeply comforting for her, and also empowering. The reconnection to her family, as well as being able to memorialize her mother, get some rest, and achieve some distance from her life in New York helped her feel stronger. Hiroko told me over Zoom from Japan that she had decided to break up with Charlie. Secretly relieved, I inquired as to what prompted this. She told me that her grief changed her perspective on everything in her life, and that she finally could see that Charlie had revealed some major red flags when her mother died with the way he treated her. I couldn't agree more. When she confronted Charlie about her feelings, he minimized her concerns about the relationship. As she spoke, she sounded strong, determined, and empowered in a way we had worked on together. I was so proud of her.

Upon returning to New York City, she was able to make swift changes in her life. She moved out of the apartment she shared with Charlie and moved to a neighborhood she'd always wanted to live in. And, yes, we processed the grief that inevitably came with the loss of her relationship to Charlie (yes, we can grieve decisions *we* make, too!). But, while she was grieving, she also pursued hobbies she had left behind and joined a volleyball team. She was talking openly with new friends about missing her mother. She was more open, honest, and present to her life. She lit up as she told me that one of her new friends had talked her into a writing class, where she had created a book of poems dedicated to her mother. She shared that she was taking her mother along with her on the adventure of her life, and she felt like she would be okay after all. I was humbled by Hiroko's ability to stay open to her grief, to keep going even when she felt she couldn't, and at the same time make the changes she deeply craved in a country and a city where she was *rebuilding* a life on her own terms.

The Tower card had been right after all.

When Grief Feels Complicated: Prolonged Grief Disorder

As we have talked about in every chapter thus far, grief is unique and can be complicated for some of us, and then additionally unique is each loss we may subsequently suffer during a lifetime. The grief experience follows no set timeline, adheres to no predictable milestones or markers. It is fluid and amorphous at times, rigid and sharp-edged at others. It is its own creation, ruled by no one and nothing, especially time. In 2021, the diagnosis "prolonged grief disorder" (PGD) was introduced into the *DSM-5*. The *Diagnostic and Statistical Manual of Mental Disorders* (*DSM*) is a volume published by the American Psychiatric Association (APA) that defines and classifies mental disorders. PGD is characterized by intense and persistent grief that causes problems and interferes with daily life. In order to be diagnosed with PGD, the symptoms must be severe enough to cause problems and stop the person from continuing with their life. Since COVID-19, I have worked with many people who, for reasons ranging from experiencing a traumatic loss or several losses at once to not being able to go on without one of the most important people in their life, have not been able to see their grief lessen within a year. This in and of itself is *not* problematic, nor pathological, unless and until they tell me that their suffering gets in the way of functioning (such as going to work or school, losing friends and support systems, or isolating for long periods), and they *want* to be able to find relief, function, and/connect to others better. Everyone is different in the way they grieve and seek healing. I honor that, with the hope that you do begin to find relief in the severity and longevity of your intense grief experience, even if just a little at a time.

My professional view on this diagnosis is that it's a double-edged sword. On the one hand, I do *not* advocate for the pathologization of a universal human wound, nor the medicalization of treating grief, outside of wanting the medical field to be more grief-informed. Grief touches everyone at some point, and we often have unrealistic expectations about how long grieving can or should take. On the other hand, as a clinician who sees too little support and attention given to mental health services and needs, I find relief in anything that gets money for research and has more and more people talking about it, and of course, hopefully more insurance panels being more accommodating. I have long wanted to see grief be destigmatized, so that policies, such as bereavement leave, for example, will get the opportunity to be further investigated and hopefully changed.

Here's what you need to know: Very few people grieving in the world today actually would be diagnosed with PGD. Sometimes, for some people, they can get very derailed by rumination, meaning that most of the day they can't get past the scenario where something was different and their loved one didn't die, but in a way that involved persistent, intrusive, and immobilizing yearning that cannot be self-soothed. For some, they relied fully on the person who died. Some people may have experienced multiple losses at once. And, there are losses that are traumatic and sudden, and for which time cannot help someone wrap their head around the loss. For some people, this can exhaust their support system, risk their job security, and lead them further into an isolated darkness. This is the time where professional help, and sometimes even medication, is a path that can really help someone find their way back to themselves again. I don't judge any path that supports and guides someone back to mental wellness and being back in the world over time.

Whatever your experience, trust that feeling "stuck" in grief is normal, and often misunderstood. Don't add to your burden by thinking that there is something wrong or broken or shameful about your experience. Not all grief requires a therapist, specialized treatment, or medication, but all of those are absolutely an option for you if you would like or, frankly, need help navigating a life-changing loss. You deserve healing and you deserve the support you need to get there.

Somehow, We Keep Going...

There has been a lot in these chapters that has been heavy and confronting of some hard inner truths and pain, I know. How are you feeling? I wish I could have made that lighter, or heck, I wish you didn't have to read these pages. But, we are here together, and the most brave and loving thing we can do for ourselves is to show up as honestly as we can to our grief experience—whether raw, tired, overexposed, overwhelmed, frustrated, and spent. Because there is room for it all.

On the grief path, it can feel like there is this huge compromise. It's like having our sandcastle knocked down and washed out to sea. We didn't lose just the castle or what the castle represented. Every one of those grains of sand represented something else to us. Something important, and now something is gone. And here society is, telling us we can be sad and feel the grief as deeply as we need to, all the while staring at its watch and letting us know our time to tend to our deepest human wound is going to swiftly come to an end, according to some invisible outside rule.

So, then, when we are overwhelmed and barely able to keep our head above water, how is it that we are expected to go on? What does that look like? Where is the starting line? How will we keep going when we are too tired to take another step?

I don't actually have the answers to those questions, as I, too, carry my grief like stones in my pockets. I can say this, though, based on my years of sitting across from courageous humans who somehow, even exhausted and emptied, show up to another day in one way or another as best they can after enduring loss: We go on simply by . . . *going on*. We find the will. Hour by hour. Day by day. One tiny little step at a time. Even if that looks as simple as eating three meals a day and drinking water. It may mean putting your grief aside and focusing on your kids, significant others, friends, pets—do yourself a favor and allow in the change of mental scenery from time to time. Maybe it grows to mean connecting more to your own needs and caring for yourself as ferociously as you love what or whom you have lost.

Know this: It will all ebb and flow. There will be good days, better days, and horrifyingly turbulent days, where the pain of the grief pangs threatens to take you down. Try your best not to judge yourself or your life based on those days. They are not your whole experience. They are not permanent. It's one day. During the hardest moments, you just have to do the next best thing. One small, gentle thing at a time, even if that means just getting out of bed or taking a shower. On the hardest days, your best course of action is to focus on caring for YOU, body, mind, heart, and soul, as best you are able—and when you feel up to it, staying connected to the people around you who can tolerate your painful, intense emotions and give comfort and love where the wound hurts most.

Some days, *rest* is the work. Some days, feeling the crushing sadness or immense emotions will be the work. The "work" lies in allowing it all—the feelings, the space, the physical howls from deep within your bones, as well as the shutting out of it all and streaming a show, the ice cream runs, the game nights and happy hours. ALL OF IT. All of it is the work of grieving, and all of it is the path toward whatever healing it is that we seek.

And, together, we will just keep on going.

PART TWO

NAVIGATING THE OUTER WORLD WITH GRIEF BY YOUR SIDE

CHAPTER 9

The Platitude Trap

"Grief is a cruel kind of education. You learn how ungentle mourning can be, how full of anger. You learn how glib condolences can feel. You learn how much grief is about language, the failure of language and the grasping for language."
　　　—Chimamanda Ngozi Adichie, *Notes on Grief*

When I first experienced my griefall, I remember wishing I could wear a pin like the one they have at meditation retreats that says, "Shh, I'm in grief." I didn't need people to say anything—a simple hand on my shoulder, a hug, a knowing glance, or even just respectfully backing away with a hand on their heart would have been acknowledgment enough. Too bad that's not how it really went down. Instead, despite the best efforts of people around me, I was overrun with platitudes of the best sort. "Your mother is now your spirit guide" was a particularly interesting thought to hear from an atheist friend of my mother's at her wake. And even the common "may her memory be a blessing" platitude just didn't land. I didn't really understand what it all meant, not really anyway. Sometimes, I wondered if there was a class offered anywhere entitled "Grief as a Second Language," because I was totally at a loss when it came to feeling connected to anyone.

I wanted something comforting to penetrate my weary and hallowed heart and I just wasn't getting it. This is not to say I didn't have any support at all, because I was immensely supported by people I loved, as well as people I didn't expect to be so present and loving, but overall, I still felt alone in my experience. I think that's just what grief does to us—it tosses us out to sea and we have to tread water, hoping for a lifeboat or a hand to reach in and grab us. Authentic connection feels *that* life or death at times.

It's hard enough to endure the grief that follows your loss and then go into the grief experience when you're just navigating it on your own. To get out of bed every day to the same reality saturated with your loss, to what feels like an overwhelming task of feeding and watering yourself, trying to literally just get through hour after hour until the end of the day nears and you get to go back to bed. And sleep, well, that's a whole other animal of epic proportions, am I right? But, when we have to go out into the world and interact with those who either don't know what we're going through, or don't know what to say if they do know? Yeah, no thanks. Hard pass on that. Which leads me to where we find comfort with the outside world.

Because steering one's way through the world after a loss is difficult, I want to help create a little road map, normalizing how it might feel and what you might come across. People in our family, friend group, or community are our first moment of connection with the outside world; it's how we begin to process our loss, with the help of comforting connections. That's why it's so vital that we get it right when we are connecting—to make sure it's sincere and not just empty, expected words of condolences.

We've all been there, getting it wrong at times, not knowing how to connect or what to say, but really, really wanting to. So, there's no shade at those who really care. I know there's so much *platitude panic* out there on what to say and how to say it sometimes. I just want us to start somewhere. I want us to be able to speak about loss and grief and all the messiness that comes with it with one another and really come through with authenticity and sincerity in our support. It makes all the difference. The reason, though, I want to talk about platitudes in particular, as we start our journey together into the outside world, is that after a loss, platitudes are one of the first interactions we have with the outside world responding to our grief and it's the first point of contact where we may feel embraced or dismissed.

The first part of this chapter is for you, my reader, to help traverse the outer world after your grief. Platitudes will be your first line of contact after your loss, and despite the best of intentions, they may have a hard landing for you. They may make you feel more alone and isolated, or they may actually feel like they are minimizing the hugeness of your loss. No doubt, there will be three groups of people you come across. (1) The people who avoid you (always hard no matter what). (2) The people who just get it, don't have to try too hard, and are able to be present with you and your grief no matter how weird, emotional, or withdrawn you're acting (thank the sweet lord for them!). (3) The people who have good intentions, perhaps, but say and do the most unhelpful things. This is not a judgment on those who fall short, but a call to action for *us all* to do better for one another, which is why the second half of this chapter is for them. You have more than enough on your plate—I'll take it from here. But first, let's talk a little more about platitudes.

The Platitude Trap

Platitudes are fairly mindless fillers for the emotional space we're afraid to occupy. This is where the platitude trap lives, and when we fall into it, we lose the opportunity for deeper connection, when that's the entire point of the platitude to begin with. We also opt out of breaking the stigma around grief as an emotional contagion, of sorts, which then leaves the griever feeling even more alone. And the trap gets deeper.

My gripe with platitudes is simple: They do not give us permission to grieve and they cut off the possibility for real connection. It's not anyone's fault, but there is never really an opportunity for a bridge between hearts when there is a ready-made response to loss. People try and it doesn't mean people don't care—they do...we just have a strange way of showing it sometimes. Grief is one of those times.

Gripped by uncertainty and desperate not to make it worse by saying the wrong thing, we resort to prepackaged, preprogrammed words. In doing so, we reveal our avoidant attitudes around loss and grief, and express more indifference than caring. For example, when we offer artificially upbeat platitudes about, say, a lost loved one "being in a better place," what we actually convey is more like, *I'm sorry you've been infected with grief, but can you please not infect me with it?*

As unhelpful, even damaging, as platitudes can be, as I mentioned earlier, we've all been that person, clumsily fishing for words that will bring comfort to someone with a grieving heart. I know I have been the giver of useless, unhelpful platitudes, because I had no idea how hurtful or unhelpful those words really were, or had no idea what to say instead. Like most of us, I was terrified of the empty space across from a hurting human, so I borrowed expressions I'd heard on TV or from family members years before. I wish someone had told me that my platitudes were most likely to either hurt them or fail to reach them altogether. Despite how horrifically embarrassing that would have been, I'd have learned and taken that lesson with me. In that spirit, I extend my compassion for our humanity and not being able to always get it right when it comes to grief.

So, what is it about grief and loss that makes people so dang uncomfortable? As a nerdy history buff, I wanted to know more. The word *platitude* has been around since the early nineteenth century. It comes from the Latin root *plat*, meaning "flat," and means "the flatness in something." While the word can be used literally, it is more commonly used to mean the dullness or lack of significance in something. Isn't it then so ironic that we use them for the most important, sometimes the most painful time in someone's life?

Below is a list of some of the more popular, albeit very impersonal platitudes most of us have heard, and yes, even said ourselves. In this list I've added my internal dialogue's honest response to them. It is a touch snarky, but it's really for effect. The goal here is not to shame or blame any of us for saying platitudes, but to notice how they unintentionally but ferociously miss the mark, making it more about the comfort of the person giving than receiving. Bringing awareness to how we show up for grief for ourselves and others, as well as how others show up for us, is a step that is missing when it comes to getting support.

Let's take a moment to appreciate just how badly some of these canned phrases miss the mark (please forgive my snarkiness in advance):

Hall of Fame: Worst Offending Platitudes

They are in a better place (Do they feel that way, now that they're there? Because I really want them here again, in *this* place.)

God doesn't give you more than you can handle (Really? Who says? Who says I should believe this is a personal test of my strength?)

Heaven just gained another angel (My all-time favorite of the hollow platitudes)

They wouldn't want you to be upset (Did you talk with them and they told you this directly?!)

You're still young (Which has nothing to do with literally anything)

You can have another child (I wanted this one, thanks so much)

Everything happens for a reason (So, am I being punished by this loss, then?)

Be strong (For what or whom? My heart has just been ripped out and I'm standing here listening to your crappy platitude, so I'd say I am already strong!)

You have your whole life ahead of you (Objection, lack of foundation— how the heck do you know and what does that have to do with the here and now?!)

They aren't worth crying over (Says who? Also, do I really need a reason to cry?)

You were too good for them anyhow (Yet, still I am here devastated)

You can get a new pet and love them just as much (I'd rather have my old pet. They were my family, thanks.)

Don't worry, you will find love again (So my love is like a car I can trade in? Because honestly, all I want is the love I've had.)

Just move on (Thanks! I would never have thought to do that!)

The unifying problem with these platitudes is that they implicitly ask the griever to meet the consoler's needs, rather than the other way around. It's as if we're saying, "I am uncomfortable with your grief and sadness and other big emotions related to this loss. Please get back to normal ASAP." It's like they are begging us to make *their* discomfort stop! People often want to stay away from loss because they don't want to "catch" our grief, like it's some kind of emotion-borne virus. The farther away they stand, literally or emotionally, the less chance they have of being "infected" by the loss. Grief, however, isn't the plague—it's life and love, and our truest humanity. Our collective avoidance and fear around our grief just makes grievers feel more isolated, and worse, ashamed of what is misinterpreted as "weakness." We have to do better.

To be clear, our avoidant attitude toward grief is a societal issue, not a personal failure. If I grew up hearing that snow was the worst possible weather event, it would make sense that when a friend told me that "it snowed last night at my house," I might react with "Oh my god, how awful! I am so, so sorry!"—even if they loved snow, or needed it to prevent wildfires the next year. The same is true for grief, especially when it involves death. When we grow up hearing only one attitude toward death and grief (namely that it's something best avoided, spoken of in hushed, hurried tones only when strictly necessary), it makes sense that we carry that belief system into adulthood.

The core problem is that we still fear our dark, challenging emotions—our own and those of other people—so we try to stuff them down or away or into some box we hope never to find again. This then continues a cycle of distancing and inauthenticity and disconnection.

And let's be honest here: We use platitudes with ourselves, too. If we aren't practiced in validating our feelings and/or they are not validated by the outside world, we may shut down and even try to persuade ourselves that the platitudes ring true, when in fact, they don't. Essentially, we're invalidating our own grief, shaming ourselves for feeling the emotional intensity we do. This reaction is understandable. As humans, we crave a sense of belonging. If something puts that at risk, we may go into survival mode, convincing ourselves to accept the crappy crumbs of half-hearted (and/or hard-hearted) caring that come our way, even going so far as to deem it adequate or loving. This connects us straight back to our self-gaslighting we explored earlier together.

What We Hear vs. What We Need to Hear

I remember being at my mom's funeral and hearing someone tell me that my mom was in a better place. Internally, all I wanted to say was, *"Oh, have you been to this better place? Did I miss the Yelp review?!"* Instead, I thanked them and kept it moving down the condolence line. Truth was, I was in a free fall, and I just wanted someone to reach out, snatch me out of the air, to stop the sickening weightlessness of my griefall. It wasn't their fault that they couldn't reach me, but we both fell into the trap, and the potential for connection was lost.

Grievers should never have the additional task of trying to make sense of and take in comfort from platitudes that sting—and let's face it, some sting more than others. Remember, platitudes like the ones I mentioned are more about the discomfort people have around grief and nothing to do with you. They do genuinely care.

At the absolute core, people enduring loss crave connection, belonging, patience, compassion, knowing we aren't alone, and space to define what our loss represents to us and our feelings around that. We need people to *see* us. And, despite the popularity of platitudes over the years, there is something better we can give to one another: *authenticity.*

Let's be more mindful of our language—all of us, for everyone's sake—when it comes to how we communicate our caring to people who are experiencing grief. Our words matter more than we may know.

Our Own Gripe with Grief

One common question I like to ask my clients when I hear them either agreeing with a painful platitude or using it on themselves is, "How did you look at grief and loss before you experienced your own? Did you stay silent or offer up some words you thought might be comforting? Did you find yourself super uncomfortable around loss?" Some of my clients told me that they never really thought about it until it was their reality. I can understand that, because why would we know what to say or how to act around loss if we hadn't yet been faced with it? No matter your answer, it makes us look at our own relationship with grief and reevaluate how we show up for others, and for ourselves.

I invite you to look at some of your older beliefs around grief, so we can know how deep in the platitudes you might be. Again, if you're deep into them, please don't blame or shame yourself! We've all been taught to say them. The goal here is simply to recognize the pattern, understand why it's harmful, and break the cycle, both with yourself and others.

Let's Check In: How Platitudes Land Within Us

I'd like to explore some questions below to look at why platitudes may have seemed useful in the past and to look closer at your own history with grief and to examine your own true feelings around loss. I find that these reflections of our very early belief system around grief can help us to understand our own potential grief biases, which inevitably can help us get closer to our true feelings about our experience.

How do you feel when you're around someone who is grieving? Do you, at least to some degree, wish you could get away from them and/or their grief?

Were you taught to avoid or suppress big, dark emotions like sadness, regret, anger, and others?

If you have used platitudes to connect with someone when they are hurting, do you know why you said them? Were you taught that was the thing to say? Do they accurately reflect your beliefs and hopes?

How have you ever wanted to reply, or even actually replied, to grief platitudes?

If you could be really, really honest, what would you say to someone who responds to your grief dismissively with a platitude (even if it is well-meaning)?

What would you like to hear from others instead of a platitude? What would be meaningful or comforting?

There are no right answers to these questions. Each of us has different needs, which are often influenced by family modeling, culture, religion, and our psychological state. None of your needs or expectations are wrong. Your emotional connection needs may change from day to day or hour to hour, so don't be surprised if sometimes the platitudes make you feel worse on some days and less so on others.

Inevitably our belief system around grief also has a lot to do with how we were taught to perceive outside support—or lack thereof. If you were taught to "take what you can get," you may feel you're supposed to appreciate platitudes (at least someone noticed your suffering). If you were taught that getting support is a sign of weakness, you may feel you're supposed to grieve in isolation and hide your vulnerability. If you were taught to seek out and accept support when you need it, standing up for your needs may feel easier. If you were taught that any kind word is the right word for you, you may not be fazed by any platitudes that come your way, nor are you moved by them. They just become a thing to say and a thing to hear. The end.

Far too many people are not taught to advocate for their own needs, and this could complicate the grieving process when we are trying to navigate the outside world after a loss. But I believe that grief can be a powerful conduit for connection when done authentically, and I believe that we can transform platitudes into bids for help and meaningful connection.

Heaven Has Another "Angle"

My client Kirsten was over the moon about having a baby when she turned thirty, but when she had a miscarriage at thirteen weeks, she plunged into a deep and very understandable state of grief. Pregnancy loss is a collection of little losses alongside the major loss itself. It's grieving the future you formed during the pregnancy, the expectation of being a parent to this specific child, the identity of parenthood itself, as well as the hopes and dreams for this new life, to name just a few. It's (yet another) intense, multilayered form of grief.

I asked Kirsten nearly every week what she needed on that day or in that moment, not only because it changes every day, but also because she wasn't taking herself or her own well-being into account. Her husband, Jeff, was ready to share the news online, but Kirsten wasn't yet feeling strong enough. She had shared every stage of her pregnancy in her social media feeds, announcing the pregnancy immediately upon finding out (and right before her loss) at twelve weeks. In her posts, she detailed her latest hack for morning sickness, recounting the fatigue and the mood swings she experienced before knowing she was pregnant, and enjoying the suggestions and support from her followers. Everyone was so excited for her, she wasn't sure how or when to share the news of her loss. She wasn't sure if she'd get the support she needed and didn't know if she was ready to handle that. She now regretted sharing her pregnancy journey online. "I feel like a failure, and worse I feel like I jinxed it," she told me one day. *Ouch.* That was a big burden to carry.

A few weeks later, Kirsten came into our session and pulled out her phone. She had posted the news of her loss on social media and had received a plethora of poorly constructed platitudes that she began reading to me. "Ten people told me that heaven got another angel. And this person, look, Gina, she couldn't even take the time to spell check her shitty comment. She said heaven got another 'angle.' What the hell?! All of this just makes it so much worse."

Hearing her, I once again wanted to scream from the rooftops, *Look, people, heaven has plenty of angels already, okay? Let's retire that one, please!*

After we discussed in depth all the complicated emotions she was feeling, Kirsten decided to try to post again. Together, we crafted a post asking friends and family not to give her platitudes, but to share similar stories around suffering through miscarriage. She asked for space and respect to grieve, and also asked people to check in on her without feeling they needed to offer comfort as she continued her grieving.

It worked! Kirsten came in a week later and showed me some responses. She told me that despite the intensity of this situation and how devastated she was, she felt less embarrassed and less alone. The grief and trauma of her loss was naturally still up front and center, but Kirsten felt more *seen.* That was the point.

I can't promise it will always be neat and tidy, or even as easy. It depends on the people we have around us, the community's belief system, and our authentic sense of closeness with them, but it's still worth it. Humans are clumsy and prone to stumbling in highly charged emotional situations like grief—so they, and we, get it wrong *a lot.* As a result, when we're feeling vulnerable, asking for what we need feels like a scary gamble. I get that. Especially when you're in the griefall, uncertain what you need or want, or not fully tuned in to your own emotional experience, it may feel easier to say nothing and accept the scraps of attention you get when something fiercely painful happens in your life.

The more practiced we become at understanding what we are feeling, the easier it can be to tune in to what we may need. Once we know what we need, the work lies in finding a way to ask for those needs to be met in a way that helps *us* more personally.

But, if we can help it, or change it in a safe way, it can be worthwhile to reach out however we feel comfortable, and maybe instead of taking that risk, you stick to the few people you know and trust to show up for you. I'd also recommend sharing your feelings and experiences with a professional, who can walk alongside you and provide gentle guidance and support during this unique and personally devastating time of loss. You are worthy of being cared for how you need it.

So, right now, I am going to take a moment away from you and talk to one of your loved ones. I want to help them to support you in a more authentic way to everyone. It's not easy to *be* the one supporting a griever, and we both know it's not easy *being* the one grieving. So, hopefully this note to your loved ones below can help us come together.

A Note for Your Loved Ones

Hi there! I'm Gina. We haven't met yet, but I've been helping the person who shared this with you through a painful time in their life. First of all, thank you for your energy, effort, and love toward this person. They could really use your support right now and, since you're reading this, I'm guessing you want to show up for them. So let's talk about how you can do that.

Connecting with someone who's grieving can feel challenging and awkward. We don't always know what to say or do, we're worried we'll say or do the wrong thing and make it worse, and what feels good to them one day may not feel good the next. (Trust me, it's confusing for us grievers, too, no matter how many losses one has had, because feelings and needs change all the time!) What I want you to know is when you're sincere and you care, it shows and it helps, because what grievers need is an authentic, compassionate connection.

With platitudes like "They're in a better place" or "It was their time," people miss the mark. Albeit unintentionally, but they still do, and often by a long shot. We may not know what someone needs to hear at any given moment in their unique grief journey, but what we can be sure of is that showing up is the most important thing. Showing up *as authentic you?* Even better!

Not knowing how to show up is not your fault, but I assure you that connecting more honestly will bring you closer to the person who needs you and, in the end, you'll feel really good about it, too. If you find yourself completely at a loss for the right words, there is absolutely nothing wrong with just saying that. "Hey, I have absolutely no idea what to say, but I care and I am just so sorry for your loss." Excellent! Bravo!

If you want more ideas, you can find more detailed suggestions on page 176, but remember that there's no single perfect thing you can say. Do your best to show up with love, put your discomfort to the side, and remind them that you're there. Just showing up means more than you might realize. Thank you for caring for someone in so much pain.

Compassionate Consolation

We already know what platitudes are, but let's talk for a minute about "compassionate consolation." When we think about consoling someone, it's because we want to reach them, right? We want to find a way to connect and comfort. Seldom do platitudes provide that comfort or connection when haphazardly tossed our way. For someone grieving, being consoled with authenticity and compassion is a connection that can quell the sting of early grief. It can help us feel less alone, and more apt to reach out, if we feel validated and seen.

For someone who loves and cares about someone grieving, I want you to think about whatever you say or do as coming from a place of compassion and connection. If you thought about simply connecting authentically and compassionately, what would you say and how would you want to connect? Let's look at the difference between a hollow platitude and compassionate consolation to make sure you're going to get this right!

Platitude vs. Compassionate Consolation

Platitude:	Compassionate Consolation:
"They are in a better place."	"My heart is with your heart right now."
"I know how you feel."	"I don't know exactly how you feel, but I am here to listen."
"Be strong. They would want you to be strong."	"I am here to listen and support you. You don't have to be strong right now."
"Something good will come from this, you'll see."	"This all just really sucks and I am deeply sorry you're having to go through this."
"I know exactly what you're feeling."	"I have no idea what you're feeling, but I am here for you. Would it be okay for me to bring or drop off a meal this week?"
"You have been expecting this, though, right?"	"I'm so sorry for your loss. This is absolute shit."
Silence or changing the topic.	"I've never dealt with grief before, but I love you and want you to know you're in my heart."

People ask me all the time, "Gina, what's a go-to to say to someone who is grieving?" And, here's the thing—I don't have one. I just want you to show up as *you*.

Not a wordsmith, but good at getting shit done? Awesome! Show up and offer to do laundry, run errands, bring food, whatever tangible and helpful activity you can think of. Imagine this: The person who has just lost someone or something major in their life, they are in some foreign land where literally nothing feels the same and everything feels off. What soft, loving spaces can you create? What tenderness or care can you offer?

Having the people around them still act like themselves? That's normalizing and loving. The words don't *really* matter (I mean, don't be insulting or mean), it's more about how you show up and how you can help bring comfort and connection to them. Sometimes, it's not asking "How are you?" but asking "How are you *today*?" And, for some people, platitudes that I scoffed at earlier will be just the thing they need to hear—it's all about the authenticity and heart associated with the words and gestures you bring forth.

The needs and feelings of someone grieving will shift and change, so my advice is to check in knowing that there is a strong possibility that if they were on solid ground yesterday, it might not be the case today. It's a delicate little tango, the grief dance, and being an outsider can be as confusing and exhausting as it can be to the person grieving. Be gentle with yourself, of course, and remember that just being authentic with the aim of connecting is the name of the game.

Can you see the difference sincerity can bring? Authentic connection can be the balm we work into the cracks of our hearts when we are in the midst of our deepest grief. However uncomfortable it can be for both people to confront loss, having someone share from an authentic heart and be present in the pain of loss allows love to flow again. That's all we crave when we are bereft. We know grief will

never go away, because that's not how love works, but with genuine, compassionate support, we can feel our needs being lovingly and
tenderly held in a way that eventually allows us to invite life in once
again.

The Moral of the Platitude Trap

In general, the most important thing for someone navigating the outside world after a loss is being able to authentically connect during our
darkest moments to the people around them. It's about learning how
to ask for what you need, redirect those who don't get it, set your platitude boundaries, and grieve however you need to without feeling the
pressure of the outside world tossing verbal Hallmark cards your way
(no offense to Hallmark). I am not saying it will be easy. You will go
back and forth on what feels good and what you may need. You may
not know the answer to those things for some time, so the best you can
do is go with what feels connective and comforting in the moment,
because with grief, the moments change.

The initial immersion with the outside world is the clumsiest part
of the grief process. There aren't any reference points, because it's too
unpredictable. We learn a little more as we go along, but don't be too
hard on yourself if you find yourself placating the platitudes and not
being able to redirect or triage the exhausting conversations. Just keep
taking care of yourself as best you can in any given moment. That's all
I ask.

Lastly, for those who attended Compassionate Consolation class
within these pages, thank you for being present with some uncomfortable guidance from me. It wasn't a judgment on my part toward you,
but rather a call for help. I promise it wasn't to chastise you into sub-
mission, but to gently nudge you in the direction of feeling more connected to the person who you actually want to connect to.

We need more connection and less discomfort around grief, and if someone grieving can ask for what they need and I can have someone learn from these pages, we are one step closer to changing the grief narrative for generations of future grievers. Bare minimum: I don't want to see "Heaven got another angle" in any comment sections on social media, okay? Okay.

CHAPTER 10

The Delicate Tango of Needs and Boundaries

" 'No' is a complete sentence."

—Anne Lamott

Because grief can be so disorienting and confusing, it makes sense that we have trouble navigating how we should be in the world now that everything is different. How do we communicate what we need, what we want, and what feels okay, especially if we are feeling so unimaginably off-kilter?

I imagine your life has been upended by loss. You're surrounded by people. Maybe texts and calls are coming in. Facebook and IG messages line your notification settings on your phone's home screen. Some people post comments. Others say things to you in person. The platitudes are rolling in. You feel overwhelmed. It's surreal. You feel comforted. Then overwhelmed again. No, comforted—or maybe both? Nothing makes sense. Nothing reaches us.

The world gets smaller. And darker. You hear yourself talking to loved ones, but you feel disconnected, like your voice belongs to someone else. Everything is too loud. Then it's too quiet. You want to be alone, but not for *that* long. You want to be with people, but only certain people. You need time alone, but only so much. Round and round you go, dancing the delicate tango we all do when we find ourselves in the grief club.

My mother used to tell me, "If you want it, you gotta ask for it." Still sound advice, I'd say, but what happens if you don't know what you want or need? Sometimes, after loss, knowing our needs when everything feels like it's on shifting ground can feel impossible.

In so many ways that slowly assert themselves after loss, you're not the person you were before your loss. There's a hole in your life that you're trying to adjust to, like how your eyes feel after you've turned off a light. Where is this all leading you? Who will you be a week, month, or year from now? What will your life look and feel like then? No one wants and needs those answers or craves that certainty more than *you*. In these ways, grief can seem like a tsunami, striking suddenly, destabilizing everyone and everything in its wake. While you will eventually discover that *all* is not lost, the fact is, nothing will ever be the same, either.

Even more disorienting, the world around you surges on. Friends, family, and colleagues who are used to you being present in their lives, both physically (by, say, meeting that friend after work) and mentally/emotionally (by being interested and involved in their lives), may feel confused when you suddenly don't seem to be the person they've known. At times they may feel abandoned and try to be helpful by telling you that going out "will be good for you," or that it's time for you "to move on." However well-intended these comments may be, none of this is helpful. Grief is changing you and your needs and boundaries, and that's completely normal.

Inevitably, in the midst of this profound uncertainty, we face all kinds of interactions, invitations, and expectations with varying levels of anticipation and trepidation. It's not just about dodging the platitude trap. It's about craving connection while also feeling deeply unsure about even being around people. How much aloneness is good? How much is too much? Should you go to that concert? Agree to go on that date? Invite a friend over or reply to that text message? Go to work or take time off? These questions are so much harder to answer when you're navigating grief because from one day to the next, even one moment to the next, your needs and boundaries shape-shift.

My goal for you in this chapter is to help you come closer to understanding your own needs while grieving. It's hard—they can change a lot and not always make much sense. It's important to start with understanding our own needs before we can set boundaries or ask for our needs to be met.

Your Changing Needs for Alone Time and People Time

One moment, you're terribly lonely; the next, you're desperate to be alone. Suddenly, your friend's standard *want to meet after work later?* text feels more fraught than you ever imagined. *Do you* want to meet after work? More importantly, *will you* want to when that time (several hours from now) comes? This hesitation isn't about moment-to-moment moodiness, it's about emotional intensity that ebbs and flows in ways you can't control or predict. When your insides feel like a dead zone vacuum-sealed by sadness and other challenging emotions, you simply don't have the energy to engage; conserving your own oxygen is all you can manage.

Inevitably, there are also times when you may think you have the energy, but then realize you still lack the ability to participate in the ways that social norms suggest you should. "Regular" conversations—about trips, family, friends, work, someone's day, and more—can feel tedious, even pointless, when all you can think and talk about is the smile you'll never see again, the hugs you can no longer exchange, and the stories you long to tell to the person you've lost. Trying to be upbeat and interested in what others are saying can be a struggle when your grief devours the space that used to be available to other people. Just when you feel ready to connect with someone again, grief sweeps in, consuming the extra room inside you.

These ups and downs are undeniably challenging, but also natural, normal parts of grieving. One of the ways this can manifest is as a growing need for time to yourself.

The Tightrope Between Solitude and Community Around Us

Being in a supportive social community can be life-affirming and even life-saving when we are in the throes of overwhelm. It's important to have authentic, caring people in our lives who can help us just experience the grieving process however it arrives in any given moment and be held and seen in this time. Being witnessed and validated in our grief can be a comfort we didn't even know we needed, but even with the most amazing people around us, it's natural to want some alone time to rest, process, get things done, or just be with our emotions. It's very natural that we will be exhausted after being in contact with so many people within our friend circles, community, and workplace. We are having to feel the loss, process the loss, negotiate our lives within the loss, and also navigate the loss with the outside world—that is a LOT. If you find you're just tired in every way, it's okay to step away, to put your phone on DND, or to let people know you will just need a little space right now. There is nothing wrong with needing some solitude after a loss, and this is an important form of self-care, too.

Truth be told, you will need both solitude and social support in different measures over time. Only you will know when you will need that alone time, because you will feel the antsy pull of wanting to be away from people. In turn, you will feel the swell of aloneness sweep over you when it's time for people and love and comfort and support.

That craving for more alone time is sometimes expected, even understood, but only to a point. It's a reality that may reflect our cultural discomfort with aloneness in general. We live in a culture that's still oriented toward extroversion, and to some degree being alone, at least "too often" (whatever that means!) or for "too long" (according to whom?) is sometimes judged as a weakness or flaw. It's as if there's some universal voice whispering to us, *Are you alone by choice or are you just a loser?* Eating alone, being out in public alone, attending a performance alone—these simple, solitary acts often make people feel uncomfortable, as if they're the "odd one out" attracting unwanted attention simply because they're by themselves.

When you're grieving, this additional attention may feel like the last thing you need. The same goes for being asked to explain *why* you don't feel like being out, or around other people. (*Is being alone some kind of crime? Are you the Aloneness Police?* Both are questions I've been tempted to ask at times!) These judgments and expectations, whether spoken or unspoken, can feel burdensome because again, you're emotionally, mentally, spiritually, and physically maxed out.

Being alone won't always be what you want or need. At times you may crave connection, yearning to feel heard and seen and held at a deeper and more intimate level than before. I'll never forget arriving at my mother's funeral and looking out the window of the car from the parking lot. It was cold outside, and the entire group of my friends was standing there waiting for us to arrive. To get there, they'd had to step away from work (and family) for at least a full day, take a train ride and then a long taxi ride to get to the funeral home. Yet here they all were, there before me, ready and available to support me on this incredibly trying day. I was so moved that I could hardly speak. I felt so loved at a moment when I really needed it. Their presence meant everything. It still does.

When Your People Don't Show Up

Deep experiences of grief can bring people together faster and more deeply than typical everyday encounters. The same is true in reverse, however. Almost without exception, people going through loss discover that some of the people they thought would be there for them, in fact, are not. It's heartbreak piled on top of grief, culminating in the ultimate "true colors" moment when we least need it and feel least able to handle it. For this reason and many others, people sometimes experience shifts in their social circles and social lives when they're grieving, whether temporarily or for the long haul. It's never an easy time to navigate these types of changes.

Grief and Our Social Life

People often assume that grief and joy can't possibly coexist. So it follows that if a griever does, say, go to a club one night, that must mean she or he is "over it." Suddenly, simple desires like wanting to attend a concert, go dancing, or plan a fun night with friends feel like a risky move. Will someone judge you for not "grieving right"? Assume that you're good now and stop checking in? Does having one good day mean that you're not allowed to feel the pain of your loss anymore?

The reality is, we experience grief and life all at once. In fact, that's both the plus and minus of grieving: Life does, and must, go on, at least on a practical level, which can also mean that we may laugh and dance and cry and yearn, all at once.

However, it also means that our feeling up to, say, going out with friends one night is *not* an indication that we've "moved on." It's an odd, and frankly painful, double standard. We want people to charge through their grief as quickly as possible, but then seem to judge them for not grieving "enough" or the "right way."

I'll invite you to remember that grief is not just an emotion. It's the journey we undertake after loss, and there is space for *all* of your feelings. Moreover, you are allowed to take a break from your grief! With so much pain as the baseline of our day-to-day experience, we each need to seize whatever enjoyment we can, whenever we feel able to experience it. Allowing grief to ebb and flow, alongside life, in tandem with our sadness and our joy, is an inherent part of grieving fully and authentically.

Just as there is no magic threshold that you'll step over someday and find yourself "done" with grief, joy, fun, and laughter are not permanently "gone" from you or your life, no matter how much it may feel that way on some days. Having any kind of fun doesn't mean you've moved on and finding yourself in some fit of laughter doesn't mean you're not still grieving. Oh, and for the record, as far as I know, there's no rule against going dancing while grieving.

The push-pull dynamic—wanting to be alone, then not; wanting to be around certain people, then others—can feel jarring, but the only way through it is to flow with it, even when it feels crazy-making. Remember, there are no rules around grieving, only a process that asks for our trust and surrender as our needs ebb, flow, and change course over time. With that in mind, let's look at some strategies to help you navigate the dance more easily, with family, while dating, in long-term relationships, and at work.

How Do We Track Our Ever-Changing Needs?

In the meantime, there are ways to navigate your changing needs, even when they can feel unpredictable. Although this time can be exhausting and overwhelming, remembering that your needs are ever shifting is going to be crucial. Be gentle with yourself when navigating your needs and boundaries.

Let's Check In with Ourselves

The key to balance is getting to know ourselves and checking in often. The anxiety I see most often is around our needs and wants shifting a lot and not being sure what we may want in any moment.

Whenever you feel unsure about interacting with people or staying alone, I want you to start by asking yourself these questions:

1. **What are my intentions?**

   Are you searching for a distraction? Do you miss this particular person or group? Does going out sound like fun for once? Do you want to "make up" for saying no to so many previous invitations? Check in with yourself and make sure your intention feels aligned with your grief journey and your overall mental health.
   - Do you have a history of distracting yourself from hard things?
   - Do you trust yourself to be able to change your mind and respect that choice?
   - Have you been taking care of your own emotional and physical needs lately?

2. **What are my expectations?**

   Are you envisioning a specific outcome? Or just hoping to enjoy yourself? Again, be honest about any expectations you have, especially if those expectations are loaded or dependent on others' actions or reactions, which is often a setup for disappointment.
   - How likely do you think it is that you'll regret this tomorrow?
   - Is this self-sabotaging?
   - Is this numbing out?
   - Is this inhibiting your safety?

3. **If I'm being truly honest with myself, what do I need right now?**

   When we are in a state of confusion, it may sometimes feel easier to just go along with other people's needs and desires. Other times, doing that may push us beyond our boundaries; this can have its benefits when, for example, doing something you initially didn't want to do ends up feeling surprisingly good. Are you, for example, people pleasing, buffering from the pain, or protecting yourself from sharing too much? It really comes down to taking your own emotional pulse, listening to what feels good in your body now, in this moment, and making the next best choice. To get clear with yourself, you might ask:

- Have I always just pushed through when I didn't want to just to please others?
- Can I make it a habit to check in with myself and my needs before making any decisions?
- Can I trust that I don't have to make more than one decision at a time so as to not overwhelm myself further?

A Plan for Making Plans

When you can't always plan according to your changing needs, you *can* plan for change. Amanda experienced this kind of confusion around her changing needs when she was invited to a close friend's wedding months after losing her husband. Wanting to support her friend and herself, she'd deferred the invitation to be in the wedding, but promised to attend the ceremony and reception. As the day drew nearer, though, even the thought of shopping for a dress felt torturous.

When Amanda and I talked about how she would navigate the situation, she realized that she needed a way out if, on the day of the wedding, her grief felt too overwhelming to be around people, much less at a wedding. She had lost the love of her life, and as happy as she was for her friend, that hole in her heart still felt shockingly raw.

I suggested that we develop a series of backup plans—Plans A, B, and C. I've done this for myself, and with many of my clients. It's fairly straightforward: Plan A is your best-case scenario—you're having a good day, this is the closest to what you imagine you'd want to have the capacity to do. Plan B turns down the volume a bit, and Plan C is often an exit strategy.

For Amanda, Plan A was letting her friend know how much she wanted to be at the wedding, but also, how deeply she was still grieving the loss of her husband. Amanda then explained that she would be present at the wedding if she felt able to attend without disrupting her friend's happy day with her grief. Her Plan B would be attending as much of her friend's ceremony and reception as she could. If, for example, the "I do's" felt too overwhelming to witness, she would allow herself to skip that and instead attend the reception, or whatever part of the reception she felt up to. Finally, her Plan C would be to skip the day altogether and instead take her friend out for a celebratory spa day at some later date when they were both available and excited to raise a glass to her friend's nuptials.

Once she had these options in place, Amanda felt less anxious about her friend's wedding. While none of it felt easy, she now felt like she had some measure of control, which also meant she could respect and honor her own limitations and allow in the grief experience in a way that felt more tolerable for her moment by moment.

Regaining some sense of control over your emotional boundaries is especially important when you're grieving, since the journey may temporarily narrow your *window of tolerance* (that we discussed in chapter 4), which is the zone where your nervous system is relaxed, calm, and able to engage. When this window shrinks, as it often does in response to extreme stress like grief, it's harder to manage your emotions, interact with others, and function effectively in any number of situations. This is normal, and an indication that you need more TLC at the moment. Your only job is to heed your fluctuating needs. One way to do that is by preparing in advance, as Amanda did, which can make your overall experience feel a little less overwhelming.

Managing Family Expectations

Setting healthy boundaries can be challenging enough, but doing this with family can be considerably more intense and complex. After all, these are the people who have known you since forever—and the ones who are the most adept at pushing your buttons (and they are masters at that, aren't they?!). Even the most loving and supportive families have unspoken rules about what is and isn't done, and what is and isn't okay. When we're grieving, those long-established understandings can feel jarring or even disruptive.

For example, when Robert's best friend Stephan lost his battle with cancer, it was a devastating loss for his whole extended family. The two had been best friends since childhood, and Robert's parents had always viewed Stephan as a de facto son. Insisting that this was a time to come together more often, Robert's mother began hosting weekly (instead of monthly) Sunday dinners that would last hours and involved a long two-way commute for Robert.

Each week, Robert's siblings, cousins, aunts, and uncles were at the dinner, wanting to support him, talk to him, hear how he was doing. What had once been a joyous occasion—seeing his loud and loving family—had become a weekly exercise in mental/emotional overload. As much as he appreciated his family's desire to support him, the way his mother was doing it didn't feel helpful or healing. Above all, Robert felt like he needed space.

"When I told her that, she accused me of being ungrateful," he told me, looking off to one side, shaking his head. He looked so utterly exhausted that a part of me wished I could tuck him in and let him sleep. "She said most people would do anything to have a big, loving family like ours. Then she reminded me that they're all grieving his loss, too." On a deeper level, Robert had always felt smothered by his mother's constant need for affection and attention, but had never felt able to communicate those boundaries.

We'd all love to feel fully seen by our family members, but the truth is, that isn't always possible. Even more so than most, loving family is sometimes about accepting them as they are. There are of course cases in which major chasms can be discussed openly, even lovingly healed, but that isn't always the case. The history and connection that's shared between family members is long-standing and unique, and certain family relationships may not successfully adapt to changes that veer too far out of a long-established familial comfort zone.

When you're navigating grief, it's important to acknowledge, if only to yourself, how your own family's dynamics feel to you at any given time. Do you feel comfortable in your own skin when you're with them? Do you feel overwhelmed or like you have to censor yourself in certain ways when they're around? Do you feel supported or unsupported, loved or unloved with them? If it's several conflicting feelings at once, that is completely normal. If your feelings change from one moment and one visit to the next, that's also normal.

Once you're clearer on the different ways you feel around your family at any given time, you can begin to look at how best to manage the situation. Robert decided to focus on how to handle his mother's Sunday dinners. He had begun to dread the weekly gatherings so much that he was having trouble sleeping. "I used to have this nightmare about suffocating and it's been happening more often since the dinners became weekly," he explained. "I always wake up in this panic."

Knowing that his mother would be hurt by his need for space, we talked about Robert maybe needing to accept that he might not be able to please her *and* take care of his own needs at the same time. She might be upset by his request for more space, but eventually she would get over it. Once he felt ready, he made a plan to talk to her again about him taking a break from her Sunday dinners. While their conversation wasn't easy, he was able to create a healthier boundary around attending the family dinners on a monthly instead of weekly basis. It's never easy to communicate boundaries with family, as there are built-in expectations sometimes that can make some family members go on the defensive. As for Robert, eventually, his mother did accept his need to heal in his own way, and several other family members (quietly) expressed their relief that the get-togethers were returning to a monthly schedule.

Grief and Family: How to Access Your Needs

In Robert's case, his Plan A proved to be sufficient, but it's a good idea to establish your A, B, and C plans in advance. Here are three questions to consider when you're ready to do that before communicating your needs to family:

- *Does my family know and understand the extent of my grief and/or is it safe to share it if not?*
- *Have I dreaded family events in the past, and either (a) been happy I've gone afterward or (b) canceled but wished that I hadn't?*
- *Am I able to communicate my needs in a way that makes me feel heard and validated by family?*

Dating While Grieving

As a therapist, I usually avoid giving direct advice, but I do lay down concrete guidelines around dating—namely, to avoid it altogether when you're feeling emotionally fragile. It's simply too likely to set you back in your grief journey. When you're already struggling to get through most days, you don't need feedback that may range from mildly hurtful to downright destructive.

When Hana first came to me, she felt like she was on an emotional roller coaster ride. Still grieving the loss of her fiancé, she'd avoided dating for more than a year. Recently, however, she'd been on a first date that had shocked her in a way she'd never imagined. Her date had not only been open to her grief but comforting when she'd gotten emotional talking about her loss. For the first time in a long while, she'd begun to imagine a future that wasn't entirely bleak or lonely. Perhaps she could be in a warm, loving relationship again someday. Perhaps she could feel hopeful again.

When her date reached out to her to schedule a second one, she felt more hesitant than she expected, suddenly unsure how ready she truly was to "get out there." Not wanting to turn him down, Hana discussed with me how she might establish some healthy boundaries with this man who had seemed supportive, but whom she still barely knew. On their second night out, she decided, instead of discussing her grief, she would try to focus on "normal" conversation and see how that felt.

When Hana arrived at our session the following week, she was visibly overwhelmed. The date had been surprisingly enjoyable, and since that night, he'd been texting her often. She should be happy, she said, but then hesitated, her facial expression turning suddenly taciturn. "I like him, but I just can't," she said, finally letting her tears flow. He was a great guy, she explained, and their time together had given her a new outlook on her future—but she didn't feel ready to be physically or emotionally intimate with him. In fact, enjoying this man's company had made her miss her fiancé even more. After each date, she'd stayed up scrolling through old photos of her and her lost love, sobbing into her pillow for hours.

Hana's self-awareness was admirable. Grievers sometimes confuse dating with healing, assuming that going on a date may also feel like a way to "prove," both to yourself and others, that you're "doing okay." All of that is entirely understandable, since on some level, grief is an inherently isolating journey that often has us grasping for reassurance. Of course we crave connection, warmth, and understanding to buffer against the pain of our losses! Who doesn't want to feel cared for when we're hurting so deeply? But I'll say it again: There is no magic threshold you can force yourself over—no date or event or life milestone that will give you a shortcut to bypass grief.

Although dating can be a positive distraction at other times in life, it can feel incompatible with grief. Why? For one thing, when you're feeling especially emotionally fragile, you're more likely to gravitate toward people who are *un*healthy for you to decide to hook up with, but find that may leave you feeling emptier or more disconnected, if you are in the throes of grief. If a date is insensitive or scrutinizing, that feedback may set you back, causing you additional pain on top of your already acute grief. Also, dating is about getting to know a new person and allowing them to get to know you. At a time when your needs, wants, and emotions are so profoundly in flux, this kind of give and take can be especially fraught.

Even if you do feel up to dating, be aware that grief has major impacts on a relationship dynamic. I see it play out with clients all the time: The person who is grieving needs more caring and consideration from the other person. For a new, or newer, dating situation or relationship, that need is even more likely to create an imbalanced dynamic whereby the griever receives the majority of the attention and nurturing. In some cases this dynamic may feel good in the short term—to you and, in some cases, the other person as well—but that level of imbalance isn't a stable foundation for a mutually supportive relationship. Unfortunately, the patterns established early in the dating phase can be hard to break down since those patterns become a couple's baseline for how the relationship operates. That norm then creates expectations that aren't always obvious to either person.

As time goes on, these issues invariably begin to bubble up to the surface. Let's say, for example, you become accustomed to the other person reacting to your emotional needs first and foremost. Then later on, he or she needs you to pay more attention to their needs, which leaves you feeling abandoned. Renegotiating each person's role at that point in the relationship can be overwhelming, because again, both of you have been operating within an unhealthy dynamic without being consciously aware of it. That's a *lot* of emotional baggage to begin accumulating before you've even begun a committed relationship!

Grief and Dating: Creating Boundaries

Let's explore how to create boundaries that support your needs and allow you to back away from dating until you feel ready to connect in a more balanced way.

- *Delete the online dating apps while you are tending to your own needs. Sometimes, it can feel good to swipe in the moment, but it takes energy to get to know someone. It also may mean being confronted by questions about your life, which you may not be ready to share while feeling vulnerable.*
- *You are not obligated to share about your loss. Even if you're asked, YOU get to decide when and how to share your experience. It's a privilege to know you, pain and all.*
- *Protect your boundaries if you become triggered by either the prospect of dating or while dating. It doesn't matter how many meetings there have been, you are allowed to communicate your needs and say no to anything that doesn't feel comfortable.*

Long-Term Relationships and Grief

Grief demands that we focus on ourselves—and conversely, a healthy, loving relationship must be a two-way street. Let's be honest, that's pretty tough to do while we're grieving. The tension between "me" and "we" always exists in relationships, but often gets considerably more intense when one or both people are navigating grief. Every relationship is unique, so there are no universally applicable rules around managing grief while in a long-term relationship.

Even when there's compatibility between two people, timing and reciprocity matter. It takes time and hard work to build the well of deep trust and emotional safety that allows long-lasting relationships to thrive. Couples that have more years of experience enduring life's stress tests together may find the grief journey difficult, but ultimately more manageable. For others, timing is just part of the equation, though; long-standing committed unions can and do struggle during the grief journey. While that additional uncertainty can feel scary, it can also highlight the need to create a new balance between "me" and "we."

As a general rule, and especially when grief is acute, both people in any committed relationship need to feel supported. However, leaning too heavily on a significant other puts an unfair burden on the other person, as well as the relationship. That's why it's important to continuously assess your needs and seek additional support outside of your relationship whenever necessary. This might look like couple's therapy, or leaning more heavily on friends or family for support, so you can get the care you need while also preventing you from acting *out* your needs.

Grief in a Long-Term Relationship: How to Assess Your Needs

As grief turns your world upside down and inside out, your relationship, too, will change. Here are questions to continue asking yourself as your needs and boundaries shift:

- *Am I communicating my needs and wishes to my person clearly?*
- *Does my person understand what I am experiencing and feeling?*
- *Is there anything specific that I need right now that I am not getting?*
- *Am I giving myself permission to take the space I need to tend to my grief as it calls to me or am I pushing it down and ignoring it so as to not inconvenience my person?*

Grieving While Working

Work can be one of the most challenging places to grieve. While some workplaces and bosses will be more tolerant of your emotional ups and downs, others will have zero patience for it. As a result, managing grief at work, whether you work in an office or from home or elsewhere, can be a very different experience for each person. First and foremost, try to take the most realistic possible assessment of your company's culture and the people—your boss(es), closest coworkers, and clients. Does your workplace culture allow any time and space for personal needs and priorities? Is your boss ever willing to express his/her own vulnerability? What about your colleagues? Highly competitive company cultures can be especially challenging environments to function in when you're grieving, since vulnerability may be interpreted as weakness and used against you.

Working demands that you contribute and produce for the good of the whole, which means that people's individual needs aren't always a top priority. Perhaps you find you do not have the same capacity for your work that you had pre-loss. This is completely normal, though it may require some accommodation, or even big changes on your part. Take note of how you are feeling, and find the right support as needed. Trying to work and remain connected to the work environment as a whole may feel extra challenging when you're grieving.

Grief at Work: How to Manage Your Changing Needs Under Pressure

Some workplace cultures or careers that allow for some of your grief to seep into your every day may run out of patience sooner than you expect or feel ready to accommodate. Let's look at some ways to cope with grief at work:

- *Continually assess how much vulnerability you can safely show at work. If, for instance, your regular absences to cry in the bathroom are increasingly being noticed, even scrutinized, take note of that.*
- *When you can't openly express your grief at work, I recommend scheduling time to grieve. Yes, I said schedule. Add it to your calendar the same way you'd add a meeting. This may sound odd, but knowing that at, say, twelve p.m. or six p.m. you can go somewhere—the bathroom, on a walk, home, etc.—to cry or look at photos of a pet or loved one—can help you to focus on your job better during the workday, while knowing you will attend to your feelings as soon as you can.*
- *Negotiate additional time off if and when you need it. Even an extra day or week can help to relieve the pressure by giving you additional time to grieve. Make it a point to get clear on your workplace bereavement policy/FMLA guidelines, and advocate for what you need.*

As with all parts of the grief experience, your ability to and interest in engaging with different people and situations in your life may feel easier at certain times and less so at others. Above all, be true to you and your needs and boundaries, no matter how often and how much they change. The people who truly care about you will be there for you, whenever you feel ready. Most important of all, *you* will be better able to be there *for yourself*—which is sometimes the best gift of all.

CHAPTER 11

Performative Emotions Only Belong on Stage:
How to Be Real About Your Grief with Yourself and the People Around You

"Authenticity is a collection of choices that we have to make every day. It's about the choice to show up and be real. The choice to be honest. The choice to let our true selves be seen."

—Brené Brown, *The Gifts of Imperfection*

When you're grieving, it can seem like your every emotion and action is being scrutinized by the outside world. The people around us would prefer that we just keep going when hard things happen, to keep showing up and not to miss a beat and prove, at least outwardly, that we're "okay." Our culture will do almost anything to avoid darker, heavier emotions, both inside ourselves and in others. Not surprisingly, we all learn how to "fake" what we feel because that fake feeling is more socially acceptable than what we're actually feeling. This pressure can be so intense that we resort to playing roles, mostly unconsciously, to allow others to feel more comfortable with our emotions. There are so many moments we are forced to fake how we feel, or feel afraid we'll be shunned if we show our true feelings, that we disconnect from how we actually feel. I can't count the number of times I've asked a client how they feel and have gotten a shrug or an "I don't even know any-more" in reply.

Don't believe me? Let's do a little experiment together:

How many times have you wanted to cry, scream, or be quietly numb and someone told you to cheer up or smile—so you faked it and did what they wanted?

How many times have you wanted to laugh, but then didn't because you thought it would be weird to laugh because you're grieving, and aren't you supposed to look like someone who's grieving?

How many times have you walked down the street and thought of some-thing that brought up a swell of emotions, but you felt you couldn't really express them because you were in public?

I'm going to guess you said a hearty "yep" or "too many times to count" to most or all of those. We've all been there. We do what we "should." But think about that for a moment: We're experiencing some of the most intense emotional pain we've ever experienced, and we're focused on *making other people comfortable?* Yikes. Performing emotions you don't feel may be a necessary coping mechanism in the midst of an immediate crisis, or in specific situations like at work or sometimes in parenting, but otherwise, it comes at a significant personal cost. When we don't express our honest emotions, we risk not being able to know for ourselves when things have become so painful that we're on the verge of a personal crisis. To get through grief—and arguably life also—we must be able to feel what we feel, when we feel it, without having to worry about how it comes across to the people who aren't in our shoes and aren't invested in us, our lives, and our well-being.

We Have to Feel Safe to Be Honest

Back in chapter 3, we got more honest about our feelings with our-selves, learning to let them show up, and giving ourselves permission to feel whatever we were feeling—the pain, confusion, anger, laughter, whatever comes up—without judgment. It's one thing to feel what we feel when we are alone, but what happens when we are around other people, or feel pressured to not express ourselves fully? What happens to the permission to feel what we feel then? Throughout this chapter, we're going to take that a step further and look at what gets in the way of being authentic when we express our grief to others, and out in the world.

Some of the hiding we do is conscious, and some of it isn't. The way we saw hard emotions modeled when we were kids has something to do with it, but whom you surround yourself with now matters, too. Giving yourself permission to feel what you feel without cutting yourself off or gaslighting yourself is the crux of healing. That essentially means this: Whether you judge your own feelings, and how you judge them, matters—a lot.

A Reminder About Emotional Safety

Many of the reasons we learn to perform our emotions are directly related to how emotionally safe we feel with the people we're talking to. Many times, we get overly used to hiding our true selves and feelings and do so even when we don't have to. That said—and this is a big one—if you do not feel safe in your current circumstances, it's essential that you put that safety first.

I know you've heard me talk a lot about safety, and maybe it's felt too repetitive at times. I assure you, I will never stop reminding you to put your emotional safety first. No one can tell you if and when you feel safe to be vulnerable. Revealing tender parts of yourself to folks you know might reject them, or may not be able to listen or support in the ways you need, may not be the right choice for you. If you do not have the environmental or relational safety you need, I want you to know that you are safe to practice here with me, and encourage you to seek new supports for yourself, whether through a hotline, a free support group, a therapist, or perhaps an online community. It can take time, perseverance, and patience, but I assure you there are people, places, and communities that will work their way into being a trusted space for you.

The Subtle Art of Taking Emotional Inventory

Depending on your upbringing, culture, religion, community, familial modeling, and personality, you may find that when you're in unknown territory (like, right now maybe), you tend to lose yourself in the expectations of others. You may not even realize you're doing it in the moment.

Straying from the societal norm of being "fine," if not downright upbeat, can be unsettling. Ironically, performing emotions we're not feeling sometimes seems easier, or at least less likely to result in others judging us negatively and maybe even rejecting us. In the long term, though, faking feelings leads to fake personal interpersonal connections, as well as disconnection from ourselves. Ultimately, it's only by feeling our authentic feelings that we can truly know ourselves. Then and only then can we form genuine, caring connections with others.

My hope is that you can inhabit your authentic feelings with the people who love you and make you feel safe, and in order to do that you're going to practice inhabiting your feelings here with me.

- To start, get out a little slip of paper and write down the one word that best describes how you're feeling right now. Don't think, just write (or say silently to yourself) whatever comes to mind. Breathe deeply and quiet your body for ten seconds. What other emotions come into your mind? Write those down. Keep writing if you want to. This is about getting clear about how you are feeling right now *in this precise moment*. (P.S. If nothing comes up right away, don't worry. This is a practice, and sometimes just noticing that you aren't able to access what you're feeling is enough.)

My client Lauren was a graduate school student in New York City when she lost her brother, Michael, to leukemia. During our first session, she told me she wasn't able to express her grief and even felt embarrassed by it. That's something I hear often, especially from new clients who are already overwhelmed by their grief, and understandably hesitant to open up. I may be highly qualified and come recommended, but at first I'm still a stranger.

Without wanting to assume too much, I began to parse out the details: *How attached and close was she to her brother? What was the history of the relationship as a whole? What other adversity had she contended with and overcome or not overcome? And, most important, does she feel safe expressing her emotions, thoughts, and opinions?*

I soon learned that Lauren had been very close with her brother, but they'd grown apart when she left Chicago for business school at NYU. Recently she'd been feeling like she was living two parallel lives—one where she was depressed about her brother's death and missing him like crazy, and another where she was pretending to be a grad student in New York City, living her best life—*as per Instagram*.

"Do you feel you can't be open about your loss to *anyone* around you?" I asked.

"Not really. I mean, I can, but I think people get sick of hearing the same thing over and over," she replied matter-of-factly. "At home, it's my parents' loss and that's more important than mine. In New York, it's just my friends, who are busy, and they seem to not really want to ask or hear about Michael. They tell me to just be happy and so I do try. Sometimes it works, sometimes I feel so much worse."

Hearing her talk, it was hardly surprising to me that she felt alone in her grief. Partially, she was shoving it away, but she also seemed to be surrounded by people who were intent on avoiding her emotions. She explained that she'd been the kid who needed nothing, "trained" to be low maintenance because her brother was sick for so long. Throughout much of her childhood, Lauren's parents hadn't had the bandwidth to meet anything more than her basic needs.

It broke my heart hearing her minimize her own deep pain, simply because she thought that was expected of her. The reality is, we all need love, attention, and validation. When that isn't available from a young age, we may internalize the idea that we don't matter—that our thoughts, emotions, needs, and desires aren't and *shouldn't be* a priority. To cope, we learn to take up as little space in our relationships as we can, prioritizing other people's needs and desires over our own. After all, life experience has taught us that by working overtime to meet others' needs—while denying our own—is how we "earn" love and friendship. This relationship dynamic ultimately causes us more pain, and often unconsciously attracts people who care mostly about themselves. The excruciating reality in cases like Lauren's is that, in the midst of intense grief, loneliness, and heartache, there's often a need to break away from at least some of these fundamentally imbalanced, unhealthy relationships. Until she believed that her grief—and all of her emotions and thoughts, needs, and desires—mattered, the cycle of suppressing her needs for others' sake was likely to continue.

Lauren and I had some new terrain to cover, so we set out to find her inner waterways—that place where her emotions could ebb and flow naturally, as they were meant to. Over the next few months, Lauren would enter my office, make a beeline to the couch, and throw her body down with such force that the pillows would somersault. Then she would sigh loudly, as if carrying the entire emotional weight of New York City in her Rothy's tote bag, and smile at me, like she was on top of the world. *A sigh and a smile, huh?* She'd keep that smile on her face until I said four simple words: *"How are you feeling?"*

Fine Is a Four-Letter Word

What we don't want? It's not helpful to you if you just say all is "good" or "fine" (unless that's sincerely your truth). The point here is to find either one of these (or some iteration of them) to use as an answer when you don't know what to say, but also to want to try to share how you're really feeling.

Performative emotions only serve to protect you in a moment. In the long run, you're only taking yourself further away from your truth. Truth leads to understanding. Understanding leads to connection and, ultimately, to healing. There can't be healing without truth. Catch my drift here? We need your truth. YOU need your truth.

What surprises a lot of people is that radical truth-telling should always begin as a solo venture. In other words, it starts with telling the full truth to *yourself*. One of the simplest (note I did *not* say easiest!!) ways to start is to pause for a moment before you answer a question like "How are you?" and actually figure out how you feel.

If your knee-jerk reaction is "fine" . . . Pause. Are you really? What does fine look or feel like for you? Just because someone expects you to say that you're "hanging in" or "okay" doesn't mean you have to be. Are you listless? Feeling fragile? On edge? Exhausted? Anxious? Sad? Do you feel lighter or heavier today? What sensations come up in your body? What emotions show up if you take a beat to really check in with yourself?

Once you know how you feel, the next step is to share that authentic answer in reply if you feel safe enough to take that risk. It might feel scary, because you may not be sure what to say (especially if you have never had to do this before), but being able to be honest about our feelings helps us to be more honest about our needs and to find the connection we so deeply crave in our grief.

Authentic Replies to "What Happened?" and "How Are You?"

If you feel at a loss or uncertain how to reply when someone asks "What happened?" or "How are you?" here are a few of my favorites to get you started:

- "Thank you for asking, but I am not really able to talk about it right now."
- "Honestly, it's been really fucking hard. I am not doing well and I really can use some extra support from you to get through this."
- "I'm grateful for any support at this time. It's a roller coaster and every day feels like a whole range of emotions."
- "At this moment, I am _____, but it changes."
- "I feel okay right now, but this morning I was feeling pretty _____."

Verbalizing our needs is very complicated terrain. First, we have to identify if we feel safe enough to do so. This may look like your need not to get into the emotional space where you will be destabilized. This may be finding safety in a person or community. This may even be stating that you don't feel safe. This may look like verbalizing your need for connection and support in the moment. This may look like being clear about your discomfort in sharing details with anyone you don't feel safe with. I say this a lot in my practice—YOU are the captain of your ship. You call the shots when it comes to what you need and how you want to proceed with people or obligations. Remember, your needs will shift and change, so what may feel good one moment may not in another. There's nothing wrong with you if this happens, and also please don't feel that you have to explain it to others. This is how grief rolls, unpredictable and ever changing.

Verbalizing Your Grief Needs

- "I could use some company tonight. I just don't want to be alone."
- "I want company, but I get easily overwhelmed these days. How about we order in and then I may have to end the night early and just go to sleep."
- "Your asking so many questions can feel overwhelming to me right now—can we talk about something else for a bit?"

Verbalizing Your Grief Boundaries

- "I don't feel comfortable sharing my feelings about this right now, as it's really deeply personal."
- "I don't feel safe."
- "I would rather talk in person than over text, because so much gets lost in translation and it just doesn't feel private."
- "Thanks for asking, but I just can't go there right now."
- "Hey, thanks, you know, I can talk for five minutes, but then I have to go."
- "Thank you." (Sometimes, that's all you have to say. You don't have to add any more if you aren't comfortable.)

Permission to Put Your Grieving Needs First

So many clients tell me about the people in their lives who try to pressure them to feel better faster, who ask intrusive questions, push them to get back into the world before they are ready, and request that they behave differently in order to make others feel comfortable. As we've seen, that's not only off base, it expresses a lack of caring around the truth of how the griever is feeling. Some clients come to my office and talk about how exhausted they are from having to show up to some event or listen to a friend tell them that they are ready for my client to be "better again" and to "move on." Yeah, I seriously hear this all the time. It's outrageous to me that anyone has to be in a position to defend their grief while in the midst of grieving. It's like someone being told to hurry up and stop bleeding after a wound. It's difficult to navigate the grief experience all the while being needed or having obligations in the world. It's a delicate balance for sure to live while grieving, but abandoning the grief journey because others need it to be wrapped up just isn't a healthy and kind option. There. I'm glad I got that off my chest.

With that said, I often find myself giving clients very specific permission slips as reminders that they are the one grieving and, thus, allowed to keep their needs at the forefront of their current grief journey. The following list is a starting point, so feel free to add your own. Come back to it whenever you feel pressured from the outside world to do, be, or feel any way other than how you are right now, in the most painful time of your life.

These permission slips are really about offering yourself patience, respect, and care when it comes to interacting with the outside world. If you don't know where to begin, read these reminders below and put a check mark next to the ones that ring the most true for you right now.

Permission Slips for Honest Grieving

- You are allowed to feel your feelings fully and authentically.
- You are allowed to show up however you need to show up to the world.
- You are allowed to share your *honest* feelings with anyone who feels safe to share with.
- You are allowed to keep your grief story to only the people whom you want to tell.

- You are allowed to put your body, mind, and spirit first, even if someone around you says otherwise.
- You are allowed to cry for however long it takes. Anytime. Anywhere.
- You are allowed to *NOT* text back or call back depending on how you feel.
- You are allowed to *NOT* respond to any social media messages that make you feel uncomfortable.
- You are allowed to create boundaries to keep you and your grief feelings safe from anyone you do not trust to hold them with care and gentleness.
- You are allowed to rest and refill when you are emotionally exhausted and overwhelmed.
- You are allowed to say *"no"* as many times as you want to anything that doesn't feel good.
- You are allowed to *NOT* answer intrusive questions from anyone you don't know well or trust.
- You are allowed to be as honest as you want about how you feel at all times, so long as you feel safe.
- You are allowed to grieve for however long you grieve. Period.

Grieving is exhausting enough without using your precious energy to perform emotions. Instead, protect your energy and save it for the endurance you will need to keep on going. Find your people, and then let those people in. Allow yourself to be carried by the love and support of secure relationships when you are at your most fragile. Try as hard as you can to show up for your grief—and its endless detours—with your whole self. Your whole self is the one who cries, screams, wails, laughs, gets physically ill, gets overwhelmed, is forgetful, dramatic, and exhausted, scared, and confused, and maybe even relieved at times. It's also the self that eventually learns how to pave a new path out of a shattered heart. This is the way. And, you're not alone. Whatever your feelings, there is room for all of them here.

Navigating Social Media: The Good, the Bad, and the Power of Privacy Settings

I still remember the first time a "memory" that I wasn't prepared for came up on my social media feed. It was a photo of my mom and me at a family event a year prior. I put a flower in her hair and thought it was cute. I took a photo while she held a glass of prosecco and smiled happily. As I looked at the photo, my heart leaped into my mouth, and I felt heat rise all over my body. *The unexpected grief triggers.* It was almost like I lost all feeling in my body for a moment. I was equal parts re-traumatized and equal parts so happy to see her smiling face on my screen. "Hi Mom," I said aloud, feeling the heat of unexpected tears roll down my face. "I miss you *so* much." I closed the app, wiped my face, and went on about my day, but make no mistake: *It shook me.*

This might be your very first experience with loss, and with something this traumatic and life-altering. This might be the first time you share something on social media that feels hard and confusing. There's no perfect guide for this moment. How do you show up honestly for yourself, but also make sure that you're not putting so much of your much-needed grief energy into managing other people's reactions and expectations of how you should be at this moment in your life?

What you do need to know is this: YOUR needs come first—online and off when it comes to your grief experience. You don't owe anyone on social media platforms anything—not your story, not your emotions, not your deepest truths. Not unless you *want* to share it, or you get comfort, connection, and solace from connecting online in that way. Social media connects millions and disconnects just as many—all within minutes, even seconds. It's shaped how we live on a daily basis. It also breeds envy, resentment, judgment, and greed. It is responsible for plummeting self-esteem and escalating isolation and loneliness.

Now, I'm not one of those therapists who hates social media—at its best, it's a place of community, or at the very least some entertaining dances and ridiculous, but spot-on memes. There is often so much good that can come from people banding together over a cause, or in support of one another online. I've seen it for myself with my own social media platform. It can be a place to make like-minded new friends, to learn more about yourself, to feel less alone, to connect with other people struggling with loss, and to find a way to express yourself to a group that really, really gets it. It can make us feel connected. I do truly believe that when done with intention and authenticity, as well as immense discernment, social media can be a great source of empowerment. The substantive interactions can sometimes really soften the landing when we are in the throes of early grief, most especially.

That said, I'm hard-pressed to think of a place where we are more performative than online. We compartmentalize, sharing only the parts of us that will get likes or shares or views or be entertaining—a literal highlight reel for public consumption to satisfy our need for affirmation and acceptance.

As a result, social media while grieving is a bit of a wild card. Sometimes, it can be this amazing community of friends and strangers all coming together and giving validation and love. Sometimes, that can really be a lifesaver when you're in the throes of anxiety, depression, or just not even wanting to go on. And, sometimes, it's a land mine, as Lauren experienced when she wrote a drunken post one night about her grief. While her post received a lot of likes and hearts, not a single one of her "friends" posted a heartfelt or validating comment in reply, or followed up with her offline.

The experience left her feeling ashamed and unwilling to share her vulnerability again, when in fact what she needed was friends who genuinely cared not just about "magical life" Lauren, but the sad, lonely, and grieving Lauren, too. Like many of my clients, she needed more people in her life who didn't expect her to perform only the emotions they found palatable. She needed what we all need—more authentic connection with people who sincerely care about *all* of who we are.

Knowing how fraught and personal our relationships to social media are, I have only three Golden Rules: (1) You don't owe anyone an update, (2) Choose your people and places carefully, and (3) When in doubt, use those privacy settings.

You Don't Owe Anyone an Update

For some, social media is a place where they want the entire world to see what they do moment by moment. Maybe it's become a place of community if, for example, you've been going through the illness of a loved one for a long period of time, you have perhaps created a support system of people who know, understand, and acknowledge this difficult time for you—and this can bring comfort when you lose that person.

Let's be real, most of us have too many faux friends and spend too much time and energy on people we show only bits and pieces of our real selves to. Like so many of my clients, Lauren began to realize that her IG feed, which featured her "living it up" and loving her "magical life," was more like a mask she was putting on to please everyone *but herself.* She wanted people to think she was okay, and that pressure she put on herself to prove she was moving on caused more harm than good for her mental health.

So, why do we feel this pressure to share and update? Why do we succumb so easily to performing so others might see us in a certain light? Social media has somehow quietly taught us that a curated showcasing of our lives is much more appealing. It moves so fast that if we aren't posting or sharing, the algorithm literally forgets us and puts us at the bottom of the heap... and when we are grieving, the last thing we need is to be pushed to the bottom and not seen. Many of my clients talked about the fear of disconnection if they didn't post, and although I can understand that fear, during the hardest times in our lives, authentic connection is what makes the most difference. I want you to remember that when you are about to post; not just the *what* of your share, but the *why*, too.

Choose Your People and Places Carefully

When my mother died, I didn't hesitate to post the news on my Facebook page. I felt comfortable being vulnerable there because I'd always kept that community tight. It was a place where I'd always shared my truth and received support, so sharing my loss and my grief journey felt natural, even important. This isn't the case for everyone, however, and often people's experience online is shaped by how they relate to social media in general.

When you're grieving, as I said earlier, it can be important to step back and consider your relationship to social media, and your social media communities. How well do you know your social media contacts? Do you usually share your personal truths online? If so, do you feel heard and supported by your community? If your social media community consists of people who feel more like followers than true friends, you may want to hold back on posting your most intimate, vulnerable thoughts and feelings. This is a time to honor and nurture yourself first and foremost. You can broadcast the news of your loss later, when you're feeling less fragile, or not at all. In the meantime, focus on expressing your vulnerability to people who know you and care about you on a deeper, more personal level.

When in Doubt, Use Those Privacy Settings

I don't know if we always know this: You do not have to allow everyone in. You don't even have to allow all of your IRL friends in! That cousin who always wishes you happy birthday but doesn't know anything real about your life, nor cares to know? Maybe not your target audience for an authentic, compassionate post-breakup consolation. Most people will want to hear your news, and many may react to it, but that isn't the same as authentically caring about you. Trust has to be earned and then lovingly maintained over time. You are allowed to save your truth only for those who you know care about the *real* you, the *all-of-you* you. Pick and choose who gets to see the vulnerable parts of you, mute the others, and give yourself a lifelong permission slip not to share with people who don't add value to your life.

Let's Check In: To Post or Not to Post

Let's take a closer look at how social media is playing a role in your life right now. I know that sometimes social media can feel like the easiest way to connect with a large number of people at once when we have something to share, but that's not always the most helpful thing to do. Pausing to check in with yourself before posting can be a powerful exercise to do whenever you're thinking of sharing vulnerable parts of yourself, like grief. Taking inventory of your social media use while in this vulnerable place of grief can help you manage expectations/limitations and protect yourself from feedback (or lack thereof) before you're ready for it.

Before posting, stop and notice which platforms you post on, the types of posts you usually put online, and the kinds of reactions you're looking for when you post something.

- Are you on more than one social media platform?
- Who are your followers on different platforms?
- Are you more open and honest on one platform over another?
- Where online do you feel seen and heard?
- Where, if anywhere, do you feel safe sharing vulnerability?
- What do you expect to get out of online support?

- Do you feel pressured to share more than you normally would on social media? If so, can you honor your own limitations and boundaries as needed?

  The clearer you can be with yourself, the better you can discern how, where, what, and even whether to share about your grief journey.

Social media is never going away, and if anything, more and more of our lives will wind up being conducted online. Each new platform seems to ask that we share more and more intimately. Whether it's online or in person, I want to say loud and clear that you should not have to perform your emotions for anyone. You have the right to stay true to your needs and desires when you're in a vulnerable emotional place. I mean it! It has to be a non-negotiable for you to protect your heart. If you don't want to share, but feel pressured to do so, you have my permission to say nothing. If you do want to share, then by all means, share! I only ask that you try to take a daily inventory of how you are feeling about connecting to others, how much you feel up to sharing, and adjust your boundaries and profile/s to protect yourself if you begin to feel overexposed in your grief.

Above all, know that always, and especially during times of grief, you can surround yourself with just the people who have earned your trust and who truly care about you. How you show up in the world is entirely up to *you*. Please don't forget that.

CHAPTER 12

Carrying Our Loved Ones with Us

"That's really all they ask of us—our parents; our
lovers, husbands, and wives; our children and dear
friends. That we carry them gently in our lives as
they carried us in theirs."

—Rabbi Steve Leder

Our society loves the phrase *"moving on."* It's often used flippantly,
even a little callously, as if we can suddenly decide that grief—as well
as trauma and other hardship—no longer affects us, like we get to
wake up one day and skip off to the magical land of I'm Over It.

I've heard the phrase "moving on" so many times in my therapy
practice, in fact, that it became part of the title of this book. We want
to move forward. We want to feel "normal" again—to feel whole, and
for the pain to evaporate. But the way we think we do that is to cut
things loose as though our feelings and needs were no more than sand-
bags on a hot-air balloon, weighing us down until we can sever the
ties and float back into the sunrise and live happily ever after. But I'll
say it again: There is no "back." There is only forward, and by now
you know I don't believe when there is deep love and attachment, followed by loss, there's any such thing as "letting go."

Although rituals of remembrance are not exclusive to death-
related loss, this chapter is going to lean more toward losses that
occurred through death or ambiguous loss. Relationships can be so

complicated, and we have been honest with one another throughout these pages about how we feel and have felt about whom or what we have lost, so I leave it to you to decide if you want to carry them forward with you, and how you want the connection to feel.

How we grieve and how we continue our relationship to whom and what we have lost is about our connection to someone or something significant to us. Whatever or whomever you lost, those are yours to feel and keep how, when, and why you choose to. No one should ever ask you or expect you to "move on" from feeling connected, whether or not that connection is for someone who's still on this earthly plane, or not. Your grief is yours, just as your love is yours. End of story.

Continuing Our Bonds

Let's look at loss solely from an early psychological perspective. It was Sigmund Freud who set a precedent that the path of grief was moving on. For the majority of his career, Freud believed that to help people adjust to loss, the treatment had to focus on detachment. His Model of Bereavement went on to explain that the role of grief is *detachment* from a loved one. For the majority of his career, Sigmund Freud believed that grief was the process by which we let go of our attachments to our loved ones. In fact, his Model of Bereavement asserted that we only feel the intense pain and sadness (as he called it, "melancholia") that most of us associate with grief when we fail to detach fully from our loved ones. The role of the therapist, then, and our objective as grievers was to increasingly relinquish our connections to our loved ones and losses.

However, in 1920, Freud lost his daughter Sophie to the Spanish flu. After this, he began to rethink his own theories on grief and mourning, which underscores the idea that you can't really and truly understand grief until you yourself are grieving. After Freud's loss, he wrote a letter to Sophie's best friend, Ludwig Binswanger, saying this about his grief: "We know that the acute pain we feel after a loss will continue; it will also remain inconsolable and we will never find a replacement. No matter what happens, no matter what we do, the pain is always there. And that's the way it should be. It's the only way to perpetuate a love we don't want to give up."[1]

No matter what happens, no matter what we do, the pain is always there. And that's the way it should be. Freud conveyed a fact we grievers have long known to be true when it comes to holding on to our loved ones: "It was (and is) a stubborn bond that one refuses to abandon because it's our way of holding on to the love of a loved one."[2]

Unfortunately, Freud's earlier model is what stuck around in most of our Western societal consciousness, and to this day detachment is our gold standard for healing from grief. In many ways, sure, it's easier for *others* if we just keep going and detach, and no one has to know how to help or support or be on the path of grief with us for this indeterminate amount of time. But that's not the way toward true healing and connection.

Thankfully, I am not alone in my frustration with this emphasis on detachment, and after decades of dissatisfaction with the outdated way of approaching grief, researchers began to look differently at our human relationship to loss. In 1996, Klass, Silverman, and Nickman published *Continuing Bonds: New Understandings of Grief.* This publication was the first real challenge to the old way of thinking about grief and loss, and it validated what so many people felt—that our relationship continues after loss. In its essence, this new Continuing Bonds Theory argued against the need for detachment as an emotional "remedy" to grief. Instead, it focused on expanding the attachment and relationship inside us as a way of nurturing a sense of connection to the person or thing we've lost.[3] Wanting to have a bond with our loved ones is natural, not pathological, so this research and progression in the grief world has been welcomed as a model for those of us working in and managing grief.

Continuing our bond with our deceased loved one is an individual choice, of course, and a journey that may evolve and change over time for you. There is no right way to continue our relationship and there is no predetermined idea of what this should look like. It's your loving relationship and you get to choose how and what you decide to carry forward with you.

What Do You Want to Carry?

As grievers, we may sometimes feel that our job is to find ways to keep all the good with us—the moments, the memories, the mementos—and keep them somewhere safe so we can take them out and relive the love again, even if it is accompanied by grief. For some, though, this desire can often be fraught with emotions that range from love, joy, and gratitude to inescapably dark sadness, longing, and regret. While, yes, life does continue—day turns into night and again into day—throughout it all, we are needed, and we are relied upon. We must continue on. Every griever inevitably faces the same question: If we know that we can stay connected to our loss for as long as we want—even as long as the rest of our lives—then what does moving forward look like?

Your answer will be as unique as your connection to what has been lost, so I ask you this: Do you want to carry your loved one forward with you? What do you think that will look like for you?

When my mom died, I wasn't sure what that would look like. I hadn't thought of it before. There is no dress rehearsal for grieving or on imagining how our relationship with our person will morph and change. How could we really prepare, and how could we really know? As Chimamanda Ngozi Adichie so appropriately said in "Notes on Grief," "Grief is a cruel kind of education."[4] Isn't that the truth?

You might feel immense comfort in the idea that grieving allows people to perpetuate their connection to a lost loved one. Lauren, from our last chapter, described that the freedom to continue her bond with her deceased brother brought a sense of purpose, as well as comfort. She could now imagine him as her biggest cheerleader, alongside her on all the job interviews and career milestones. Another client said she envisioned her deceased father as a sort of guardian angel, as he was always overprotective of her while he was alive. Others, though, may find it brings a burden of its own, depending on the relationship or circumstance they're grieving. Whatever works, whatever brings comfort and a sense of being able to move forward without the deepest, most intense grief-sting threatening to last forever? I endorse that.

There is also no rule against doing whatever works for you at any given time, and no rule that says you only choose once. Maybe it's wearing your grandmother's necklace, but down the road you want to wear something else that feels meaningful to you. Or maybe it feels like too much to have a picture of your beloved dog as your lock screen wallpaper right away, but in a few months you realize you'd be glad for the reminder of fond memories. We don't have to forget the hard stuff or wrap the relationship up in this beautifully curated package. We get to create a remembering ritual, or not! As Dr. Clarissa Pinkola Estés, who wrote *Women Who Run with the Wolves*, once said, "wisdom is in whatever works." The freedom to create a ritual as unique as your connection or that serves the highest good for your healing and well-being is what matters most.

When Detachment Is Necessary (and Healthy)

While many people want to bring their deceased loved ones with them, I also want to honor that some relationships are so painful or traumatic that you may specifically *not* want to bring them forward. This is completely okay and may even be the best, healthiest thing for you. No one knows the truth and history of your relationship or your feelings like you do. Honor your grief experience.

Why Do Anniversaries Feel So Hard?

Anniversaries can bring up a vivid reexperiencing of our grief in its many forms. It can be so overwhelming, both emotionally and physically, either before, on, or right after the anniversary date. You may even notice that you have no specific grief reaction for many years, but find yourself confronted with a reminder of your loss, and the grief can be reawakened. These days can be birthdays, wedding anniversaries, work anniversaries, death anniversaries, or important event days that you celebrated together. It's a day that holds special meaning for you, and elicits a sense of loss whenever the day or time of year comes around.

Important anniversary days can feel so hard and it can feel sometimes even more overwhelming leading up to the anniversary of our significant loss. Sometimes, we get lost in our own world, but notice we may feel more anxious or "off" without knowing why, until we look at the calendar. Our body does remember...

Our bodies really do remember these important days, holding the memories and felt sense (a bodily awareness of a memory, person, situation, or event) of that day/time/moment. Whether it is the day of the loss or other important days that remind you of your loss or loved one, you may find yourself experiencing anxiety or feelings of depression, because thoughts and feelings around your loss are being reactivated. I've had some clients come to a session feeling really "off" or anxious or sad and not be able to pinpoint why, but upon poking around, we come to find out it's an important day they shared with their loved one, whether it was a birthday, death anniversary, or a day of special meaning that they shared.

If you, too, find yourself unexpectedly feeling tense, "off," out of sorts, sad, angry, anxious, or more exhausted, remember that a full spectrum of emotions and even physical reminders can reemerge with anniversaries, important dates, and even change of seasons. Even if it's a day you have dreaded all year, or find yourself feeling so much anxiety over, it can be a day that you choose to spend however you need. Read that last part again: however you need.

What Can We Do to Take Care of Ourselves?

- Honor your grief experience however it comes.
- Give yourself grace and space to change your mind and play it all by ear.
- Rest, lie in bed, and watch reruns of your favorite show.
- Schedule time to devote to honoring the memories of your loved one in a way that feels special to you.
- Distract yourself—if you need a break from the overwhelming emotions that arise, it's okay to take breaks from feeling so much and keep yourself busy that day.
- Surround yourself with people who "get it" and can be present and nourishing for you.

There is no "right" way to do this day, and it can change from moment to moment. There is no right way to feel and no right way to experience an anniversary, as it's whatever feels most nourishing, meaningful, or helpful to you. As I always say, go gently and take good care of your heart and body on these days. Like in all the activities we've done together here, pay attention to why you're doing it, and what feels the most nourishing and comforting. It may change from moment to moment, day to day, or year to year, but the authenticity should remain the constant.

Reawakened Grief

It's hard to avoid triggers. Hell, even the word *trigger* can feel like too much. I hate it myself. Alas, it gets us right to the heart of the matter—that sometimes, something will pop up, a sound, a smell, someone who looks like them; sometimes, it's a memory or a song on the playlist. It can be a million little moments that can pick us up and take us back in time like some grief-colored time machine, where we are reminded of all we had, but then, all we lost.

Grief wounds can reopen when we least expect them to, even after we feel like we've worked through them or have no other losses to mourn. Think of this reawakened grief like a bad cut that looks and feels healed... until it accidentally and unexpectedly slams into a sharp, hard surface and, just like that, pops open anew, forcing the body into a new round of healing. Coming alive even after we feel sure it's been sufficiently tended to, resurfaced and reawakened grief is normal and *not* an indication that your previous inner work "didn't work." Grief finds a way to attach itself to details, feelings, our senses, and memories, as well as secondary losses, especially when some of those losses were traumatic.

It can really shake us when those old feelings related to a previous loss bubble back up to the surface, but they can also be an (admittedly unwelcome) invitation to feel feelings that your body and spirit need to feel and acknowledge, some of which may have originated in secondary losses. Especially when changes arrive suddenly, harshly, or not by our choice, the loss(es) we experience are likely to have multiple layers that may accidentally encounter triggers that pry open "old" grief.

When I have been reminded of the loss of my mother—usually it feels like something stops me in my tracks and takes me back to the sometimes immobilizing experience of my fresh grief—I put a hand on my heart or I take a deep breath, and I send a quiet whisper of love to my mother. Sometimes, it can take a moment to reorient myself to the present, and that's okay. In any given moment, we can be blindsided by a grief memory or a reminder of what has been lost, and it can be hard to know what to do. After all, these moments can almost literally take our breath away.

Knowing these moments will come *is* the strategy in working with them. Or, in a cheesy clinical moment, I would say, "Prevention is the best intervention sometimes." Getting to know what may trigger us can help us prepare for them as best we can. In the moments you may feel blindsided, you can excuse yourself from the table or take a moment away from a conversation, you can stay a moment longer in your car before going inside, whatever it may be. Tend to your immediate needs, remind yourself you are also safe and cared about in the present and at your own pace, keep going.

Looking for Signs as We Go Forward

This process of continuing on/moving forward—which is part of our "healing" with grief—can feel like a double-edged sword. On one hand, we want to feel better and try to find joy in life again. However, it's never as simple as that. As David Kessler says in his book *Finding Meaning: The Sixth Stage of Grief,* "Whether I like it or not, my life is continuing, and I have decided to be part of it."[5]

As the days, weeks, and months of my broken heart began finding small ways to reassemble itself, my inner world slowly began to reorient itself to its new landscape. It's a process I've seen in countless clients, and now that I've experienced it, it is one I respect and admire even more deeply than before. It's here, in this new landscape, that we hold the density of our grief and still face a sometimes daunting decision: How do we authentically carry our deceased loved one with us as we move forward?

Inevitably, grief leaves us with so many moments of longing and wistfulness. I know I still grieve the future life milestones that my mother would never be able to witness in the way I yearned for her to. She'd never see me (finally) perfect her meatballs, or her struffoli Italian pastry recipe. She'd never see me write and publish my first book, parent, or grow old enough to appreciate her overprotectiveness.

Almost worse, she'd never be able to tell me what to keep or throw away in my refrigerator—Google never did catch up with her expertise on that subject.

When I lost those touchstones, I thought that perhaps I had lost her presence in my everyday life. The thought was devastating...until I started to notice signs. I first found her in the Enya song we both loved. How, you may ask? Well, I was sitting on the floor of the grief section in Barnes & Noble soaking up all the books I did not yet own. It was the week she died, and it was Christmastime, so they were playing holiday music. "Frosty the Snowman" had just been blaring from the loudspeaker when all of a sudden, "So I Could Find My Way" by Enya came on. Suuuuuper weird switch, right? I mean, Enya isn't exactly on today's top hits, but I digress. In shock, I got up and went to ask the man at the counter nearby if he knew how that song got on there. Looking perplexed, he said he absolutely had no idea. I smiled, nodded, and said it must have been my mom, to which he replied, "Oh! How'd she get back there to change it?" If only he knew. That moment still makes me laugh.

These days I find her in the ethereal Catholic hymns at Easter and in the minor chords of Kol Nidre's haunting melodies during Yom Kippur (I'm a bit of both). I find her in every pigeon that perches on my balcony staring in far longer than would be normal. I find her in the calls I get from friends when I need a dose of that maternal love. I find her when the lights flicker or when I get a waft of roses out of nowhere while sitting on my couch. I find her in mediums and psychics that somehow speak straight to the skeptic in me. I find her when I sing her favorite songs to her and can *swear* I feel her arms around me. I find her sometimes walking down the street in the face of a stranger who resembles her. If I pay attention, my mother is nearly everywhere—which is exactly the point. Our bond is stronger than ever.

The connection, the things and thoughts and feelings that remind me of her are here, even when she is not. Which is, in fact, the ultimate

Jedi mind fuck of grief: The meaning and symbolism of our relationship remains unique and actively alive within us, but the person or thing that gave that meaning in a real, live context is now gone, at least on the physical plane. That creates a chasm, that void we've been navigating for so many of these pages.

Let me also say that being religious or even vaguely spiritual isn't required if that's not your thing! For some people, religion is a costumed event that doesn't bring any sense of support or comfort. Others lean on religion for the community, assurance, and comfort of a connection to a larger-than-life protector and overseer, such as "God," or a clear vision of what happens after death. All of this is great, because inevitably, this is about what brings a sense of solace for *you* as you navigate your loss. Finding comfort as we continue on the grief path is an inside expedition, and a harrowing one at times. It only matters that you find that comfort in something or someone, as going it alone for the entirety of the path is not a recommendation I'd give to anyone if they can help it.

Ritual and Remembrance

When we begin to think about honoring our deceased loved ones, it can sometimes feel daunting to trust that they can be with us every day—which is where rituals of remembrance can step in. For me and so many of my clients, remembering rituals can become bridges that we build to connect our grief to our present lived experience. I believe that rituals can be created outside the box of any set of beliefs, religion, or spiritual doctrine. Through rituals that feel meaningful to us, we can visit those we love and have lost, whenever, wherever, and however we choose.

Sam, my client whom we met in chapter 1, very much wanted to honor his mother, but wasn't sure how to begin. He had never lost anyone to death before, so he didn't know where to start. I suggested we understand what he wanted to get out of remembering and honoring, so we could get closer to creating remembering rituals that felt authentic and good to him, even with the caveat that they may change, expand, or fall off in lieu of another way to honor his mom.

As you think about your own rituals for remembrance, on what you'd like to feel as you honor the memory of someone or something you have lost, you might ask yourself questions like:

> *Is there anything you already do to honor the memory of someone you love no longer in your life?*
>
> *Do you have a day of the week or day of the year that you are reminded of your loss the most?*
>
> *What did you learn about loss growing up?*
>
> *In general, how do you honor things and people who have left your life?*
>
> *Are there milestones that feel more important to honor your loved one?*
>
> *Do you prefer to honor your loved one internally or externally?*

Suggestions for Holding and Honoring

I hope it goes without saying that we can continue the bonds with and for anything and anyone who feels significant to us, even if it's not a death loss. Relationships can evolve or change over time, and we are welcome to find rituals that bring us a sense of peace for any situation that is calling for it. Calling for the connection.

The following list includes just some of the rituals that can be helpful in creating and maintaining a connection to your losses and loved ones. Of course, you can choose to do none of them, some of them, or some variation of all of them. Inevitably, the purpose is to make you feel close to them again, to honor their memory and keep their memory alive, to give you access to your feelings about them, and also to remind you that their significance in your life is absolute. It will never, can never go away.

Rituals for Connection

- Talk to them—anyhow, anywhere, continue the conversations as needed.
- Write them letters—either in a special notebook just for them, your journal, or notes you keep in a special box.
- Keep a project going that they started.
- Use social media to keep celebrating them and communicating with them—birthdays, anniversaries, or memories to tag them in is a nice way to keep connected if that brings positive feelings.
- Get a memorial tattoo.
- Create memory boxes—photos, mementos, important things that hold meaning for you can be placed in this box to peruse as desired.
- Create or choose an "anchor item" that you keep with you.
- Make their favorite meal.
- Create a charitable donation or give back to a cause that your loved one cared about.
- Create a playlist of songs that remind you of them.
- Have a religious service dedicated to their memory.
- Travel to their favorite place on a special day or eat at their favorite restaurant.
- Light a candle in their honor whenever it feels special or necessary.
- Carry a photo in a locket or ashes in a piece of jewelry (this can include pets).

In my grief journey, it eventually began to feel comforting to perform an action that helps to fill that void with the love that once lived in that space. As a trained singer, I began to have charity cabaret shows in my mother's name nearly every year from the time of her diagnosis until a few years after she died. I will continue these shows in her honor, as they have also helped me honor and tend to both my love for her and my grief in losing her.

But honoring your loved one doesn't have to be an elaborate act of devotion—unless that suits you, in which case, go for it! It can be anything that feels important to you, anything that ties you to them and allows you to hold their memory alive and well inside you. Whatever feels right for you, *that* is your path.

Kirsten, the client whose story I shared in chapter 9, yearned to find a way to remember and honor Emma, the miscarried child she had planned a life for. In her backyard, Kirsten planted and nurtured a small garden of the flowers she loved, naming it "Emma's Garden." She told me she was also planning to paint some rocks with Emma's name and decorate the garden with some of the colors she had used in the nursery that was meant for her. Through that small but deeply loving and healing garden, Kirsten was actively tending to her love and affection for her lost daughter.

Sam, my client from chapter 1, decided after our conversation to bring a yoga mat and a dozen yellow roses to the cemetery nearly every Sunday to spend time telling his mom about all the life events that are now taking place for him. He tells me that showing up for his mother this way has been the most healing ritual for him. Sometimes, he even takes friends his mom knew. They enjoy a picnic, reminisce, and discuss plans for the future.

Shira, my client from chapter 2, wears her safta's necklace and feels her grandmother is keeping her safe and leading the way for her.

Lauren, my client from chapter 11, now has a dedicated Instagram page to her brother, Michael, where she has cultivated an authentic community of followers who have endured a similar loss. Hosting that community who really gets what she has been going through has helped her, and probably many of them, find their way toward more inner peace. Lauren also feels comforted, knowing that every day she is honoring her brother's life.

Josh, from the intro, puts his hand on his heart or looks up at the sky and sends his love and remembrance to the girlfriend he loved so deeply and lost so unexpectedly. He knows she will always live within him no matter what his future brings.

Hiroko from chapter 8 has taken a trip to every country her mother loved and brought a small token of her mother's to leave in each place as a way to "allow her mother's spirit to continue doing what it loves."

These are just a few examples of how my clients have continued their bonds with loved ones they lost.

You can use ritual and active remembrance daily, monthly, or whenever you feel the urge. You can save your rituals for anniversaries, or even once in a while with no rhyme or reason to the timing. You can also change your ritual or remembrance activity from one day to the next or one season or year to the next. *It's all good.* Honoring yourself, your loss, and your journey is the point, and how you do that is entirely up to you.

Over time our way of carrying our lost loved one with us may transform, becoming less about ritual and more about honoring an "inner knowing" that we keep them within us always. All that matters is how it makes you feel.

If carrying your loved one forward in these more tangible ways I spoke of above feels foreign and uncomfortable, that's okay, too. It only matters that you find enough comfort and peace to be able to move forward in your life whenever and however you choose to.

In *The Beauty of What Remains*, Rabbi Steve Leder tells us, "understanding death—its rituals, its lessons, its gift to reshape love through memory, its grief, its powerful reminder that it is not what but who we have that matters—gives our lives exquisite meaning."[6] Over time and in our own ways we can indeed "reshape love through memory" and keep our love strong and alive.

Those we have lost are not just some void or hole within us, but rather already written into all that we will become. Which is a fancy way of saying that you don't have to drive yourself crazy by trying to remember in just the "right" way or worry about forgetting every detail. Within the love we carry, there is a safety that our loved ones, losses, and our infinite connection are each indelibly written on our souls.

"Come back. Even as a shadow, even as a dream."

—Euripides

CHAPTER 13

The Holy Grail: Integration

"I have lost and loved and won and cried myself to
the person I am today."
—Charlotte Eriksson, *Empty Roads & Broken
Bottles: In Search for The Great Perhaps*

It feels kind of silly to think of there being a last chapter of a grief book, since there's no "last chapter" to the grief journey, yet here we are. I've been honored to be your travel companion as we have honored our losses, our feelings, our bodies, our needs and boundaries, and navigated showing up authentically, knowing that our losses will always be with us in some form. As we come to these final pages together, you're likely wondering, *What's next? Where do I go from here?* I completely get that. Those questions feel appropriate, given that we've come a long way together.

For better or worse, there is no next step or activity that will make this all go away or feel magically "better." There is nothing I can say that will wrap up the pain of your loss in a neat little package and send it on its way. I can't claim that after closing this book, your grief will dissipate like sparkly fairy dust and you'll feel fully transformed.

As you know by now, that's just not what grief is.

So, what *can* I promise? I can promise that you will still feel shitty at times. You will sometimes still feel sad, angry, exhausted, forgetful, and a bunch of other difficult things. You will also still long for *what was*—and those feelings will sometimes come over you at the worst possible times. Anniversaries and other important days will still hold weight and still cause dread that may (or may not) shift over time. I can promise you will not forget your loved one by adding new things into your life. I can also promise that you will also smile and laugh again—more and more as time goes on.

My expectation isn't that you'll reach this page and be *totally healed*, moving forward fully intact, never to grieve again. What I hope is that you have gotten to know yourself better throughout these pages and feel able to look at your loss in new ways. That you're starting to allow the truth of your grief journey to experience the light of day. That you're starting to honor your grief and your loss for what it is, and for how it has changed you. Because that is how we move forward—with grief and all it reveals to us about ourselves and about our love integrated fully into our lives.

The Hallway of Grief

When I try to describe the grieving process to my clients, I often visualize a person living in a hallway, moving between two rooms. One room is the past, full of the people, places, things, and experiences that we love and are attached to, but that we can no longer live in. Yet, that room isn't ours anymore. The room ahead, at the other end of the hallway, is the unknown. It's what lies ahead after a loss or trauma. It's a room that has some of our pictures on the wall, but there is so much that's unrecognizable and new.

We'd rather not enter, thanks. We long for that other room. That's a room we know, a place where we felt good. It's a place where goodness lives in abundance, however imperfectly at times. But we also know we have to go forward into this new room. It's scary, and everything feels uncertain. The world feels harder to understand or make sense of in there. We just want to go back to the other room. And we try.

Over and over. Back and forth we go, between the before and the after, trying to find where we belong, hoping somewhere will feel more like home again. Inevitably, we go and collect whatever we can from the old room. We know we cannot stay forever. So, we look around and try not to forget what this room looked and felt like. We do all we can to replicate some of what we had before in this new room, but we know we can't. Not really. Not fully.

We don't want the new room, but we know it awaits. It has a new scent, the light enters the windows differently. It will take time to get our bearings, even though we don't want to get too comfortable. Despite the pain, we know this is where we need to be. Day by day, we come back to the room more often. Eventually, we try sitting down, sipping some tea. We enjoy the warmth of the sunlight, but still go back down the hall to the old room for a nap, and to snuggle in the left-behinds—but less and less often now. We are beginning to see that we have already carried out everything we need. Then, one day, you realize you haven't been to that room in a while and you're content just to remember it.

Little by little, moment by moment, day by day, this is how the before and after become *integrated*. We can begin to see ourselves more and more in this new place, while holding on to all the heirlooms of what was.

That is integration. Nothing goes away, it just becomes part of who we are.

How Do We Integrate Grief?

It is often said we are rebuilt and remade in our darkest, most shattered moments. It's like staring down at our broken pieces and knowing the next, but most exhausting and overwhelming step, is reassembling our parts. There is obviously no denying the gaping hole that loss leaves in its wake. Most times, it will feel impossible to know what to do with this hole, except to simply *endure* it, as you've already been doing.

In that vein, grief integration is simply this: a softening and opening toward the truth of what grief has brought into your life, and what it has taken away. Over time, you can do this by consolidating the different parts of yourself that were affected and changed by your loss. The pieces that felt broken and changed from who you were beforehand come together with parts of who you are now. This is the path toward healing the gaping wound left by the loss, a little at a time.

Throughout this book, the exercises and reflections we've done together have hopefully brought you closer to your grief story and a more honest account of your loss experience.

I believe that by looking at something honestly, we can understand it in a new way, and in the process become empowered to meet it as it comes. It's the trickle effect of healing, I suppose you could say.

My client Kirsten and I talked about the idea of integrating her grief a year after her miscarriage. By that point in our work together, Kirsten was trying to get pregnant again, and her fear of losing *another* baby was overtaking her excitement and joy about having another chance at being pregnant. Grief makes us think that there is just one or the other—joy or despair, a future or a past—when in fact there's room for all of it. The fear, the joy and hope, the remembering and cherishing, and the going forward, all exist together.

For Kirsten, integration meant making space for her joy and grief to live side by side, without letting the loss totally overshadow what could be a hopeful and beautiful new adventure. She could live with the sadness and the excitement, without having one negate the other.

Often, grief integration looks like accepting and even befriending your grief, acknowledging that it's a permanent part of your life in its unique way, even as the level of intensity shifts over time. Accepting loss as a part of life frees up space to invite in other experiences and emotions alongside that grief. A day out with friends. A date that's fun. A birthday party in your honor. Doing something you have always loved to do but stopped doing after your loss. Bringing in life (and maybe love) again, to hang out alongside your grief.

Am I on the Right Track?

As we have talked about a lot over the course of this book, loss is transformational in and of itself, and its trajectory unknown. But if we let it, it can lead us deeper into our own interior world, rearranging the dusty shelves, connecting us with new and unknown parts of ourselves. Ultimately, we have the opportunity to emerge stronger, more compassionate, connected, and even more loving, despite our heart feeling like it's been inescapably torn. And by the way, this might look different every day! While there is no set path, there are a few signs that you're starting to integrate your grief:

Signs of Grief Integration

- *You don't feel totally blindsided and in shock every time you think of the loss.*
- *You see and accept your loss as a part of your life and who you are going forward.*
- *You accept that your life going forward means moving forward without your loved one being physically (or mentally) present, but feel able to carry them forward and stay emotionally connected to them.*
- *You're able to honestly acknowledge the impact of your loss on your life.*
- *You see the difference between living in the dark abyss of grief and peering into it from time to time.*
- *You feel the intensity of your grief symptoms (e.g., physical pain, GI distress, depression, anxiety, exhaustion) lessen or disappear completely.*
- *You have rituals that keep you connected to who and what you have lost without overwhelming you.*
- *You experience the lessening of the most intense of grief feelings, while acknowledging the grief is still there and will always be with you in varying ways.*
- *You allow yourself to have the emotions and experiences as they come without judging them or allowing anyone else to judge them.*

- *You have a little more physical energy to face the day and make plans in the future.*
- *You don't feel totally overcome by the anxiety of loss happening again so that it overshadows positive feelings and connection.*

These indicators are, of course, things that come with time, and with honesty and allowance. The timeline and trajectory are personal to your experience. I'd like for you to come back to this chapter over time and see if you can relate to some of the integration indicators above or to notice anything that has shifted.

Missing and Fearing Come with the Territory of Moving Forward

You've heard me say throughout the book that moving forward isn't linear. I'm sure you've really *felt* that, too. We can talk all day about "transformation" and "integration," moving forward and carrying *with*, but none of these mean we won't also carry along with them the immense ferocity of simply *missing* our person. I'd be lying to you if I didn't tell you that I miss my mother immensely. What I miss is incalculable, because she gave so much to me in my life. I miss so many things and people no longer in my life, and that will remain with me, albeit with less agonizing stickiness, as I continue my journey. But, still, I am sometimes kicked in the gut with my longing for another moment with my deceased loved ones. I wonder how it could be any other way. All I can ask for is a new kind of spaciousness in the grief. A sacred internal beat that allows us to sit with the sadness and yearning that undoubtedly will always arise with a newfound sense of gentle allowance. It doesn't take *away* the missing—it simply allows more room for it to breathe within us.

Along with that missing is the fear we also carry—the fear of forgetting, the fear of losing *for good*. We fear we will forget their voice, the sound of their laughter, the inside jokes we shared with them, their smell, the way they made us feel. We fear that with time, our memories will fade and that time will then steal what little remains of them.

These additional aspects of our grief—the missing and the fear—are normal, even likely. And so, as we come together to take inventory and look within and ahead together, just take with you this idea that we will change along with life's motion, but it may not always *look* like "progress," okay? Every day "progress" and "healing" may look different, and I don't want that to freak you out. Just notice it. We will sometimes feel set back by the intensity of our longing, but remember, that's just your heart reminding you of your connection and love. It does not mean you're not moving forward, or not accepting, or anything else you may believe it means. When we stop and wonder who we are now, the missing and the longing and the fear of the fading . . . that's all natural. Those are parts of the whole that is our grief and our love.

Come, Sit with Me: A Final Check-In

As you continue to live your life, you'll undoubtedly brush up against this question—*who am I now?* When I speak with clients about the idea of identity, some of them admit that progress doesn't really feel good. I get that. It can feel hard to really take in the fact that progress doesn't take us back to our loved one and how we were before our loss. In so many ways, that's what some people long for, because there isn't an understandable blueprint for where this progress is going to take us and who we will become with it. In truth, our identity shifts as we grow and as we add new things, people, and experiences into our lives. In my work I'm sometimes asked what grief looks like as we, and our lives, change. Grief lives in the layers, so it's always there. As we grow and change, we will still come face-to-face with it again. As our life changes, we are asked to look at how our grief shifts and reshapes along with us.

Let's do that together now.

I want you to imagine that you are sitting on my couch right now. My office is off the lobby of a quintessential prewar building on the Upper West Side of Manhattan, with crisp white crown molding and a large floral wool rug. The couch you're on is a dark gray twill, and so deep, it feels like you could escape into it for a while. There are a few different types of pillows that can either support you or that you can hold on to, for anchoring. Across from you, and behind me, are endless shelves of mental health books, a clock, and some ceramics, some of which I made and others that were gifted to me. I am on a gray armchair with a pink-and-gray paisley pillow, and between us, there's a small glass coffee table with a rose quartz heart on it. At the right time of day, the sunshine comes through the window at just the right angle that the office looks kind of dreamy. It's a very warm and inviting space, but even more important, all of you are welcome here.

Once you get comfortable, take a deep breath in... and exhale out slowly. I want to know things like: *What's hurting right now at this moment? Where do you feel more like you're moving in place? What's feeling better? Does any part of your emotional or physical experience feel worse?*

This is a time to really feel into these experiences, whatever they may be at this moment.

I am here with you and there are no right answers. If nothing feels different, please don't judge it. Feeling the same way you did doesn't mean you're going "backward" or that you are "stuck." We're here to explore, not to judge or label. It may simply mean that you need more witnessing, care, time, love, and nourishment.

Let's Check In...

I want us to pause for a moment here together. I want us to get quiet and go within. In this quiet place, I want you to take inventory of our time together. If you are able, take a few deep breaths, and put a hand on your heart center.

When you read the following questions, I'd like you to really feel into your body and emotions that may be telling you something you don't yet know. Remember that I am here with you. You are safe, your honesty is important, and no matter your answers, we are here to explore, not to judge or label.

1. *Do you feel you have begun the grieving process or are you still at the portal gate of the griefall?*

2. *Do you feel you can be honest with others about how you feel?*

3. *Do you feel you are honest with yourself about your grief experience?*

4. *Do you feel safe allowing in the full-body grief experience as it calls out for attention?*

5. *Do you feel safe creating boundaries around your grief-related needs? For example, do you feel able to turn down social invitations that feel like too much?*

6. *Do you feel compelled to put others' needs before your own?*

7. *Are you able to see your relationship with your deceased loved one with more honesty?*

8. *Do you feel continuously overwhelmed with guilt or ruminate at length over your loss?*

9. *Are you able to look at your loss through a self-compassionate lens?*

10. *How does saying "no" feel to you now in general?*

11. *Are you able to seek out and ask for help when you need it?*

12. *Are you giving yourself grace for moving at your own pace?*

13. *What are strengths you have learned about yourself in this process?*

14. *Are there new relationships (of any kind) that feel authentic and nourishing?*

15. *Have you introduced new things into your life that feel good and are beneficial to your overall well-being?*

My hope is that the *intensity* of this experience lessens a little bit for you with the passing of time, with the tools in this book, and with deep, authentic connection in your life.

These are the ingredients for moving forward with your grief, and how that happens will be how you're meant to do it.

Take a moment and maybe take note in some way the areas of your grief process that still feel fragile to the touch. Are there areas you want to revisit? What are the places that still feel raw? My goal for you at this point in *our* work here together is that you slowly, and in your own time, and in your own way, begin to see your grief clearer, understand your experience as it comes, and find a gentle and loving way to meet your grief where it is *every time* it shows up.

Your grief is not your enemy. Your grief is your attachment doing its job and wanting to stay attached. It's your caring, commitment, hope, plans, expectations, and always, your love. So, doesn't it then make sense to treat it with the tenderness that each of those represents? Yes, I think it does.

Releasing Expectations

One of the hardest parts about my work with clients who are grieving is asking them to gently let go of the expectations they have of themselves and where they think they *should be* after loss. This also means letting go of the expectations others may have of and for them, as well. Grieving is one storm pattern we cannot forecast. We cannot predict when the heart quakes will come and knock us off the perch we spent months climbing to. We cannot control the physical cues that may come up, seemingly out of nowhere, when we least expect it, that render us dizzy or nauseous, needing to hide away or lie down or fall to our knees weeping.

Expect to still struggle for a long while ahead, while also hopefully experiencing some moments of respite, fun, and ease along the way. Don't pay any attention to what anyone else expects from you. They aren't in your shoes experiencing what you are experiencing, and you must do this *your* way.

Why Truth Is the Way

I talk about being honest a lot. Much of this book is me gently asking you to get radically honest about your before loss and your after loss, how it felt and how it feels, what it is and what it's not.

We have to do this for many reasons, one of which is so that someday, when we're as ready as we can be, we're able to clearly look ahead and eventually even make plans for the future with a truthful heart. It's only through that deep dive that we can begin to rebuild an authentic intimacy with life. If and when we allow it, grief can slowly but seriously deepen our connection to everything around us and show us the truth of what feels right and good for us, and what doesn't. It clarifies, unmasking truths that we ultimately need in order to move forward with grief and with love.

So many of the clients you met here in these pages struggled and endured a very painful grieving experience. Many of them struggled for a very long time with their loss and the experience of integrating their grief and moving forward. They felt challenged by how to integrate their loss in their lives, as they so desired to simply *move on*. One after another, they found that grief is an ending, yes, but it's not *their* end—and it won't be yours, either.

Coming Full Circle on Our Way Forward

"Grief turns out to be a place none of us know until we reach it."
— Joan Didion, *The Year of Magical Thinking*

A few weeks back, I got a surprise email from Josh, the client featured in the first pages of this book. When I met him, he was in the throes of intense grief over the death of his girlfriend, Rebecca, after the tragic car accident they had been in together. You may recall that Josh and I started to conduct therapy "our way," which meant a combination of different therapeutic modalities and an unrelenting commitment to trusting in the goodness of life again. It didn't happen overnight, or with ease. As you now know, we don't just go from the griefall to... happy ever after, or even "less devastated ever after"—that's *not* how it works.

Over time and with commitment to his life and healing, Josh began to perceive the facts and circumstances around the accident differently, and—most importantly—felt his complicated grief feelings without trying to escape them. His grief slowly began to integrate. He carried the desire to live, love, and connect again alongside the grief that still lives inside him. In order to get there, Josh had to go further into his raw feelings of guilt, and to put aside the hope that he could change what happened. Once he could fully take in that he didn't have to "let go" of Becca, and that she could be a part of him going forward, he felt ready to allow life to slowly trickle in. He began moving forward with her memory and all the ways in which his life was affected and changed by hers. The hole she left in his heart was mended, slowly, and transformed into a part of his new whole.

You've heard me going on a lot throughout this book about how the full spectrum of our feelings deserves the space and freedom to rise up and be seen, witnessed, and valued, no matter how shameful, ugly, scary, or painful. When Josh left therapy, he felt both sad and hopeful, but much less afraid of his emotions.

Four years later with his email in front of me, I was filled with joy at how he had continued to show up for his grief and his life. He had gotten married and had an adorable newborn son. I stared at the photo he had sent of his family, zeroing in on his smile for a bit, to check for genuineness. Josh looked sincerely happy and healthy, and as his email said, "terrifically fulfilled." He wrote that he has never stopped thinking about or loving Becca. He shares stories about her from time to time and talks with her about his life when he goes cycling in the mountains of Boulder, where he now lives. My heart burst for Josh's full life, given how he'd sworn up and down in our sessions that he'd never be able to love anyone else or find happiness.

I'm pretty sure we both always knew better.

And that's the human condition, isn't it? To love again, to reconnect to life, even through pain, to rediscover a sense of "worthwhileness" as we crawl on hands and knees in search of what feels evasive, even impossible, amid the rubble of heartbreaking loss: meaningful connection to self, to life, to others—to *hope*.

When a client leaves therapy, it doesn't mean that they are "cured," or that the grief and trauma are now gone from their life. A lot of my clients come back for what therapists affectionately call a "tune-up." Others stay in touch. It heartens me to hear from clients after time passes, because, therapist insider secret? *We care a lot about the relationship, too.* I love being able to witness how their life has transformed, or where they are at and how they are feeling. In this way, the therapeutic relationship can sometimes mirror some of what I talk about with grieving. The moments together may come to an end, but the relationship carries on.

As you and I get closer to ending here together, I notice those same feelings coming up for me about you: pure admiration for your ability to stay the course here with me on these country roads toward healing, for making space within yourself and all of the painful, overwhelming experiences you have felt in your grieving process, for looking so honestly at your losses as well as your life, relationships, patterns, and old wounds. It wasn't easy, I know. I am humbled and grateful that you stuck it out. That's a courageous act, and I feel truly proud to be here with you, despite how hollow those words can land in writing. I hope that you keep going, keep taking chances on happiness and love and connection and fulfillment. That's what this work is about, after all.

We Continue On...

I started this book talking about my own experience as a therapist who lost her mom, so I want to share with you where I am now, with a few years sitting between my loss and my present relationship to it.

Since the morning I first heard of my mother's death while standing on a Manhattan street corner, my grief continues to wax and wane through the years, as grief does. Losing my mother permanently changed the climate of my life, where on certain days of the year, there is a soft, sorrowful rain that seeps into everything, but inevitably makes the beautiful things in my life grow.

I continue to learn so much about death and loss from being untethered from my mothership. Grief has shifted my life in a way I could never have imagined and although I am not grateful for losing my mother, I find myself thankful for the expansion of my heart and its ability to love and connect more authentically in both life and work because of this loss. I am grateful for the ability to live in a state of gentle surrender when the grief waves come, as opposed to fighting against their tides. I now go *with* them, and that has made all the difference. Loss has prodded me to actively seek out joy, beauty, and fulfillment. One of the most powerful healing tools that I have had in my own grief is connecting to the love and joy of my mother's aliveness. In this way, my sense of her being my lighthouse remains.

About a year after my mom died, I came across a little book that I'd given to her as a stocking stuffer one Christmas years earlier. It was one of those little memory journals you give to parents/grandparents that asks them to share personal memories or wisdom that you can keep when they are gone. I hadn't looked much at her responses when she gave it back to me and nearly forgot about it until one random night perusing my bookshelf in my childhood home. Reading through it, I was grateful to have known most of her answers through conversations we'd had. The last page, though, was like a punch to the gut and a tight hug all at once. It asked, *"What do you want your legacy to be?"* To which she answered one single word: *"you."*

And maybe that's the burden and the gift of grief itself—being the legacy of those we love whom we have lost. Carrying on *with* them and *for* them.

I am forever humbled by that thought.

As much as I may have wanted or tried, I know I may not have been able to capture every part of your grief and its sticky shadows. It's impossible to encapsulate every part of the grief spectrum in a single book, but I am nevertheless grateful to have had the opportunity to be here with you to feel and engage this experience together. I hope by now you've learned a lot about yourself throughout these pages, and that self-knowledge is your first step: Understanding what's happening to you emotionally and physically can allow compassion, patience, and hope to filter in on even the darkest days.

I also hope for you that throughout this book you have found yourself more able to meet your grief with honesty and tender allowance. I hope that you continue to open yourself up to feel a renewed sense of connection to your life, your relationship to whom or what you have lost, and that you have discovered new pathways in your heart. I hope that you make new connections, try new experiences, and allow *life* in again—with all of its gritty pain, sure, but all of its beauty, too. Most of all, I hope you give yourself credit for sticking so steadfastly and honestly to this grief journey, even when the going felt more than tough. That's true courage.

Ultimately, as we end our time here together, having learned and shared, I've come to more viscerally realize that grief itself is a mystery that continues to unfold and unfurl in our lives like only a broken-hearted sojourn can. It's a brutal, heart-wrenching emotional current that can make us feel lost and unmoored, but ultimately has the potential to bring us closer to ourselves and our boundless capacity to keep going, heart open, despite it all.

I wish you peace and gentleness as you continue forward, and I invite you back to these pages any time you may need that "tune-up." Whatever you feel, whomever and whatever you lose, you don't have to go it alone.

Acknowledgments

As a reader, I've always gone to the acknowledgments section of the book first. I like to know all the beautiful people that go into the making of someone's story or work. Now, as a writer, I can understand even more fully the preciousness of having loving companionship when you want to give up, when you full-on doubt your own capabilities, when you just want to pace or snack or find whatever crazy distraction there is to take you away from having to face a blank page waiting for you (once it was singing the entire soundtrack of *Les Mis* to my houseplants just to avoid writing).

I've always had this image of writing a book as an endeavor of solitude. A passionate escape to our interior world where all the wild wisdom lives. But nope. For me, it was a lot of moments with a lot of people, and I could have it no other way. There are so many people without whom I could not have gotten through this first book-writing experience intact, and to each of them I am indebted with unrelenting gratitude. They are my walking, breathing ride-or-dies.

Richelle Fredson, amazing book proposal coach turned absolute best pal and soul twin—I owe you in return a lifetime supply of chewing voice notes, Cheez-Its, and filet mignon at our favorite spot. I couldn't possibly be more thankful for your friendship and presence in my life since day one.

My Folio Literary Management dream team—Jan Baumer and Steve Troha—agents beyond my wildest expectations. Truly, your support and friendship has been a life-changing treasure to me. Thank you for believing in me and my mission for this book. I couldn't be luckier to be represented by such unparalleled talent, who also happen to be kick-ass, brilliant, and hilarious humans.

Hannah Robinson, my extraordinary, kind, patient, saintly, brilliant editor at GCP Balance: Thank you for your tireless commitment to this book—but also your friendship, for going above and beyond, for talking me off several ledges with those "problem child moments," for baking me an unusually complicated pie, for your magic pep talks, for our eighteen-hour dinners that fly by, and most importantly, for bringing your beautiful depth of soul to this experience. My life and my work within these pages are so much richer because of you.

Rebekah Borucki, for inviting me to coauthor my first children's book (*Zara's Big Messy Goodbye*) with you, for the strawberry Pop-Tart care package when I needed it most, and for reminding me that I can do more. You are a force and a light.

Jessica Baum, all these years later, we really did it—so grateful for your friendship, for sharing Cosmo, for the "repairs," and for steering me in every right direction on this crazy journey—Tower cards and all.

Ruby Warrington, for your guidance, grace, camaraderie, and dear friendship that all began with this strange little endeavor of writing a book—what a blessing you are.

Wyndham Wood, for guiding and calming my nervous, deer-in-headlights, rookie-writer self in the early days of navigating what a book might actually come to look like.

For the sake of not having a fifty-page acknowledgment section (because I would if I could!), I will simply mention some really important people without whom my life would have felt harder and more daunting during this process (and beyond). The people around me are my greatest gifts in life. I don't take a single moment of sincere and caring connection for granted. In naming each person, I have to emphasize the big and small ways in which their companionship and support have kept me afloat. And that to each name listed below, for different reasons and seasons, there is a very, very deep wellspring of love, inspiration, joy, and immense gratitude attached:

Michelle Pigott, Stacey Lynn, Todd Obolsky, Tazkeea Choudury, Sylvia Kalicinski, Gila Kaplan, Karen Ann-Marie Duncan, Kimberly Austin, Merri Lee Kingsly, Steve Weiss, Katie DeCoste, Tiffany Yu, Yvelette Stines, Nitzalie Garced, Gyri Nysaeter, Micheline Maalouf, Laura Kovall, Sylvester McNutt, Mary Allard, Dominique Troy, Alex Mammadyarov, Faith Martyn, Tony Marytn, Nadia Zilkha, Meghan Riordan Jarvis, Dina Scippa, Kristen Boice, Audrey Stimpson, Joe Snow, Cookie Correll, Devon Reiffer, Jarrett Goetz, Nicole Puzio, Raphael Miranda, Doug Simpson, Heather Wilcockson, Georgina Miranda, Deanne Lorette, Kelly Taylor, Karen McBride, Cheryl Gellert, Michelle Madrid, Rahana Rampershad, Karen Chinca, Sara Watchko, Marian Conaty, Guy Giarizzo, Ashley Taylor, Daniel Cherniack, Christine Priegel, Nicole Stassinopoulos, Marci Mattes, and Judy Wolfe. Each of you is a true, true blessing to me.

Melissa Pfluger, sister and sidekick—I feel so thankful for our endless adventures around the world, for your flawlessly stepping in whenever I needed Rose, and for being the family that my heart so very much missed.

My amazing staff and colleagues brought light back to my life again after I lost my mother and had my other position at a nonprofit closed down all at once. What a blessing in disguise, as I was brought exactly to where I needed to be. Within two weeks of my loss, I immediately started as clinical director at the Addiction Institute at Mount Sinai St. Luke's Hospital in New York City. Our small but mighty team kept the ship going and gave incredible care to our patients. They taught what it meant to show up for people. For each of you, for so many different reasons, I am grateful (and I miss you!): Paul Rinaldi, Deanna Billington, Janice Nickens, Carmen Suero, Gail Lewis-Williams, Yenny Carrasco, Patricia Vanderlinde, Emilia Alexopoulos, Stephen Johnson,

Raul Narvaez, Rise Gibson, Ed Walsh, Aruna Parasram, Sharon Lewis, Shanta (Devi) Persaud, Antoinette James, Arpan Parikh, Ray Dooley, Millie Curbelo, Valerie Williams, and Janelle Clarke.

Deep appreciation also belongs to my dad's bereavement group, which helped uplift him and bring joy (and music) back to our family again—John Amato, Raymond Leduc, Bernadette O'Keefe, Andrea Primavera, Elaine DeCrosta, Beverly Austin, Linda DeWitt, Nancy Tripi—you've become priceless family to us over these years.

Judy and Harvey Langberg, my Boulder, Colorado, parents and loudest cheerleaders (otherwise known as my "heads of marketing"). Unfortunately, we lost Harvey to a swift illness before the book was finished. I do know he's been supporting me from the other side, just as always. His spirit will remain within the heart of these pages. Judy, you and Figgy (Figaroo) are a gift to me beyond words.

To my dad, Frank Moffa, who has been a steadfast listener and supporter (and whose belief in me was far stronger than my own). You continue to teach me it's never too late to seek out the adventure of new horizons and define our own sense of meaning after loss. For forty-five years you loved Mom, and I am fortunate to witness how that love continues to grow and evolve, despite it all.

And finally, to MFB—I am ready now, and what an adventure lies ahead! xx

Notes

Introduction

1. AmeriSpeak, *Grief: Beyond the 5 Stages* (Chicago: WebMD, 2019).

Chapter 2: Honoring Life's Many Losses

1. Pauline Boss, *Ambiguous Loss: Learning to Live with Unresolved Grief* (Cambridge, MA: Harvard University Press, 1999/2000).
2. Kenneth J. Doka, *Disenfranchised Grief: Recognizing Hidden Sorrow* (Washington, DC: Lexington Books, 1989).

Chapter 3: The Freedom to Feel What You Feel

1. Francis Weller, *The Wild Edge of Sorrow: Rituals of Renewal and the Sacred Work of Grief* (Berkeley: North Atlantic Books, 2015).

Chapter 4: My Body Was Calling, but I Was on "Do Not Disturb"

1. Gaia Vince, "Hacking the Nervous System to Heal the Bod," *Discover*, May 2015.
2. Mary-Frances O'Connor, "Grief: A Brief History of Research on How Body, Mind, and Brain Adapt," *Psychosomatic Medicine* 81, no. 8 (October 2019): 731–38.
3. "Broken Heart Syndrome," Mayo Clinic, accessed January 3, 2023, https://www.mayoclinic.org/diseases-conditions/broken-heart-syndrome/symptoms-causes/syc-20354617.
4. Mary-Frances O'Connor, *The Grieving Brain: The Surprising Science of How We Learn from Love and Loss* (San Francisco: HarperOne, 2022), xiv.
5. "The Science & Process of Healing from Grief," Huberman Lab, accessed February 2, 2023, https://hubermanlab.com/the-science-and-process-of-healing-from-grief/.
6. Gilberto Gerra et al., "Long-term Immune-Endocrine Effects of Bereavement: Relationships with Anxiety Levels and Mood," *Psychiatry Res*, no. 121 (December 2003): 145–58, https://doi: 10.1016/s0165-1781(03)00255-5.
7. "Meditation and Mindfulness: What You Need to Know," National Center for Complementary and Integrative Health, accessed February 2, 2023, https://www.nccih.nih.gov/health/meditation-and-mindfulness-what-you-need-to-know.

Chapter 5: Grief's Sister, Trauma

1. "Complex Trauma," National Child Traumatic Stress Network, accessed January 3, 2023, https://www.nctsn.org/what-is-child-trauma/trauma-types/complex-trauma.
2. "National Strategy for Trauma-Informed Care Operating Plan," Substance Abuse and Mental Health Services Association, accessed November 12, 2022, https://www.samhsa.gov/sites/default/files/trauma-informed-care-operating -plan.pdf.
3. Babette Rothschild, "Post-traumatic Stress Disorder," *Self & Society: An International Journal for Humanistic Psychology* 28, no. 5 (January 2015): 1523.
4. Judith Herman, *Trauma and Recovery* (New York: Basic Books/Hachette Book Group, 1997), 35.
5. Paul A. Boelan et al., "Traumatic Loss: Mental Health Consequences and Implications for Treatment and Prevention," *European Journal of Psychotraumatology* 10, no. 1 (April 2019), https://doi.org/10.1080/20008198.2019.1591331.
6. Lisa Shulman, *Before and After Loss: A Neurologist's Perspective on Loss, Grief, and Our Brain* (Baltimore: Johns Hopkins Press, 2018).
7. Bessel A. van der Kolk, *The Body Keeps the Score: Brain, Mind, and Body in the Healing of Trauma* (New York: Viking, 2014), 97.
8. Babette Rothschild, "Safe Trauma Recovery," filmed September 2, 2009, video, 8:18, https://www.youtube.com/watch?v=LhuzpUlaX_k.

Chapter 6: Self-Compassion and Grieving to Our Own Rhythm

1. "The Three Elements of Self-Compassion," Self Compassion by Dr. Kristin Neff, accessed February 16, 2023, https://self-compassion.org/the-three-elements -of-self-compassion-2/.

Chapter 12: Carrying Our Loved Ones with Us

1. Tammy Clewell, "Mourning Beyond Melancholia: Freud's Psychoanalysis of Loss," *Journal of the American Psychoanalytic Association* 52, no. 1 (July 2016): 43–67.
2. Sigmund Freud, *Letters of Sigmund Freud* (New York: Basic Books), 1960.
3. Dennis Klass et al., *Continuing Bonds: New Understandings of Grief* (New York: Routledge, 1996).
4. Chimamanda Ngozi Adichie, "Notes on Grief," *New Yorker*, September 10, 2020 (4).
5. David Kessler, *Finding Meaning: The Sixth Stage of Grief* (New York: Scribner, 2019), 212.
6. Steve Leder, *The Beauty of What Remains: How Our Greatest Fear Becomes Our Greatest Gift* (New York: Avery, 2021), 4.

About the Author

Gina Moffa, LCSW, is a licensed psychotherapist, mental health educator, and media consultant in New York City. In practice for nearly two decades, she has helped thousands of people seeking treatment for trauma and grief, as well as challenging life experiences and transitions. This includes work with Holocaust survivors at 92Y, as well as being a clinical director for a Mt. Sinai Hospital Outpatient Program specializing in addictions. She received her master's degree in social work with a specialty in trauma from New York University.